A GREAT EXPERIMENT

VISCOUNT CECIL, 1929

A GREAT EXPERIMENT

An Autobiography by

VISCOUNT CECIL
[LORD ROBERT CECIL]

OXFORD UNIVERSITY PRESS
NEW YORK

PREFACE

IN this volume, Viscount Cecil of Chelwood, perhaps better known as Lord Robert Cecil, has made a contribution of first importance to the history of international relations during the past generation. Viscount Cecil, and it may be he alone, is able to make this contribution to the history of our times because of his own personal relation to the events which he records and describes. Following a truly fascinating sketch of his own education and early life, Viscount Cecil plunges directly into the story of the making of the League of Nations. He has full personal knowledge of the plans and discussions which preceded the proposal to establish the League, and he traces step by step the story of its organization and its activity, as well as of its collapse which, it is firmly believed, will be followed some of these days by its reorganization and re-establishment on a more sound and permanent basis to the end that peace may be restored to this stricken and war-broken world.

Viscount Cecil tells in detail the story of the relationship of President Woodrow Wilson to this undertaking. He points with unerring accuracy but with great kindliness to the errors of understanding and of temperament on the part of the most influential members of the Peace Conference which formulated the Treaty of Versailles and brought the League of Nations into being in the only form which could then be agreed upon.

If the world of tomorrow is to make progress toward the permanent establishment of international prosperity and peace, it must first of all make sure that it knows and understands the mistakes of the world of yesterday and today. There can be no better preparation for the international studies and consultations which must shortly come than to read and to reflect upon Viscount Cecil's record of exactly what took place between 1919 and the collapse which, becoming evident in 1931, followed quickly as the tide of revolt against law, order and public morals rose in Asia, in Africa and in Europe.

Viscount Cecil is wholly justified in pointing out that the League of Nations, which failed in its largest field of endeavor, has nevertheless accomplished much in building up international co-operation in many important fields in spite of international jealousies and hostilities. The economic and social labors of the League and its proposals for world improvement have been and are of high importance. They have not succeeded on the scale which it was hoped might be the case, but, nevertheless, their record is there to be read by all. In respect to such matters as public health, working conditions for the manual laborer and intellectual co-operation, accomplishment has been very considerable, even if slow and imperfect.

It was, as Viscount Cecil makes clear, lack of respect for treaty obligations, for established international law and for every principle of public morals, which opened the door wide to the attack upon the foundations of an orderly and free civilization by highly organized, fully prepared and gigantic armed force which is now going forward in so appalling a fashion.

To those who would surrender to this invasion in the hope that they might thereby preserve some of their personal and national possessions, there is but one reply to make. That is that such a course of action means the complete overturn of that western civilization which has been more than two thousand years in building. What would take its place becomes day by day increasingly clear. The world would then be ruled by group tyranny, intent upon establishing a world-wide economic, political and intellectual despotism. Freedom would disappear from this earth for heaven only knows how many centuries. The alternative is to make every sacrifice, personal and national, for the maintenance and defense of what has been our liberal and forward-facing civilization. This has marched along through one great achievement after another and is marked by Magna Carta and the seventeenth-century revolution in Great Britain, by the organization of the Government of the United States with the Bill of Rights which is a part of its Federal Constitution, and in France by the revolution of 1789 with its motto of *Liberté, Egalité, Fraternité,* and the principles recorded in the

PREFACE

Déclaration des Droits de l'homme. Are all these great historic achievements to count for nothing? Do they not rather provide the inspiration and the strength successfully to defend them from any attack by armed force and in time to extend them to the control of the organized social, economic and political life of the whole world? Viscount Cecil is in no doubt as to how this question should be answered.

NICHOLAS MURRAY BUTLER

Columbia University
in the City of New York
February 12, 1941

FOREWORD

It is generally agreed that, at the end of the present war, it is vital that some effective reconstruction of international order should be attempted. That any ambitious Power, dominated by a tyrannical Government, should be able to plunge the nations into war and inflict incalculable suffering on mankind, is intolerable. It was to prevent this that the Great Experiment of the League of Nations was carried out. It has done much admirable work, but it has failed in its main purpose. If we are to succeed better the next time, we must know what the League is, what it has done, where and why it has failed to keep the peace and what changes in it would improve its chances of full success.

This book is an attempt to answer these questions from the point of view of an observer who had exceptional opportunities of watching the League from its foundation to the present day.

Some account of his personality is added and of how he came to be connected with the League.

My thanks are due to many who have encouraged me in my task, especially to Lord Lytton, Professor Gilbert Murray, and Mr. Noel Baker. I also owe much gratitude to Miss Freda White and Mr. Maurice Fanshawe for reading the manuscript. Among the books and papers I have consulted I should like to mention Mr. Hunter Miller's 'Drafting of the Covenant', Mr. Wilson Harris's accounts of the earlier meetings of the League Assembly, and those of the later meetings by Miss Freda White.

CONTENTS

ILLUSTRATIONS

A GREAT EXPERIMENT

INTRODUCTORY

I WAS born on September 14th, 1864, at 11 Duchess Street, Portland Place, which enabled me to claim, when I was standing for East Marylebone nearly fifty years later, that I was a Marylebone man! My earliest topographical recollection is of my father's house at Headley, on the borders of Hampshire, the garden of which became, to my childish imagination, the prototype of the Garden of Eden. It had an approach road leading upwards out of it with a white gate at the top which was to me the station of the angel with the flaming sword. Except that, in my early years, I suffered badly from eczema, my childhood was peaceful enough. I did not go to a private school — my parents holding that until they had been confirmed, children should not be sent away from home. Accordingly I was educated, till I was thirteen, by governesses and tutors in London and at Hatfield, to which my father succeeded in 1868. Our home life has been admirably described in my sister's life of my father and I need say little more about it. For the period, it was extraordinarily free from rules. We were encouraged to read any books or ask any questions we liked. As a matter of fact, books of a really objectionable character were not found in the house. But we were free to read and did read any of the ordinary literature of the day both in French and English. My mother frequently, and my father more rarely, used to read out the novels of Walter Scott, Marryat, etc.

My mother was an expert at 'skipping' passages which might lead to awkward questions. My father was less cautious, and I remember the emphasis with which he recited the full-blooded oaths of Midshipman Easy and Peter Simple. I do not know how far the education of their children was carefully planned by my parents. I have heard my mother say that she did not much believe in educational systems for, 'after all, the thing that really counts is example'. Certainly we were left to find our own feet intellectually apart from our actual lessons. But we were early taught to plan our lives. I have no doubt that our steps were tactfully guided. Certainly when I was quite young, — ten or eleven at the most — I believed that I had chosen to go to the Bar. My mother approved and probably suggested the choice. She had an exceedingly forceful personality. We were never punished in the ordinary way, least of all were we ever beaten. But it was enough for my mother to show displeasure to produce instant obedience. Such occasions happened seldom for two reasons. In the first place, my parents profoundly believed in the intellectual and moral liberty of their children. They did not wish to control them more than was absolutely necessary. They held that since the whole object of education was to enable the child to stand by himself, the sooner he practised doing so the better. To fence him round with rules and regulations was really to weaken his self-reliance. No doubt he had to be given the necessary informations so far as that could be done. No doubt he must have a high standard set before him by example. But in the end he must decide for himself what he meant to do with his life. Even in religious matters we were left free. We were taught the elements of Christianity and encouraged to ask questions or state difficulties. But there was no constraint as to our belief or practice. Attendance at church or family prayers was, if anything, discouraged when we were very young. We were taught to consider it as a privilege, a source of strength for those who were old enough, certainly not a social duty. Sermons, unless of first-rate quality, were, perhaps, over-much slighted.

Whether these principles of education would have been successful, as I think they were, but for another circumstance, may be doubtful. My father and mother were very remarkable people. We each and all of us, in spite of the atmosphere in which we lived — or it may be in part because of it — had a complete trust in both their wisdom and their justice. Both of them were delightful friends for their children. My mother's marvellous vitality and enjoyment of life, her readiness to be interested in anything and everything, her courage and crystalline sincerity, and above all the depth and warmth of her affection, made her companionship a 'liberal education' in itself. Of my father I have nothing to add to what has been so brilliantly said in the Life.

Politically I began to take notice, as the nurses say, in the early '70s. At that time my father was in a more or less independent position. He had resigned from the Conservative Ministry in 1867 and had succeeded to the peerage in 1868. On the other hand, he was not a Liberal. At that time, he disliked Disraeli and distrusted Gladstone. Indeed, I was brought up in the nursery to believe that those statesmen were two political ogres, equally dangerous for the country. There was not, therefore, much party politics talked by my elders. In 1874 two political events took place of family importance. My father joined Disraeli's second Government, and Arthur Balfour entered Parliament as Member for Hertford. A.J.B. was twenty-seven — seventeen years older than me, — but he encouraged his Cecil cousins, including myself, to treat him as a kind of elder brother, and a most delightful elder brother he was. To the end of his life he had a perfect touch with children, exerting for their benefit his marvellous gift of making the talk of others seem to the talkers much more worth hearing than it really was. He romped with us, he played games with us, he chaffed us, he laughed at our jokes. The memory of what he was to us in those years is still golden.

As for myself, I grew up in what is now called a sheltered life. No great evils happened to me beyond the ordinary accidents of childhood. I was once nearly drowned bathing, and on another occasion I fell into an underground cistern and nearly broke my neck. The greatest grievance I can remember was being made to dress up for a children's fancy-dress ball!

In 1877 I went to Eton and stayed there for four years. I must confess I did not enjoy it. It was my first separation from home, and I had no previous experience of a private school to enable me to feel, as many boys did at that date, what a relief it was to get to a public school. Games naturally filled the largest and most important part of boy life at Eton, and I was without training in cricket or fives or football. On the other hand, the things of which I heard most at home, like politics, were at Eton of little value. Probably what was most irksome to me was the existence of many rules made by masters and boys which seemed arbitrary and unreasonable. Finally, it so happened that in the House in which I was, the moral tone could only be described as bad.

I did tolerably well in my work, though I learnt little. Still, I acquired a certain number of minor prizes and took a good place in the class examinations called Trials. My last half I was captain in my house and tried, with the support and encouragement of my eldest brother who was then at Oxford, to be a reformer. I trust I did no harm. On the whole, to be candid, I seem to have wasted most of my time at school in such idiocy as the construction of Latin verses and reading the great classical authors under conditions which made it almost impossible to take the slightest interest in them. Very likely that was my fault; and the fact that my father disliked his time at Eton probably predisposed me against it.

But there were interludes which have left pleasant memories. During the later years of my time at school, my parents were occasionally summoned to spend a night at Windsor Castle, and we used to go up to see them in the afternoon. Though in fact nothing memorable happened, yet the general conception of visiting a Palace appealed to a school-boy. Then the Dean of Windsor at that time was a Wellesley and in consequence a distant connection. We did not see much of him. But he asked me once to dinner to meet Gladstone. I remember little of what passed except a discussion between the Dean and his distinguished guest, on the Disestablishment of the Church of England. Gladstone declared that the majority of the English were Anglican so that the question did not arise. The Dean denied the fact and pressed Gladstone, to know what he would do if the majority was the other way. But he got nothing out of the old Parliamentary hand! The impression left on me was that if the safety of the Establishment depended on Mr. Gladstone its position was pretty precarious. Perhaps this may be a good place to record my only other personal meeting with him. It was at a dinner-party at the Philip Stanhope's in 1892 or 1893. It was a hot night and the windows of the dining room, which was on the ground floor, were open. Accordingly we dined under the admiring gaze of the populace. After dinner, Mr. Gladstone drew me aside and talked with me as if I were the only person in the room. He had an ancient kindness for the family which he never forgot. To the end of his life he would sometimes call on my mother and was always charming to her children. On this occasion he talked to me about the bishopric of Norwich. I can see him now, bending his hawk-like gaze upon me as he discoursed in his wonderful voice with the deepest earnestness about the history of the See of Norwich and the considerations he had had in view in appointing a new Bishop, which he had just done. I, of course, knew nothing of the matter and, to speak truly, cared less. But I was immensely impressed by his personality and flattered by his attention. Of Mrs. Gladstone we saw, perhaps, rather more. Both my parents were fond of her and delighted to tell stories of her childlike candour. One which my mother used to repeat was of Mrs. Gladstone coming to her and saying: 'Do ask young —— to your parties. I do so want to get him out of the clever set!'

Then in 1878 my mother went to Berlin for a few days, where my father was attending the Congress, and took two of her sons with her, my eldest brother being already there. To us the most interesting incident was a visit to the Crown Prince and Princess at Potsdam. He was a most attractive personality — handsome, kindly, able and enlightened.

Had he lived, the history of the world might have been different.

After leaving Eton, I spent a year with a tutor and then went up to Oxford. That I thoroughly enjoyed. I liked college life and especially the endless talks with undergraduates on every topic under the sun. The debates at the Union (of which I became President), the discussions at political clubs like the Canning, the society of some of the Dons whom I 'knew at home', were all sources of great pleasure. In particular I enjoyed luncheon on Sundays with the Warden of Keble, Edward Talbot, afterwards Bishop of Winchester, and his wife. He was a Liberal like several of my other graduate friends, and I was a Tory of the straitest sect, but that in no way lessened our friendship. Austen Chamberlain used to remind me that when he, as a representative of the Cambridge Union, visited its Oxford counterpart, he spoke as a strict Free Trader and I replied to him as a Protectionist. But the dominating subject at that time was, as now, Foreign Affairs — the Eastern Question — Bulgarian atrocities — the Midlothian Campaign. On these topics I no doubt accepted the Conservative view. Anyone who reads the account[1] given of the struggle in the Cabinet a year or two earlier and the policy which finally emerged, will note two points on which my father insisted. One was 'the horror of war which always dominated him'.[2] The other was his adherence to the Concert of Europe in its various forms as a great peace-making instrument, illustrated by his insistence, for instance, on the whole terms of the Treaty of San Stefano being submitted to the Congress of Berlin. I have no doubt that in these as in other matters my father's opinion deeply influenced myself.

I made many friends at Oxford. One was Edward Grey, whom I knew slightly before. He used to be kind enough to play tennis with me though he was even then a first-rate

[1] See the *Life of Lord Salisbury*, by Lady Gwendolen Cecil.
[2] ibid., p. 189.

player which I never became. However, perhaps owing to his example, I did succeed in playing for my University (very badly!) against Cambridge. Another friend was Cosmo Lang, then a scholar of Balliol. We met at the Canning, of which he became Secretary and at the Union where he was by far the best speaker of his time. I remember hearing him in a debate to which one of the eloquent Irish members came as a visitor, and thinking Lang much the better of the two. We became great friends and allies — both, at that time, being Conservative in politics and both intending to make the Bar our profession. He, however, never practised, since he decided to take orders before he was actually called, and our paths diverged — his leading him to the Archbishopric of Canterbury — mine to Geneva. But it is a great thing for me to be able to say, as I can, that our friendship for more than half a century has never been interrupted. He is a great Christian, an impressive preacher, a dexterous and sometimes an eloquent speaker, an acute and resourceful controversialist. Of his work as an Archbishop I do not presume to judge. But I doubt not he will be deemed a worthy successor of the long line which began with St. Augustine.

I had many other friends, the most intimate one being William Carr, a man of great ability hampered by a curious manner which gave him the unjust reputation of being supercilious. For that or some other reason he never achieved a position equal to his merits, not the least of which was his marriage to a charming lady, the eldest daughter of Dr. Bright, the Master of our College, for we were both at University. The affair was proceeding while we were undergraduates together and was naturally of the greatest interest to me as his nearest friend. Perhaps, indeed, it partly accounted for my failure to achieve a better Degree than a Second Class in Law.

I went down in the summer of 1886 and was almost immediately plunged into a contested election in the Darwen

Division of North East Lancashire where my eldest brother was a candidate, at the Dissolution after the defeat of Gladstone's first Home Rule Bill. It was great fun — almost the only contested election I have ever enjoyed. My brother had got in the previous year by a majority of five votes, which he increased on this occasion to seven or eight hundred. A good deal depended on the Roman Catholic vote which supported him in 1886 on educational grounds. Six years later it went the other way and he was defeated. On each occasion we were told that it was priestly influence which decided the question.

After the Election I settled down to work for the Bar. The examination was at that time not very formidable — nor very useful. I passed it and, having kept the necessary Terms — that is, having eaten three dinners each term in the Hall of the Inner Temple for three years, — I was called in 1887. Then began the real professional education. I became a pupil of Mr. Swinfen Eady, afterwards a distinguished judge and peer by the name of Lord Swinfen. He was a very highly accomplished Equity lawyer who rightly insisted on the importance of thoroughness and accuracy. From him I passed to Mr. Joseph Walton who also reached the Bench as a Judge of the King's Bench Division. He was a Lancashire Roman Catholic and one of the most charming and admirable men that I have ever met. It was largely through him that I joined the Northern circuit and attended it for three years though without much pecuniary result. The only case of interest in which I was engaged was a charge of murder on board ship. I was asked by the presiding judge, who knew me, to defend the case without fee, which I was very glad to do. The prosecuting counsel, who was anxious to get away for the Long Vacation, came to me and suggested that I should advise my client to plead guilty to manslaughter and he would then not press the charge of murder. I hesitated, and he then began to hint that if he did press the murder charge he might very well get a conviction. It was a difficult position for a young and inexperienced man and I sought

FAMILY GROUP, 1896

Left to Right

Back row: Lady Selborne, Lord Selborne, Lord Hugh Cecil, the late Bishop
of Exeter, the present Lord Salisbury, the late Lord Salisbury, the late Lady
Salisbury, the late Lord Edward Cecil, Viscountess Cecil, Viscount Cecil

Front Row: The present Lady Salisbury, Lady Gwendolen Cecil, Lady
Florence Cecil, Lady Milner

the advice of a Leader, Mr. French, afterwards a County Court Judge. He asked me if I thought I had a case worth putting, and I said Yes. 'Then go on and never mind P——' (the prosecuting counsel), said my adviser. I acted accordingly, and in the end my man got off cheaply — there had been very grave provocation — with a sentence of three months' imprisonment.

In 1888 I was lucky enough to persuade Lady Eleanor Lambton to marry me — it was certainly the most fortunate thing that has happened to me. We went to live in a small house in Spanish Place and I went on working at the Bar. My progress in the Common Law was slow, but in one way or another I was always busy. When I left Walton's chambers I became a 'devil' of Gorell Barnes — a great authority on Commercial and Shipping Law and afterwards a Judge. My duty was to read the papers that came in to his chambers and make notes on them for his use. When he was made a Judge I went into the chambers of Danckwerts. He was, I believe, a German by origin and I think had been brought up in South Africa. He was very fat, with a bright red face and a subtle mind. He was an exceedingly good lawyer; indeed, on some branches of the law he knew all that there was to be known. He despised most people intellectually, whether on the Bench or at the Bar, and did not conceal his opinion. He used to do a certain amount of Government business and so had come across Henry James when he was Attorney General. Danckwerts did not get on with him and on one occasion when Sir Henry had rebuked him for some reason, Danckwerts turned on him saying: — 'I am not a peripatetic politician who goes about the country making speeches and then trembles to see what the papers will say of him the next morning'. In spite of his peculiarities I liked him. He was very generous and kindhearted and had a kind of elephantine *bonhomie* which was very attractive. From him I went to Sir Charles Russell when he was Attorney General in 1892. That was a great experience. Russell was in some ways an exacting chief. He expected a lot from his assistants. But he always, if possible, made use of their help and took care to give them all and more than all the credit they deserved. He would take you into court as often as he could and pointedly, in the hearing of his clients, ask your opinion on the progress of the case. He was the best advocate in my time and a far better lawyer than he was generally thought to be. But scientific and, still more, mechanical questions were a closed book to him. When I went to him he had been retained in a case about large consignments of chilled mutton from New Zealand which had gone bad owing to a failure of the freezing machinery. It became necessary for Russell to understand how this machinery worked, and accordingly he had a model of it which was placed in my room. At intervals he would come in and slowly turn the wheels round with his fingers and then ask me to show him how the thing worked, which I did, and he went away apparently satisfied. However, in an hour or two he returned in the same difficulty. The same by-play followed, with the same result, and I doubt whether he ever really grasped the mechanics involved. The case was ultimately settled. He did not find the same difficulty in other branches of applied science. In a great case in which the Government were charged with having infringed the ballistite patent by the manufacture of cordite, he led for the Crown and had with him his predecessor, Sir Richard Webster, in whose time of office the proceedings had been begun. No two men could have been more different. Russell's mind was clear-cut and definite. Though in some respects he was a sentimentalist, he hated all shams. Webster disliked crudities to such an extent that a bare statement of fact seemed to him slightly indecent. He revelled in detail for its own sake and, with an excellent memory, loved to recite technicalities more or less relevant to the question in hand. Russell aimed at the fundamental principle and perhaps did not always allow for the complications inevitable in mundane matters. I was asked by Russell to help him in the Cordite case and, since I found the subject interesting, I put my back into it. Russell made the most of all I did for him and indeed insisted on the solicitors giving me a brief. Sometimes he used me in order to run pins into his learned brother. I remember once Webster, arriving for a consultation, was greeted by Russell: 'I say, Webster, Cecil has been telling me that you're quite wrong (on some point in the case) and I think so too' — which was far from the attitude which a young and struggling barrister desired to take up towards one of the chief leaders of his profession! Nevertheless, I look back with great gratitude to all I learnt from Russell, and I was very sorry when his acceptance of a Lordship of Appeal in 1894 put an end to our association. He had a real genius for advocacy, seizing on the essential point in a case and insisting on his client's view of it with immense force and skill. There were, at about that time, many distinguished men at the Bar — Moulton perhaps the first for sheer intellect; Finlay with that steel-like vigour, greatest in reply: Clarke, with his beautifully polished style; Carson, another Irishman whose flashes of eloquence for the time carried all before them; and many others. But to my mind Russell was the greatest of them all.

When I left Russell I set up for myself in chambers in Paper Buildings. By this time I was getting into a little work at the Parliamentary Bar, which was much more remunerative than anything that had come to me at the Common Law. I also had one or two peerage cases which I found very interesting, an occasional patent action, and other odds and ends.

Meanwhile, my father's second administration had come to an end with the General Election of 1892. It had been largely concerned with Foreign Affairs. Most of the actual questions of that time have ceased to have much interest for us. But some of the principles by which Lord Salisbury was guided are still important. Thus, he was against anything like an ordinary treaty alliance on the ground that such a treaty was incompatible with our democracy, and that in no case could a promise be given even of diplomatic assistance against a named Power. But he was ready to co-operate with other Powers 'in the maintenance of the *status quo*',[1] and in 1887 he had given assurances to Germany and Italy in that sense. So, too, he rejected isolation because it was inconsistent with the safety of the Empire and because of our duty as part of the community of Nations.[2] Thus, on April 11th, 1888, he said, in a speech at Carnarvon:[3] 'We must recognize that the members of every community have duties towards each other. We are part of what has been well called the Federation of Mankind. We belong to a great community of nations and we have no right to shrink from the duties which the community impose on us'; and he went on scornfully to repudiate the 'spirit of haughty and sullen isolation'.[4] The myth that Lord Salisbury was ever in favour of 'splendid isolation' seems to have no better foundation than a complete misunderstanding of a phrase torn from its context.[5]

In 1894 we moved into a house in Manchester Square which my father took for us. About the same time I changed from the Northern to the South-Eastern Circuit, which meant that I attended the Assizes and Quarter Sessions in Hertfordshire and Essex — but I never made much of it — indeed, there was not much to make. Before the Parliamentary Committees I was more successful. In many ways it was pleasant work. A great deal of it consisted in argumentative contests with expert witnesses who for the most part frankly regarded themselves as advocates. They were sworn as witnesses and I doubt not were rigidly truthful, when they were giving evidence as to facts. But they urged arguments as well, and since arguments deal with opinions, many experts would maintain dialectical positions irrespective of their personal judgement. Evidently there was a good deal to be said against such a system, though it did not affect the Bar since they are not supposed or indeed entitled to put forward

[1] The *Life*, vol. IV, pp. 21-25.
[2] ibid., vol. IV, p. 24.
[3] ibid., p. 90.
[4] cf. his speech on November 9th, 1897, in which he looked forward to an 'international constitution' which should give a long spell of continued peace.
[5] The *Life*, vol. IV, p. 85.

their own views and must confine themselves to the presentation of the case of their clients. Some of the experts were men of great ability and readiness of speech. The theories on which they relied were therefore always at least plausible and used with great skill in these controversies on oath. One instance may be given. There was a long-continued battle between the London Water Authorities and the County of Hertford, the bone of contention being whether by the very heavy pumping in and near London, the water supplies of Hertfordshire were depleted. London maintained that the water it consumed would otherwise have found its way into the sea. Hertfordshire, through many sessions, fought — ultimately with success — to shew that every gallon taken from the wells under London north of the Thames diminished by so much the rivers of Hertfordshire. It was a most interesting argument.

The interests in Private Bills were large and money was freely spent so that not only the experts but the lawyers — counsel, solicitors and agents alike — included many men of remarkable ability. When I was practising, Samuel Pope was the leader of the Bar, his chief competitors being Balfour Browne, Pember, Littler and others. Pope was a remarkable man with great natural eloquence and acuteness. He had become very fat and disinclined for exertion so that his knowledge of the details of his case was usually slight. A member of the Bar told me once that when he was with Pope in a railway case, he met Pope in the Committee room a short time before the Committee sat and tried to give his leader some account of what the case was about. But Pope waved him aside saying: 'Never mind! I'll give them some of my fluffery!' He then examined the maps that adorned the walls of the room, as is customary, and began: 'My lords, this is a Bill to make a little railway while there is still time', and then expatiated on the growth of the neighbourhood and other similar topics!

One of the defects of Parliamentary work was that, since the Bar was not numerous, some of them had many cases going on at the same time and would run from one to another, their despairing clients pursuing them and clamouring for their presence elsewhere. This did not affect Pope. It was physically almost impossible for him to move — he was always allowed to speak sitting down — and so once he had reached a Committee he would sit there until it adjourned for the day.

In 1896 took place the Jameson Raid, a harebrained and irresponsible enterprise which never had a chance of success. The leaders were arrested and a number of them sent to England where they were tried before Lord Russell (who had become Chief Justice) and two other judges. They were convicted and sent to prison. In the following session, the House of Commons appointed a select Committee to investigate the subject and particularly how far the Colonial Minister, Mr. Joseph Chamberlain and others, were mixed up in the Raid. I appeared as counsel for Dr. Rutherfoord Harris, one of the followers of Cecil Rhodes, who enjoyed an exceedingly doubtful reputation in South Africa. My instructions were to protect Harris but not at the cost of trying to throw blame on others. There was no counsel for the prosecution, certain members of the Committee undertaking, more or less, to act as such. But as always happens in these circumstances, they had no one to get up the case for them. The result was that the Committee discovered nothing. Probably there was nothing to discover. But if there had been, they certainly would not have discovered it. Whenever they seemed to be getting near a point which we regarded with anxiety, they always drifted away from it because no doubt they did not know of its existence. A Select Committee of that kind is, I believe, almost the worst possible instrument for clearing up questions of personal responsibility. I sat on the other side of the table, as a member of the Committee appointed to investigate the Marconi allegations and found it even worse than the South African Committee.

Two years later, the Boer War broke out and lasted till 1902. It ought never to have taken place. The issues involved might have been settled but for the characteristics of some of the persons involved. No doubt President Kruger was chiefly to blame and it is far from being a mere technicality that it was he that declared war. But there was no international tribunal to which the controversies could have been referred and when negotiations broke down, war was inevitable.

War had always been hateful to my father. I have heard him say that, though as things stood he regarded it as a necessary evil, yet he could see in principle no satisfactory defence of it. It was therefore a tragedy that at the end of his life he should have been responsible for the most serious war in which this country had been engaged since the Indian Mutiny. To those who have been through the horrors of the World Wars the casualties of the Boer struggle seem almost insignificant. But when they took place, they were far from insignificant to Lord Salisbury. Coupled with the deaths of the Queen, and his wife, which both occurred before the end of the war, they undoubtedly shortened his life. He resigned office in 1902, as soon as the war was over, and died in 1903.

He was succeeded as Prime Minister by his nephew, Mr. Arthur Balfour, and almost immediately the first rumblings of the Tariff Reform controversy were heard. In its inception Tariff Reform was an Imperial Policy. Mr. Chamberlain regarded the consolidation of the Empire as of supreme importance and believed that it might be assisted by giving to its component parts a material interest in unity. He therefore proposed to erect a wall of customs duties higher against foreign imports than against those coming from our Dominions who would therefore have what came to be called Preference. This led him and his friends on to the advocacy of a general protective system, since otherwise his policy might have appeared to be the imposition of a tax on the British consumers for the benefit of the Colonial producers. To this Tariff Reform policy a section of the Cabinet and of the Party were strongly opposed, as were almost the whole of the

Opposition. Balfour tried his best to prevent a split in his Party. His plan of action was first to minimize the economic importance of moderate Protection — as to which I believe he was right — and then to devise somewhat nebulous formulae which he required the whole Party to accept. The plan was a complete failure. No one knew how far the formulae went. The Protectionists and the Free Traders were alike suspicious. But since the Protectionists were the largest in numbers, it very soon became clear that they would control the Party machine. Mr. Chamberlain resigned in order to free his hands from Balfourian subtleties, and shortly afterwards the Duke of Devonshire also resigned because, as he had once said on an earlier occasion, he became convinced that he and the Prime Minister did not mean the same thing. Other members of the Government also resigned and very soon the Unionist Free Traders organized their opposition to the policy. My brother Hugh was one of their leaders in the House of Commons and I followed him. As usually happens in such cases, the split widened. Devonshire was the outstanding figure on our side and became the President of the Unionist Free Trade organization.

In that capacity I frequently met him. He was not in the ordinary sense a very clever man. Balfour and Chamberlain were far more brilliant. But he had to a degree which neither of them ever attained, the faculty of inspiring confidence. One had merely to listen to one of his speeches to see why. He was evidently trying rather laboriously to explain what he meant. There were no fireworks. He just sought — and did not easily find — words to express his thought. From that purpose nothing turned him. And it was the same in private conversation. I remember seeing him on some business or other in the office of the Unionist Free Trade organization. He sat in the corner of the room so close up against the wall that, as he talked, the back of his head with every motion struck against the ornamental mouldings of the wall. It must have been very uncomfortable, if not painful. But he never changed the place of his chair.

His whole mind was concentrated on the question we were discussing.

For two years the controversy went on and at the General Election in January 1906, Tariff Reform was heavily defeated. Balfour's plan could never have succeeded. Both sides of it were unsound. It was bad to have a political creed the meaning of which was intentionally obscure. The trumpet was giving an uncertain sound, with the well-known result. It was still worse to make such a formula the test of Party orthodoxy and require everyone to profess acceptance of what no two of them understood in the same sense. The result was a defeat at the Polls from which the Conservative Party did not recover till the World War. No doubt the position was difficult. But if Balfour had made up his mind as to the policy to be pursued, had stated it in the plainest and least equivocal words possible and had insisted that it should not, for the time being, be made an essential part of the Party creed, the worst of the storm might have been avoided. In any case it was madness to go on for two years with a considerable part of the ablest of his followers becoming more and more indignant with the attacks made by the protectionists on those who were only standing by their old faith. Clearly, the moment both Chamberlain and Devonshire resigned, Balfour should have asked for a Dissolution.

Though this incident is outside the general purport of this book, I have dealt with it fairly fully because it was the first thing that loosened my adherence to Party Conservatism. But for the time being I did nothing more. I was President of the Conservative Association in Marylebone and remained so, not taking any great part in the Fiscal agitation. The most spectacular thing I did was to go down to Birmingham to be one of the Platform at a meeting addressed by Mr. Winston Churchill and my brother. Meanwhile, I had become busier at the Bar, especially in the Committee rooms where I was beginning to make a fair income. In 1894 we had moved into a larger house in Manchester Square and in 1904 we migrated to Grove End Road — a charming house with a large garden. In 1900 I had taken silk. In the same year I built myself a small house on Ashdown Forest looking towards the South Downs.

In the summer of 1905, I was briefed to go out to a big arbitration in Singapore for which I was given a large fee on the terms that I should pay my own expenses. The arbitration was to settle the price to be given by the Singapore Government to the Dock Company for their property, and I was for the Company. My wife and her friend, Miss Violet Dickinson, came with me, and the Arbitrators were Lord St. Aldwyn and two colleagues. My opponent was Mr. Balfour Browne. We went by Canada crossing from Quebec to Vancouver. Thence we crossed the Pacific to Yokohama, a cold, uninteresting voyage though not so stormy as, I believe, it usually is. We arrived in Japan at the close of the Russo-Japanese war. We travelled up to Tokio in the train with Prince Ito, who was responsible for the newly-signed Treaty of Portsmouth which was very unpopular. Indeed, there had been riots in Tokio and police stations had been burnt down. I remember that when we got out at Tokio I was following Ito rather closely and an English friend pulled me back saying that it was quite likely that Ito would be assassinated. Nothing happened in fact; but four years later Ito was assassinated by a Korean patriot at Kharbin.

We stayed a fortnight mainly at Tokio and Kioto. Sir Claude Macdonald was our Ambassador and, having had a great admiration for my father, treated us with the utmost kindness. He arranged for me to see the Mikado — an uninteresting interview, the most noticeable thing being that the Mikado's clothes fitted even worse than my own, the explanation given me being that his person was so sacred that he could not be measured! The Japanese whom I met were all charming — particularly the women — but not very interesting. We did the usual things, and nothing remarkable happened to us except a slight earthquake.

Thence I went on by myself to Shanghai, Hong Kong and Singapore — where I was joined by my wife a fortnight later.

By that time all those engaged in the Arbitration were rather exhausted, partly because we had sat from 10.0 till 4.0 every day, with half an hour off for lunch, exactly as if we had been in England. The climate of Singapore is not bad, but it is very hot and steamy so that we were continually in a profuse perspiration. By the time my wife arrived, the evidence was finished and the final stages of the Arbitration were adjourned to London. In the result, the Company got an award with which they were satisfied.

At Singapore we had heard much of the arrogance of the Germans. Nevertheless we and the Arbitrators went home in a German vessel called the *Ziethen* where we were very courteously treated, especially by the Captain — a charming man. We went in her as far as Suez, (stopping at Penang, Colombo and Aden on the way). From Suez we went on to Cairo. Lord Cromer was still Agent-General and his second wife was an old friend of ours. They very kindly asked us to stay at the Agency and we were there for a short time seeing a great deal of my brother Edward, who was then in the Egyptian Civil Service. After a few days we went home by P. & O., finding Lord and Lady Curzon on board on their way back from his Vice-Royalty in India — he very bitter about what he conceived to have been his ill-treatment by the Government.

My wife left me at Marseilles, going to see her sister on the Riviera, and I went on alone to London. When I arrived I found Parliament on the brink of Dissolution and a great local controversy as to the candidate for East Marylebone. The sitting member — a highly respectable Conservative and a convinced though moderate Tariff Reformer — was retiring, and the local aspirants for the seat were thought unsuitable. *Faute de mieux*, they turned to me, and I stood and was elected as a Conservative — my fiscal views being condoned.

The Conservative Government had resigned before the election, believing that the Liberal Party were so much divided that it was doubtful if they could form a tolerable Government. As a matter of fact, though there were difficult negotiations, Sir Henry Campbell Bannerman became Premier of a strong Administration. The General Election gave him a very large majority, and the Opposition was reduced to less than 200.

It was as one of this numerically feeble Opposition that I took my seat facing 'serried ranks' of truculent Ministerialists back from an overwhelming electoral triumph. We had not even a Leader, since Balfour had lost his seat in Manchester and it took some weeks before a refuge was found for him in the City of London.

My own position was complicated. On the most important issue at the Election I agreed much more with the Liberal Government than the Conservative Opposition. On the other hand, on the principal Government measures, such as their Education Bill, the Disestablishment of the Welsh Church, their scheme of Land Taxation, and to a lesser degree their Irish Councils Bill, I was decidedly against them. On other matters, though I did not feel strongly, I was quite ready to vote for the Party view. Foreign Affairs were not a Party question. Generally speaking, the Opposition supported Sir Edward Grey's foreign policy. I did very strongly and used to say to my Unionist Free Trade friends — of whom there were a sprinkling — that I agreed more with Grey than with anyone else in the House.

The Opposition continued to be very weak. A good many even of those who had accepted Tariff Reform were angry at the way in which it had been pushed in the country, and at the landslide for which they held Mr. Chamberlain responsible. Even in the absence of Balfour they would not accept him as Leader, and when Balfour returned the subtleties of his Parliamentary methods were not appreciated by the rampant Radicals. The climax came when, on a motion moved from the Government side approving Free Trade, Balfour, instead of directly opposing it, resorted to Parliamentary dialectics. It was then that the Prime Minister, still smarting under the contemptuous treatment he had endured in the previous Parliament, uttered his celebrated phrase, 'Enough of this foolery!' and amidst the frantic cheers of his followers moved the Closure. It was a great moment for him, and yet within a very few weeks Balfour, by his charm and his Parliamentary skill, had completely re-established his personal position.

Meanwhile, I was very assiduous in my attendance, and since there were so few on our side who cared to speak I was 'called' almost every time I rose. The work was very attractive to me and, with one or two friends of whom George Bowles, the son of the journalist — universally known as Tommy Bowles — was the chief, we carried on a not ineffective guerilla warfare. Nothing is less interesting than the details of past Parliamentary discussions, and I shall not enlarge on them, exciting as they sometimes were at the time. Besides, the Fiscal controversy dominated the political situation. The Tariff Reform League had been formed with large funds coming mainly from those who hoped to profit by a Protectionist policy. There was, besides, a kind of political secret society called the Confederates. One of its objects was to stir up trouble for Unionist Free Traders in their Constituencies — part of the plan, perhaps borrowed from Birmingham Municipal politics, for driving out of public life all Conservatives who refused to accept Tariff Reform. George Bowles and I were soon attacked. Bowles was given no quarter. But I was treated with more consideration. Various Tariff missionaries made efforts to convert me. Mr. Chamberlain himself made some advances. Mr. Harry Chaplin, an old-time Protectionist, asked me to dine alone with him at the Marlborough Club. It was a charming dinner. For most of the time we talked about non-controversial topics, including the merits of the Club's wine. He was on a diet, but insisted on ordering for me port, which had been forbidden to him. The procedure was delightful. He sent for some particular vintage. When it came he said that he would taste it to see that it was all right. So he had a glass and promptly rejected the wine. Another sample followed and he had another glass. In this way he obeyed his doctors in principle, but in practice was not deprived of his usual refreshment. Our fiscal conversation was to me much less attractive and led to no result. The Chief Whip, Sir Alexander Acland Hood, also tried his hand, as one who had been a Free Trader and who had found Tariff salvation. Perhaps the kindest effort was made by Bonar Law, always a good friend to me, who, hearing that there was some chance of a compromise with me, travelled down from Scotland to see me. I was very sorry not to be able to meet him. Perhaps if the Tariff campaign had not been so bitterly conducted some arrangements could have been made. But it is disagreeable to yield to threats and to make terms for oneself which would not be extended to others.

My objection to Tariff Reform was not chiefly on economic grounds. The theoretical case for Protection did not seem to me very convincing and for some reason the disputants on both sides fought shy of anything like a scientific examination of what had been its practical results. Could commercial prosperity be definitely traced to Protection or Free Trade? The evidence was curiously meagre and unsatisfactory. Countries had flourished and suffered under both systems. Slumps and Booms occurred irrespective of Fiscal policy. Perhaps it was not economically as important as both sides alleged. But the political and imperial case against Tariff Reform seemed — and still seems — to me much stronger. I do not believe that the policy of Preferences has increased the solidarity of the Empire or is likely to do so. The pecuniary advantage conferred by it is not large, nor does it seriously affect the bulk of the peoples of the Commonwealth. Moreover, self-interest is usually a disruptive rather than a unifying force, particularly when it is combined with idealistic motives like Patriotism. Each section is tempted to believe that in the name of Patriotism they are being asked to allow an undue pecuniary advantage to some other section. How often does one see a bitter family quarrel over just such issues! On the other hand, Preferences have greatly increased the international difficulties of the British Empire. As long as there was complete Free Trade, the jealousy of other countries was mollified. Now there does seem some force in the complaint that it is unfair for one State to exclude even partially all other countries from so large a part of the Earth's surface as that occupied by the British Empire.

Nor are these the only consequences of the adoption of Tariff Reform which seem to me to have been of doubtful advantage. Protection has increased a tendency in our politics which has been growing in importance — a tendency to make our political divisions depend on the possession of wealth. The rich men are almost all on one side. Compare, for instance, the condition of the House of Lords now with what it was fifty years ago. In the crucial division on such a Party measure as the County Franchise Bill in 1884, the Conservative majority in a very full House was no more than fifty. In a House of anything like that magnitude the majority would run nowadays to several hundreds. Not only is the preponderance of regular Conservatives very large but even in the 'Liberal' Party, which in name constitutes the largest part of the Opposition in the Upper House, many of the more wealthy members are almost as reactionary as the Diehard section of the Tories. That is doubtless due to other causes than Protection. Indeed, it would be perhaps more true to say that the triumph of protection was a symptom of a fundamental alteration in the political centre of gravity. There has been an almost revolutionary change in that respect. For something like two centuries the chief political power was gradually absorbed by the landowning class. As Disraeli was fond of pointing out, that was the true meaning of the Revolution of 1688 and the same process continued well into the nineteenth century. For the last half-century or more the Landowners have been progressively ousted by the mercantile magnates, and as the latter have gained power they have become conservative. The City of London, which a hundred years ago was still a Liberal stronghold, is now the impregnable fortress of extreme Conservatism. And as the old Liberal moneyed class are moving to the Right, their place on the Left is being occupied by Labour. Indeed, the two processes are complementary to one another.

In domestic matters the consequences have so far not been serious. At one time it looked as if the drift towards Socialism might develop into a class war with a communistic tinge. But in practice, the Trades Unions have shewn themselves extremely cautious.

In external affairs there is more room for anxiety. It is inevitable that the mercantile class whose training must be to attribute the greatest importance to commercial and financial considerations will bring the same point of view into the direction of external policy. The belief that by Tariffs the Empire can be cemented together is only an example of this attitude. In Foreign Affairs there seems to me signs of the same trend.

Whether I was right or not in my fears as to the direction which Tariff Reform would give to our policy, the belief that it would, in that sense, lower the standards of our public life was the foundation of my opposition to it — and my feeling on the subject was not lessened by the methods employed to push it forward. At one time, indeed, I thought of making some kind of terms with the Liberals and even wrote to Mr. Asquith on the subject. But nothing came of it.

By entering Parliament I had abandoned my practice in the Committee Rooms. Nor did I get any substantial increase of my other law work; so that I became more and more absorbed in the House of Commons. Then came the struggle over the constitutional position of the Second Chamber. It had been long threatening and when, after rejecting most of the important Liberal measures, it was decided to throw out the land taxes of Mr. Lloyd George, the storm burst. The ground taken by the Conservative leaders could not have been weaker. The land taxes seemed to me unsound economics and financially foolish. But in themselves, and apart from 'principle', they were not serious. For the House of Lords to challenge a fight with the House of Commons on a budget question and one which affected the property of very many Peers seemed to me extremely rash. I went to see Balfour and urged this view as strongly as I could — without effect. Parliament was dissolved. Both my seat and that of George Bowles were threatened by the Tariff Reformers. The position had become intolerable. We were, I suppose, two of the most active members of the Opposition. We had fought side by side with our Tory colleagues in all other Parliamentary contests. And yet, because we were not ready on the Fiscal question to change our views, we were continually exposed to the most harassing of all opposition, that from one's own political friends. I decided, therefore, to accept an invitation to stand for Blackburn as a Unionist Free Trader, with George Bowles as my colleague. At the last moment the Marylebone Tariff Reformers, or some of them, relented and begged me to stand again. But no offer was made to Bowles and I obviously could not desert him. So we both went down to Blackburn and, after a very lively contest, were heavily defeated by Philip Snowden and Sir Thomas Barclay.

The Liberals came back with a large majority, and produced their scheme for the reform of the House of Lords, which that body naturally rejected. There was another election, and this time I stood for the Wisbech division of Cambridgeshire against Neil Primrose. Under the pressure of the Constitutional crisis, Tariff Reform retired to the background, but I was nevertheless defeated. The Liberal majority in the House was not diminished and the Parliament Bill was again brought in. The Conservative Leaders lost their nerve and, under threat of a wholesale creation of Peers, they advised the acceptance of the Bill. Why the Conservative Leaders should have provoked this battle and then, when it had produced its inevitable result, should have run away, passes my comprehension. A good deal was said about not destroying the Second Chamber. But in fact it has been just as efficiently destroyed as it would have been by being swamped, and has, besides, lost all belief in itself. Not one third of its members ever attend its debates — generally much less. Certainly if it ever does have to face a revolutionary Government of the Left, its assistance will be valueless.

I was now out of Parliament and so took little part in the fight over the Parliament Bill. I joined an organization called the Halsbury Club, led by the undaunted ex-Lord Chancellor. There was one dinner at which he made the principal speech. He traced all our troubles first to the Reform Bill of '32, and then, casting further back, to the Revolution of 1688, and finally to the destruction of the Privy Council by Henry VII!

Meanwhile, the Government set about passing Home Rule and Welsh Disestablishment under the new procedure. At the same time Mr. Lloyd George introduced his Contributory Pensions scheme. A vacancy unexpectedly occurred in the Hitchin Division of Hertfordshire, and I was asked to stand. There were some misgivings among the Tariff Reformers, but Tariff Reform was no longer in the front rank of political questions. Mr. Chamberlain's health had given way and Mr. Balfour had resigned from the Leadership of the Conservative Party. He was succeeded by Mr. Bonar Law — a compromise between the supporters of Mr. Walter Long and Mr. Austen Chamberlain. He was intellectually superior to both of them but without much political experience. He was a brilliant speaker of a rather unusual kind — excelling in striking epigrammatic phrases rather than in elaborate argument or emotional appeal. For me, the choice was fortunate. Bonar Law believed that in the early days of his political life I had warmly praised him to Balfour. He was deeply grateful to me for having done so at a time when, as a *novus homo*, he conceived there was much prejudice against him in Conservative circles. I had no recollection of the incident, though it may very well have happened. Anyhow, he always stood by me and, as his Tariff Reform orthodoxy was unimpeachable, that was a very great help.

I was elected for Hitchin, and was lucky in being able to repel an attack by Mr. Lloyd George about my attitude at

Hitchin to the Insurance Bill, then the chief measure before Parliament. That gave me a certain position in my Party and when the so-called Marconi scandal took place, I was put on the Select Committee appointed to investigate it. The Committee was nominated by the Party Whips in proportion to the numbers of the Parties in Parliament, and after a long enquiry, rejected, by a strictly Party vote, all the allegations against members of the Government for having improperly dealt in Marconi shares. A minority Report, for which only the Conservative members voted, while not making any charges of corruption, animadverted strongly on what was considered the grave want of discretion shewn by the Ministers impugned. I had a good deal to do with the drafting of the minority Report. The whole incident confirmed me in the view that, for what was in the nature of a judicial inquiry, no tribunal could be worse than a Select Committee of the House of Commons.

This was by no means the only cause of political disquiet. There was the Suffrage movement. On that question I had been always in favour of giving the vote to women on the same terms as men. That had been my father's opinion and he had collaborated with the Radical, John Stuart Mill, in their support. In the same way, in following his lead I found myself voting with Mr. Keir Hardie. That was all right. But our position was complicated by the action of the so-called 'militant suffragettes', who, under the leadership of Mrs. Pankhurst and others, were convinced that their cause would never be fairly considered by the House of Commons unless the Members were compelled to give it attention by violent and illegal action outside. This led to considerable disorder and ill-feeling. None of the constitutional supporters of the suffrage could possibly accept that doctrine and we therefore collaborated with Mrs. Fawcett, who had long been the leader of the law-abiding wing of the Suffragists. Unfortunately, there was just sufficient truth in the Suffragette position to give them a certain measure of Parliamentary success. What would have been the ultimate result it is difficult to say. Before anything had been definitely achieved, the war of 1914 broke out. All the women of both sections threw themselves vigorously into war service and Mr. Lloyd George, who had always been a suffragist, made that the not very logical but entirely convincing reason for giving them the vote when peace came.

Besides the Suffrage controversy, there was a great railway strike and there was still great bitterness over the outcome of the Constitutional struggle. Above all there was a vehement agitation in Ulster against the Home Rule Bill, with threats and counter-threats of rebellion and armed repression. In Europe for a long time past there had been forming two hostile groups, Germany, Austria and Italy on the one side; France, Russia and, with some ambiguities, the British Empire, on the other. Each group was arming with more and more vigour. From time to time the German Emperor startled the world with violent speeches. The Balkans were in their usual condition of turbulence. The whole situation is described in Lord Grey's *Twenty-Five Years* and many other publications. Possibly if, in 1912, we had succeeded in convincing the German Government that, if Germany attacked France, we should go to her assistance, war might have been avoided. But the Cabinet — and probably their Parliamentary supporters — were not prepared for so drastic a declaration. Accordingly when Lord Haldane went to Berlin in 1912, though he certainly warned the Germans of the danger of the course which they seemed to be contemplating, he did not feel justified in speaking the only kind of language which Germans understand. As an American diplomat once said: 'It is no use telling the Germans anything unless you hit the table at the same time!' That, no doubt, is the principal reason why the recent policy of appeasement failed. It is melancholy that in 1938 we should have committed just the same fault as we did in 1912. As I write, it is still uncertain whether it will have the same result.[1]

No doubt the Germans believed that our domestic diffi-

[1] Unhappily it has.

culties were much graver than they actually were. The kind of language which was being used about political controversies here, particularly about Ireland, might easily have persuaded the Germans that, when it came to the point, we should not be able to fight. When, therefore, the murders took place at Serajevo, they and their very incompetent Austrian allies believed the day had come to which some, at least, of the German army had long looked forward. I must admit that, till the last moment, I was an optimist. Like most people, I had very little idea of what modern war was like. But even with my very imperfect conception of it, I could not think that the statesmen of a highly-civilized Europe would plunge their countries into the 'orgy of lust and cruelty' which such a war must mean. However, I was quite wrong, and all we could do was to secure that the whole force of the country should be utilized to obtain as early a victory as possible.

I was fifty years old when the war broke out and therefore over military age. Accordingly I joined the Red Cross and went to Paris to help to organize what was called the Department of Wounded and Missing. Owing to the vast numbers engaged and the terrible destructiveness of modern weapons, it was constantly unknown whether a soldier reported missing had been killed or captured, wounded or unwounded. Naturally the relations were in the deepest anxiety, and the Department made what enquiries were possible. It was depressing work and did not often produce results. One feature of it was noticeable. We received large numbers of letters. Those from the more educated writers were bare enquiries. But there were also many from people who found writing laborious but yet expressed themselves with a natural and human pathos which was terribly moving. Altogether my work with the Red Cross made me hate war even more bitterly than I had done before.

We began our work at Paris, then we moved to Boulogne and finally to London. Most of our workers were women, one of the chief of them being Gertrude Bell, that most gifted and charming woman. Her energy, vitality and acuteness were extraordinary. But her greatest attraction was her warm-heartedness. She was devoted to her father, Sir Hugh Bell, and to her friends, so that she suffered extremely during the war. Her early death in Mesopotamia was an immense loss to her friends and to her country.

I went on with this work till the first Coalition was formed in the summer of 1915. In that Government I was offered and accepted the position of Under-Secretary for Foreign Affairs, with a Privy Councillorship — an unusual arrangement — made, I fancy, by Bonar Law. My Chief was Sir Edward Grey, who treated me always with the greatest kindness.

The ordinary work of the Foreign Office was at a standstill. Everything was concentrated on negotiations with the Allies and Neutrals about the conduct of the war. A very large part of the work concerned the so-called blockade. It was really much more than a blockade. It was the organization of all sorts of economic and commercial pressure on our enemies. The chief object was to deprive Germany and her allies of all imports essential for carrying on the war. This could be done in two ways. Firstly, by directly intercepting such imports — and for this purpose the Tenth Cruiser Squadron was thrown across the North Sea so as to block all ships going to German ports. But that was not enough. The trade was very soon diverted to the neutral ports of Holland and Scandinavia, consigned to merchants residing in those places and afterwards transmitted to Germany. The neutrals evidently had a right to import goods for their own consumption. How were such goods to be distinguished from goods really going into Germany? At first all sorts of difficulties arose. It was doubtful how far the old principles of blockade applied as defined by international law. Then there were complications about what constituted contraband. Then there were questions as to the right of search. It was impossible to search effectively all the vessels in the North Sea and the right to send them into the nearest British port to be searched was contested. Various devices were employed to get over these difficulties, especially the difficulty of ultimate destination. In Holland we organized a society to which goods were consigned and which undertook that they should not be sent on to Germany. In the Scandinavian countries we had to rely at first on assurances given to us by the native importers, which were not always to be trusted. Similar difficulties about goods consigned to Swiss importers were met by the constitution of a society on the lines of the one in Holland.

None of these devices were perfect, though they were more effective than was believed by our critics. Later in the war we adopted a procedure which was much more watertight though its legality was contested by some of the neutrals. It consisted in rationing the neutrals, as it was called. On this system we worked out by careful comparison of pre-war statistics how much of each commodity had gone to each neutral in time of peace for its own use, and we stopped everything in excess of that amount, whatever was its alleged destination. Then, to get over the difficulty of search, by arrangement with the ship-owners we supervised the cargo taken on board at the port of loading. If it was satisfactory from the belligerent point of view the ship was given a certificate — called a navicert — which passed the ship through the lines of the blockading squadron. If it had no navicert it was taken into a port and searched, involving great delay and loss. These two plans undoubtedly increased the stringency of the 'blockade'. But it is very doubtful whether they could have been safely adopted earlier in the war. Our great diplomatic anxiety was about our relations with the United States. In that country there was a considerable body of opinion which resented any interference with the very large profits made by American interests out of trading with Germany. That was particularly true of cotton and meat-packing. Besides this, there was a very natural jealousy of what was called British 'navalism'. The result was a continuous stream of protests from the Government of the United States, based on what was at least a sustainable view of the rule of international law. Luckily for us, in the American Civil War of

1860-64, the North had to cope with the same kind of difficulties as those we had to face. The Federal Government had declared a blockade of the Atlantic ports of the South. Therefore blockade-runners took their cargoes to Mexican ports from whence they reached the Confederates by land. The American Courts, relying upon what was called the principle of continuous voyage, laid it down that the ultimate destination of the goods was what mattered and the fact that they passed through Mexican territory made no difference. Sheltering ourselves, therefore, under the great authority of American jurists, we day by day tightened our commercial pressure on Germany.

Another method of pressure was to stop German exports. Unless Germany could export she could not get the money to pay for her imports except so far as she had investments or credit in neutral countries which could be utilized for that purpose. Early in the war we succeeded in cutting off German exports, which was technically a simpler matter than the direct arrest of the imports. We further attempted to destroy German credit in North and South America. This we did by 'black-listing' firms suspected of assisting Germany, which then were deprived of the trade of ourselves and our allies. I am not sure how far this plan was of real use, and for some reason which I never followed, it caused great indignation in America. However, we persisted, and when the United States came into the war, I believe they dealt with the 'black listed' firms far more drastically than we had done or could have done. There were many other ancillary devices we employed for strengthening our pressure. One of them arose from the quasi-world monopoly we had in certain goods, the most important of which were bunker coal and jute. Almost all the coaling stations were in our hands and so was the supply of jute, and only those who agreed not to trade with Germany were supplied. Then we controlled all the submarine cables and this enabled us to establish a censorship of messages which dealt with German trade. This also was, in my judgement, of comparatively little value from a blockade point of view and was a very sore point with the Americans.

Apart from these international arrangements, the official organization of the blockade was at first very complicated. It was without any directing chief and was distributed over several Departments such as the Foreign Office, the Admiralty and the Board of Trade, while other offices like the Treasury and the War Office occasionally intervened. There were co-ordinating committees, but in spite of them differences of opinion as to policy occurred which could only be settled by reference to the Cabinet. After one of these, Grey insisted that I should be given Cabinet rank and put in charge of the whole Blockade operation, which Asquith agreed to. I should like to say here how very much I admired Asquith as Prime Minister. He was always ready to see one and to give advice. He understood the point in a moment and gave his opinion clearly and decisively. No doubt he was too apt to treat himself as a Judge in Cabinet, listening to both sides and then deciding, instead of himself initiating policy. But to a junior colleague like myself he was delightful; considerate, rapid and unshrinkingly loyal under all circumstances. The Grey proposal was carried out, and gradually a large Blockade Department came into existence which worked smoothly and efficiently. In spite of what was sometimes said outside, my relations with the Lords of the Admiralty were always excellent. I was very pleased to receive letters and other communications from the chief of the Admiralty Trade Department and others, warmly approving of the Blockade operations.

Sir Edward Grey was often attacked for not being sufficiently drastic in blockade matters, and I came in for a certain amount of similar criticism, mainly from people who were only acquainted with one aspect of the question. These critics forgot that a serious quarrel with the United States might have been fatal to us. Had their Government pressed strongly the American view of belligerent naval rights, our blockade would have been gravely hampered.

Moreover, we drew considerable war supplies from America, the loss of which would have been a great and perhaps fatal handicap to us. To a lesser degree the same was true of Sweden which had a monopoly of the iron ore which made the best steel necessary for ball-bearings and other vital parts of war machinery. And there, the Court and the official classes were pro-German, though the Popular Party under Branting were pro-Entente. Sir Edward Grey was very conscious of these difficulties and was, besides, extremely keen to remain on friendly terms with America so that we might have her support when we made peace. He was therefore anxious to keep within the limits of our rights under International law, an anxiety which I shared. There were two ways in which our blockade policy might have failed. We might have allowed it to become ineffective. This we never did. On the contrary, it was far more effective than any previous economic warfare had ever been and undoubtedly played a great part in the final victory. Or we might have tried to ride roughshod over neutral rights — as we were constantly urged to do — and have thereby lost the support of a large part of international public opinion — an asset of incalculable value — or even driven some of the neutrals into the arms of our enemies.

In September 1916, as I relate in the next chapter, I took my first step in the advocacy of the League of Nations. A month or two later, the Asquith Government came to an end and the second Coalition, under Mr. Lloyd George, was formed. I have nothing to add to the many pages that have been written about that event except to record the profound personal relief it was to Grey to leave office. He never liked office. All the personal questions and compromises inevitable in party Government were very distasteful to him. He had no ambition. He loathed war and his health and, particularly, his eyesight, were getting worse and worse. On the day that the Liberal resignations were settled, he asked me whether I thought it was wrong of him to be glad to go! I replied suitably, suggesting that perhaps I ought to resign as well, believing, as I did, that the attacks made on him and on Asquith were undeserved. But he thought there was no reason for me to do that. Throughout the crisis I had been acting with Austen Chamberlain, Walter Long and Edward Carson. We therefore went together to see Mr. Lloyd George and explained that we were not anxious to go on in office and if he preferred to do without us we would readily stand aside. He was good enough to say that he valued our co-operation, and we all agreed to go on. I remained in my previous position, Balfour taking the place of Grey to the great indignation of the Northcliffe press. The new Government had a kind of double Cabinet — a large one, of which some twenty-five, including me, were members, which seldom met — and a small War Cabinet of five or six which met almost every day. The Foreign Secretary was not technically a member of the War Cabinet but he generally attended it and when he was away I did. It was in many respects a very useful body. To it were summoned not only the Ministers concerned but any official or other person whose advice on some special question was desired. The result was that the room was commonly full to overflowing and, since it often happened that the agenda was not strictly followed, the discussions ranged over a large number of topics. Sometimes an official summoned for one item in the agenda was kept waiting outside the Cabinet room for a long time and then, perhaps, was told that his business could not be taken till the following day. Something like this happened to a Minister waiting to report on a mission to Russia, who deeply resented being kept 'on the mat' as he put it.

It certainly was a method of work which consumed a great deal of time. But it gave life and vigour to the administration which were of great importance to the war. On the whole I believe it would have worked better if the personnel had been confined, generally speaking, to Ministers. Officials, and especially most officers of the fighting forces, who were not trained to express themselves easily in speech, were sometimes at a great disadvantage as, for instance, in the case of men like Sir William Robertson, Lord Haig and Lord Jellicoe. Sir Henry Wilson was a marked exception. He could hold his own with any Parliamentarian.

At the end of 1916 a Ministry of Blockade was created and I became its first Minister. As I retained my position in the Foreign Office, this made no difference in my work. In January 1917 I helped to draft the statement of the War Aims of the Entente Powers which included, at the suggestion of the French, the liberation of the people of Czechoslovakia. The spring of that year was the real crisis of the war. The submarine pressure had become very dangerous to us, the German naval authorities believing that within six months we should be forced to make peace if it was pressed without reserve, which was done. That brought the Americans into the war and almost at the same time the Russians went out of it. The actual fighting on the Western Front was indecisive. Then came the great effort of the Germans in 1918 which did not ultimately succeed, the arrival of the American troops and the series of German defeats at the end of the summer culminating in the breaking of their home front as the result of the combination of defeat and blockade.

In the early part of 1918 I had become Assistant Secretary of State for Foreign Affairs, and handed over the Blockade to Leverton Harris. He was a charming man of great ability, but the strain of the war was too much for him and when a perfectly unjust and venomous attack was made upon him in the Press he resigned his office and died a few months later.

Then at last, in November, came the Armistice and the end of the War.

CHAPTER II

THE MAKING OF THE LEAGUE

(1) EARLIER EFFORTS

HALF way through the World War, in the autumn of 1916, I submitted a memorandum to the British Cabinet in which, after calling attention to the terrible slaughter and destruction already caused by the fighting, I set out the outline of a plan for preventing its recurrence.

The actual proposal only contained three clauses. By the first, the territorial provisions of the post-war treaty were only to last five years. At the end of that time a fresh conference was to be called at which a more final settlement might be possible. This suggestion did not become part of the Covenant of the League, though a proposal for something like it has recently been revived. The other two clauses proceeded on the conception that the great thing was to secure an interval for public discussion between the occurrence of a serious international dispute and the outbreak of war. That was no doubt a reminiscence of the desperate attempts made by Sir Edward Grey in 1914 to induce Austria to agree to refer her dispute with Serbia to an international Conference. Many have held, including Sir Edward himself, that if that could have been done war might have been avoided. Accordingly from this earliest British germ of the Covenant to its final draft the principle was always included that international disputants should be forbidden to resort to war until all other means of settling the dispute had been tried. As appears from the document itself, which will be found in Appendix I, it was felt that the thing to aim at was the prevention of war, leaving the remedy of grievances to be dealt with by negotiation, arbitration or international conference. In order to secure that, sanctions against an aggressor were regarded as essential, though in this document reliance was placed on economic rather than on military measures.

Fundamentally there was nothing very new in these proposals. From the earliest times reasonable men have protested against the folly and cruelty of war. At intervals these protests have resulted in proposals for the substitution of some organized international procedure to take the place of war in the settlement of international disputes. So long as the Roman Empire lasted as the effective government of the civilized world, disputes between equally sovereign Western States scarcely existed. They were all included in the Pax Romana and, as has often been pointed out, the conception of a single world authority was regarded for many centuries as obviously right and indeed essential. Long after it had ceased to be a veritable instrument of world government, the Holy Roman Empire filled the imagination of men quite as vividly as the idea of the independent sovereignty and equality of States does now. The Empire declined and fell and an attempt was made to stretch the powers of the Catholic Church so as to prolong in some degree the political control of Rome. The plan failed, nor is it necessary here to examine into the causes of its failure. The point is that down to the Reformation there was a system of international control and the settlement of international disputes, with its sanctions of interdict and excommunication, imperfect no doubt but still a witness to the universal conviction that some method of disposing of international disputes otherwise than by haphazard slaughter and destruction, was necessary.

With the Reformation the international position of the Papacy even in Europe was necessarily modified. Less and less did it continue to be the practice of the Vatican to express opinions or, as it would now be called, to take sides in international disputes.[1] The Holy Roman empire was little more than a name; its ecclesiastical counterpart had ceased to attempt the enforcement of peace and Europe was left

[1] This was written before the recent action of Pius XII.

without any international authority to guide or control its nations. To many people this seemed an intolerable condition of affairs. They instinctively rejected the view that the moral law had no bearing on the action of nations as such; and they felt that international chaos could only lead to the destruction of western civilization. The horrors of the Thirty Years' War served to confirm this apprehension. Accordingly when, in 1625, after the war had already lasted seven years, Grotius published his great work *De Jure Belli et Pacis*, it was hailed with general acceptance. For he taught that the relations between nations were and ought to be governed by the principles of International Law, which fundamentally rested on the propositions that all States were sovereign and independent, and all had equal rights however much they might differ in power. It was on the basis of this that subsequent writers on International Law built up the present structure. It was never displaced and though the practice of nations fell far short of its precepts, there was, till recently, no serious dispute as to the existence and moral authority of such precepts. True, there have been many who have denied that any international law properly so-called exists, since there is no means of enforcing it. But that is largely a question of words. In any case here were a number of principles and regulations which had been either formally agreed upon or generally accepted by the whole or almost the whole of the civilized nations of the world.

That was a great step forward, but it was not enough. On this point I cannot do better than quote the Introduction to the Final Report of the very authoritative Committee which sat under the late Lord Phillimore's chairmanship in 1918.[1]

'International anarchy was not checked, and the protest against it became more vocal with each successive epidemic of war. The Thirty Years' War, the wars of Louis XIV, and

---

[1] Quoted in Wilson's *Origins of the League Covenant*. The Committee consisted of Lord Phillimore (Chairman), Professor Pollard, Sir Julian Corbett, Mr. Holland Rose, Sir Eyre Crowe, Sir William Tyrrell and Sir Cecil Hurst.

those of the Revolutionary and Napoleonic period were all accompanied or followed by more or less academic projects for establishing perpetual peace, all of which, in greater or less degree, looked back to the mediaeval system. In spite of the wholly changed condition which the development of the national State had set up, they were planned on the old foundations and were dismissed by practical statesmen as dreams that ignored the fundamental factors of the problem.

'All these schemes were, in fact, the work of political philosophers. Even the "Grand Design" of Sully's memoirs cannot be regarded as an exception. Though the memoirs sought to attribute it to Queen Elizabeth and Henry IV, it is known that the negotiations the memoirs profess to describe never took place. Recent research has shewn the whole story to be apocryphal. It is even doubtful whether the detailed exposition of the "Design" was the work of Sully at all, and not that of the Abbé, who edited the later volumes of the memoirs. They were not issued until twenty years after the fallen minister's death, and bear internal evidence of having been composed after the outbreak of the Thirty Years' War. Even if the germ of the "Design", which appeared in the earlier volumes, can be attributed to Sully, it was the work of his disappointed old age, and can be placed no higher than the plan for perpetual peace which Napoleon expounded to Las Cases at St. Helena as having been the key of his whole policy.

'The latest of the series of schemes which Sully's memoirs inaugurated was the plan for a "confederation " of Europe by means of a congress which the Abbé de St. Pierre brought forward during the negotiation of the Peace of Utrecht in 1715. Political philosophers were inclined to regard it with approval: and the congresses of Brunswick (1712 — 1722), Cambrai (1724) and Soissons (1729), illustrate the hold which the idea obtained upon the minds of practical men. But they also illustrate the difficulty of giving practical application to the Abbé's proposal that all differences between the contracting parties should be "settled by arbitration or juridical decision". Statesmen were obsessed by the idea of a balance of power as the only means for mitigating or preventing war; and their attitude towards the Abbé's scheme is sufficiently marked by Cardinal Fleury's comment: "You have forgotten, Sir, the preliminary condition. You must begin by sending a troop of missionaries to prepare the hearts and minds of the contracting sovereigns".

'The Cardinal's criticism touched a fundamental weakness in these early projects. Since the European system had become a collection of sovereign national States, the problem was to find a bond of union, which would restore the conception of a European family, while preserving the individuality of the State. The Abbé's plan was really to expand the constitution of the Holy Roman Empire so as to include the whole of Europe, with the Emperor's place taken by a rota of sovereigns; and Leibnitz' main criticisms of the scheme were that it deposed the Emperor, and, unlike the Empire, provided no appeal from subjects against their sovereigns. The possibility of a conflict of interests between princes and peoples was obscured, but not removed, by the Abbé's curious phrase about a European "republic" consisting of sovereigns. Few monarchs had yet divested their minds of the feudal conception that the State was the private property of the prince. A confederation could therefore only take the form of a confederation of princes, not of peoples, and the Abbé even recommended his scheme on the ground that it would strengthen the power of princes, inasmuch as it would guarantee them not only against foreign invasion, but also against rebellions of their subjects.

'It is not possible, however, to prove that democracy, had it existed and exercised sovereign rights in the first half of the eighteenth century, would have been less tenacious of them than were princes; and we must rest content with the historical fact that the proprietary notion of the State did give the sovereign a personal interest in the extension of his sovereignty which acted as a deterrent to all schemes for preventing it. Nor can it be doubted that acquisitiveness exerts a greater influence upon the individual than upon the community; and the examples of the United Netherlands, Switzerland, and Poland created the presumption that less autocratic forms of government were, either from principle or from weakness, more pacific than monarchies like those of

Louis XIV, Peter the Great, Charles XII, Frederick the Great, Joseph II, and Catherine the Great.

'The ideas of this period showed little development until the democratic movement of thought began to infuse new blood. Till then men continued to harp on the analogy of the Swiss Confederation and the United Provinces, though in 1760 the Abbé de Mably put his finger on its weak point. "Neighbouring nations", he said, "are naturally hostile, unless their common weakness forces them to league in a confederative republic." In both those instances confederation was the outcome, not of any idea of instituting a reign of peace, but of a sense of common danger so strong as to overcome particularist sentiment. Against this objection, however, Rousseau urged what he hoped from democracy. If peoples were free, he contended, they would not go to war.

'This line of thought may be taken as culminating in the project for perpetual peace with which Kant attempted to round off his *System of Politics*. It is marked by two advances. The one is that under the influence of Bentham it had come to be recognized that for any such plan to succeed the proprietary theory of the State must give way to one based on the interests of the people. The other was due to the successful formation of the United States of America. For although that was also a confederative republic to meet a common danger, it was on so large a scale that it seemed to bring the idea of something approaching a federal union of Europe within the range of practical politics.

'Bentham himself never advocated any such scheme. His mind was working rather on the lines which led eventually to the Hague Tribunal, and in his *Principles of Morals and Legislation*, 1789, he went no further than to put forward a plan for the institution of an International Court of Judicature without coercive powers. It was left to Kant to apply his theory of "the general interest" to the older conceptions of a league of nations. This Kant did by postulating a constitutional, or, as he termed it, a republican conception of the State as the essential condition of the success of the scheme he was proposing. But probably no one better than himself knew how hopeless was the attainment of that condition at the time, at least in Central Europe. For Kant, then, his plan may have been intended as a Benthamite pamphlet, but, little as Kant seems to have believed in it, Bentham's ideas had fertilized the ground too widely for it not to take some root, and, under the stimulus of the Napoleonic wars, a strong growth sprang up which aimed at something far more comprehensive than Bentham himself regarded as practicable.

'In its initial phases the French revolution seemed destined to justify the thesis — shortly afterwards expounded in Kant's *Essay on Perpetual Peace* — that a free people would not be likely to make war, but would rather form a nucleus for an expanding federation of free peoples bound by a covenant of peace (*feodus pacificum*) as distinguished from an ordinary treaty of peace (*pactum Pacis*). At the outset the revolution was distinctly pacifist. The early revolutionaries also anticipated Kant's thesis by endeavouring to apply to alien peoples the principle of pacific union which had been so successfully applied to peoples of kindred race and institutions in America.

'It soon became apparent, however, that, whether or not Kant's anticipation would hold good for a system of established democracies, it would not apply to a people in revolution who had still to establish their liberties in the face of the scarcely concealed hostility and suspicion of neighbouring monarchies. For the old rivalry of princes as a cause of war was substituted the rivalry of two political ideas. Apprehension on the one side and revolutionary intoxication on the other engendered for a time strife between nations as bitter as anything the old order had seen. Still, the belief in the natural pacifism of democracies, or at least the belief in the virtue and practicability of a new international system based on an accord between free peoples, was not lost. The outcome of the new series of wars was the fresh line of effort to secure perpetual peace which is associated with the Emperor Alexander.

'In 1804 Alexander made overtures for an alliance to the British Government, and, while disclaiming any attempt to realize "the dream of perpetual peace", he advocated the formation of a league in which governments were to be "founded on the sacred rights of humanity", the "prescriptions of the rights of nations" were to be established on "precise principles", and no war was to be begun "until all the resources which the mediation of a third party could offer have been exhausted". His envoy, Novosilitzof, said to Pitt that his master's aims might be "reduced to a single one only — that of restoring the equilibrium of Europe and establishing its safety and tranquillity on more solid bases". Pitt gave a guarded assent, and, in the Anglo-Russian Alliance of the 11th April 1805, a secret article was included providing for "the establishment in Europe of a federative system to ensure the independence of the weaker States by erecting a formidable barrier against the ambitions of the more powerful".

'Alexander's nebulous projects had little influence upon the practical agreements by means of which the four Great Powers — Great Britain, Russia, Prussia and Austria — effected Napoleon's overthrow; but in September 1815 he induced his Prussian and Austrian allies to sign with him a still vaguer document, the "Act of the Holy Alliance". It was little more than a confession of legitimist faith; its signatories avowed their belief that the principles of the Christian religion were binding upon States not less than upon individuals, and mutually pledged themselves to regulate thereby their domestic and their foreign policy; they described themselves as vicars of God, to whom all sovereignty belonged, and their peoples as but branches of a single Christian nation; they promised one another "aid and assistance on all occasions and in all places", and undertook to admit to their fraternity all Christian sovereigns who made the same profession of faith. The Pope and the Sultan were not invited to sign, and Great Britain politely refused. But most Christian princes gave in their adhesion. The Act, however, contained no executive clauses and created no organisation; and the universal union held no congresses, passed no further resolutions, and left the practical work of guaranteeing European peace to the narrower, but more specific and effective, combination of the four Great Powers in the Quadruple Alliance.

'This other association had been founded by the Treaty of Chaumont (10th March 1814), which was renewed with some modifications at Paris (30th May 1814), Vienna (25th March

1815), and again at Paris on 20th November 1815. Castle-reagh called the original "my treaty" and it aimed simply at "the re-establishment of a just equilibrium" and at "maintaining against all attacks the order of things that shall be the happy outcome of our efforts". By "equilibrium" it may be remarked, Castlereagh meant not a simple balance of power between France and her enemies or between any two systems of alliance, but "a just repartition of force amongst the States of Europe". These efforts produced the Final Act of the Congress of Vienna (9th June 1815) and a series of amending treaties concluded in the autumn after Napoleon's return from Elba and final defeat at Waterloo. During this period Alexander made various attempts to expand the Quadruple Alliance into a universal union and the terms of Castlereagh's treaty into an unlimited obligation, and the proclamation of the Holy Alliance was an effort on his part to stampede Great Britain into the common fold. But the only practical step he achieved was the incorporation in the final treaty of the 20th November 1815 of an article providing for the periodic meeting of the four allies in Congress.

'At the first of these congresses, held at Aix-la-Chapelle in 1818, Alexander renewed his endeavours to graft upon the Quadruple Alliance the principles and universality of the Holy Alliance. Castlereagh objected that a limited alliance for certain defined purposes was one thing; a universal union committed to common action in circumstances that could not be foreseen was another. "Till", he wrote to Lord Liverpool on the 19th October 1818, "a system of administering Europe by a general alliance of all its States can be reduced to some practical form, all notions of a general and unqualified guarantee must be abandoned, and the States must be left to rely for their security upon the justice and wisdom of their respective systems and the aid of other States according to the Law of Nations". He was, however, convinced by experience of the utility of periodic congresses. "It really appears to me", he wrote to Liverpool, "to be a new discovery in the European Government (sic), at once extinguishing the cobwebs with which diplomacy obscures the horizon, bringing the whole bearing of the system into its true light, and giving to the counsels of the Great Powers the efficiency and almost the simplicity of a single State." He was, therefore, glad to concur in the admission of France to the circle, thus converting the Quadruple into the Quintuple Alliance.

'The success of this Alliance in maintaining peace, in spite of its insecure foundation upon a legitimist and anti-national basis, was considerable. The "single State", however, soon broke down owing to the divergent views of its constituent governments. It could only succeed so long as it was animated by a common will, representing a compromise between the reactionary views of Metternich and the comparative liberalism of Castlereagh. Alexander held the balance; but it was upset when a series of liberal or revolutionary manifestations in Germany and elsewhere, followed by a mutiny of Alexander's own guards in October 1820, alienated his mind from liberalism and threw him into the arms of Metternich. Castlereagh foresaw that the Alliance would "move away from us without our having quitted it". France was reluctant to see order re-established in Italy by Austrian arms; Great Britain was reluctant to see it restored in Spain (and still more in the Spanish colonies) by French arms. A schism commenced at the congress of Troppau in 1820. Russia, Austria and Prussia resolved to bring back "into the bosom of the great Alliance", if need be by force of arms, any State which broke away from its constituted authorities. The breach thus created was widened at Verona in 1822. Great Britain and the United States drew together in 1823 over the Monroe Doctrine, which denied the legitimist claim, and France was finally withdrawn by the revolution of 1830. The Quintuple Alliance was thus reduced to the three original signatories of the Holy Alliance, Russia, Austria and Prussia, a circumstance which tended to perpetuate the confusion between the two. In this form, as a triple alliance of the three autocracies, it continued to combat progress until the revolutions of 1848, and even survived in the intervention of Russia at Austria's invitation in 1849 to suppress the nationalist rising in Hungary. The common impulse of those revolutions in 1848, coupled with the commercial and industrial internationalism of the free trade movement which was illustrated by the international exhibition of 1851, provided a more democratic, or at least more popular, basis for future attempts to prevent international conflicts.

'The success and the failure of this "Confederation of Europe" during the period of the congresses may be explained either by its methods or its objects. So far as its methods are concerned, it is clear that the plan of a simple declaration, embodied in the Holy Alliance, effected nothing. The universal union was unsubstantial until it had lost its character by being transformed into the remnants of the treaty-bound Quintuple Alliance, and the simple declaration remained nothing more until its vague professions had been reduced to Metternich's concrete and reactionary programme. The effective and useful work of the "Confederation" was done through the congresses of the Great Powers who signed the specific engagements contained in the second Treaty of Paris, but it is to be noted that many of the important disputes which they settled were not within the declared scope of those engagements. With regard to its objects, the "Confederation" was formed to guarantee peace, was then perverted into an engine for repressing reform, and thus became an effective provocation to revolution. So far as any moral applicable to existing circumstances can be deduced from an experiment conditioned by those of a century ago, it would seem to be that any attempt to reconstruct a similar system must be limited to a policy upon which there is a substantial measure of agreement among the Powers, and must possess sufficient elasticity to provide for future developments in the public opinion of the world.

'The period which followed the breakdown of the congress system was marked by frequent wars. It was also a period when nationalism with a democratic impulse, which had been the main cause of the dissolution of the Quintuple Alliance, showed increasing activity. But, apart from the wars of liberation in Greece, Italy and the Balkans, nationalism cannot be held responsible for the unrest. European warfare was mainly the creation of militarist governments, and even the wars of liberation might be considered as the outcome of the vicious and unstable system which those Governments had insisted on setting up. It can hardly be questioned that popular representative Governments have on the whole been more alive than autocracies to the impression that aggressive war, even if successful, may prove to be a greater evil than any reasonable compromise that would have averted it.

'It was mainly to arrange such compromises that the Concert of Europe came to take its place in the international system. Its successes and its failures are of such recent memory that a detailed examination of them has seemed unnecessary. But as a new device for preventing war which was independent of any treaty and trusted entirely to fostering a spirit of co-operation to preserve peace or to localize wars, it is to be noted that it borrowed from the Quintuple Alliance the feature which Castlereagh regarded as its most valuable invention — that is, it sought by conferences to give "to the counsels of the Great Powers the efficiency and almost the simplicity of a single State."

'In this, like the congresses, it failed. Though the spread of democratic nationalism seemed to many to have paved the way to success, there were still obstacles — legacies of 1815 and others — which it could not overcome, and one at least was insuperable. In Germany the people were persuaded that the national State depended for its security upon a military monarchy, and, so long as this creed was held in the most powerful military State in Europe, successful co-operation was as impossible as it became after Alexander I's relapse into absolutism.'

(II) THE COVENANT

It will be noticed that the Phillimore Committee say that any attempt to build an organization for peace 'Must be limited to a policy upon which there is a substantial measure of agreement among the Powers'. That is no doubt true. In one sense, it is obvious. Such a system can only be set up by a Treaty, and a Treaty involves the agreement of its signatories. But it must be more than a formal assent if the peace machinery is to be effective. It must be a conviction deeply and sincerely held that the civilized world cannot afford to go on with —

'The good old rule,
The simple plan,
That they should take who have the power
And they should keep who can.'

Certainly it seemed in 1918 that such a conviction existed. The facts which made the basis of the proposals set out in the Cabinet Memorandum of 1916 had become much graver since that time. The tale of slaughter and destruction had enormously increased. It is safe to say that there had never been anything in history comparable to the total figures. With this destruction had gone the complete dislocation of the system of confidence and credit essential to modern trade and commerce. It was clear that it would take many years before Europe, at least, could hope to recover normal prosperity. On the other hand, there was little prospect that the territorial and financial arrangements possible in the atmosphere of the Paris Conference could endure. The war was over, but the war mentality continued. One vein of sanity ran through the whole confusion of fear and passion, and that was the vehement desire for the erection of some barrier against future war. So far there was a genuine agreement even among the negotiators at Paris, and still more amongst the peoples whom they represented. Disillusioned statesmen might say, with Clemenceau, — 'I like the League, but I do not believe in it.' But popular feeling in its favour was strong enough in their countries to prevent them saying so openly. The great mass of the peoples of the world, then as now, longed for peace and were ready, I am convinced, to make great sacrifices to secure it. No one who remembers the delirious joy with which the news of the Armistice was greeted in London or the unprecedented enthusiasm with which President Wilson was received in the capitals of Europe as the embodiment of the Peace Idea, can doubt the strength of the hatred of war which swept over the civilized world in 1919.

The problem to be solved was — how could this powerful sentiment be translated into a practical constitution which, in the words of the late Lord Salisbury, could 'by its great strength secure an enduring peace'? By the time the Conference met, many schemes had been evolved in the different countries. An account of them will be found in the Phillimore Report. They differed in many ways. But I believe in every one of them will be found provisions forbidding war as the result of an international dispute, until, at least, every means for settling the dispute by peaceful means had been tried. That was true in this country of the first official memorandum on the subject in 1916; and the provision was re-affirmed in every version of what afterwards became the Covenant, put forward on behalf of the British Government.

After the Memorandum of 1916 had been laid before the Foreign Secretary,[1] he agreed, at my suggestion, to the appointment of the Phillimore Committee, who drew up what may be called the first British Draft of the Covenant. That contained the embryos of Articles 5, 7, 12, 13, 15, 16, 17, and 20 of the Covenant, as finally agreed to, — that is to say, it contained articles as to Procedure and the seat of the League, as to arbitration and the submission of all international disputes either to arbitral decision or to the consideration and recommendation by the other members of the League. In the winter of 1918, General Smuts, who agreed with the leading ideas of the Phillimore Committee, issued a brilliant pamphlet in which he supported the conception of a League with the powers proposed by the Phillimore Committee, and added a plan for an international Secretariat — a most valuable suggestion which later became Articles 2 and 6 of the Covenant. He also proposed that the States which had formed part of Russia, Austria, Hungary and Turkey, and had been separated from those countries, should be transferred to the League of Nations and administered by mandatory States selected by the League. In this form, General

---

[1] The Foreign Secretary in September 1916 was Lord Grey. As a result of the political crisis he was succeeded by Mr. Balfour in the autumn of that year. I remained Under Secretary for Foreign Affairs, with Cabinet rank, in both Governments, becoming Assistant Secretary of State in 1918.

Smuts' proposal could not, unfortunately, be adopted. But the mandatory idea was retained and applied, by Article 22 of the Covenant, to territories which had belonged to the defeated Powers and which were 'inhabited by peoples not yet able to stand by themselves'. The General also proposed to nationalize in each country 'the factories for the production of direct weapons of war', and the abolition of conscription. These suggestions also fell by the way, to the lasting injury of the world. Meanwhile, the Imperial War Cabinet considered, amended and approved generally the Phillimore scheme, with the Smuts additions, subject to one change. It will have been noticed that so far no proposal for international disarmament has been made. It is true that in the original draft of the Cabinet Memorandum of 1916, a proposal with that object had been included. But it had been criticised very severely by Sir Eyre Crowe, and I had been so shaken by his arguments that I had omitted it from the Memorandum as presented to the Cabinet. When the matter came before the Imperial War Cabinet, the Dominion statesmen — especially, if I recollect rightly, that bluff, outspoken Briton, Mr. Massey of New Zealand — strongly objected to the omission, and it was agreed that some provision on the point should be included.

When the war came to an end, I resigned from the Government over the question of the Disestablishment of the Welsh Church, though I continued to act as Assistant Secretary for Foreign Affairs during and after the Election of 1918, until I went to Paris. Indeed, it so happened that, owing to the illness of the Foreign Secretary, Mr. Balfour, I was for a great part of that time acting Foreign Secretary. At the 'coupon' Election I stood and was elected as a supporter of the Government, and the Prime Minister, Mr. Lloyd George, was good enough to appoint General Smuts and me as the British Representatives to deal with the League of Nations questions at the Paris Peace Conference. Lord Balfour attended the Conference as Foreign Secretary, and Lord Curzon acted as his Deputy in London.

Meanwhile, the elaboration of the British draft of the Covenant had gone on in the Foreign Office. Debates on the subject took place in Parliament. In particular there was one in the House of Lords on June 26th, 1918, in which Lord Curzon made a speech explaining the ideas of the Government on the subject and stressing their proposals for enforcing a moratorium before the declaration of War.

Some little time before this, I had been appointed Chancellor of Birmingham University in succession to Mr. Joseph Chamberlain. The honour was a very great one, both because of the office itself and still more because of the great eminence of its first holder. Mr. Chamberlain had been the creator of the University and had devoted much of his time and energy to it. So long as the war lasted it had been impossible for me to be installed. But as soon as it was over, the ceremony took place. Part of it consisted in the giving of Honorary Degrees and I like to remember that among those whom I was allowed to select for that honour were Mrs. Fawcett, Sir Austen Chamberlain and Lord Hankey. My robes were those of my predecessor which, owing to the great kindness of Mrs. Chamberlain, were lent to me for the occasion. They have since been presented by her to the University.

I had to deliver an address and chose for my subject the League of Nations. In order to be sure that the Cabinet approved of the scheme, the address had been written out and submitted to a Committee of that body. It was received respectfully rather than cordially, but at least no objection was raised to it. It had a similar though a warmer reception at the Birmingham meeting. There was nothing fresh in the proposals in the address, except that great stress was laid on the importance of public opinion as the chief instrument for maintaining peace. It was also insisted that the Central Powers, Germany and Austria, should from the outset be members of the League.

It may be said, then, that by the end of 1918 the British

Government had accepted the main principles of the Covenant. The next step was to ascertain the views of other Governments and especially of President Wilson. At that time he occupied a world position of immense authority. When he visited London on his way to the Peace Conference he was received in the streets with tremendous enthusiasm. In the celebrated Fourteen Points which he had declared should be the basis of Peace, he had included a demand for the creation of a League of Nations. Accordingly I tried to see him on the subject while he was here. But he was only here a short time and was very busy so that the best I could manage was a brief conversation during a State reception at Buckingham Palace. At such a time he naturally could not be prevailed on to express any opinion; and I had to go to Paris early in January 1919 without knowing what was in the mind of the individual whom Monsieur Clemenceau habitually referred to as Jupiter.

I reached Paris on January 6th, 1919. I was not one of the chief British Delegates but a special adviser on League questions. As such, I immediately got in touch with the American delegation to the Peace Conference. The President was already there but was not available. I saw Colonel House and Mr. Lansing, the American Secretary of State, more than once. The Colonel was an old war acquaintance. He was at that period a trusted personal friend of President Wilson and had visited England during the War as his unofficial representative. A very strong supporter of the League, he with the President represented the United States on the Committee or Commission of the Conference to which the question was referred. He was a high-minded and clearsighted American, devoted to the President and profoundly convinced that a good understanding between the British Empire and America was vital for the peace and prosperity of the world. If men may be divided into those whose ambition is to do something, and those who want to be something, he emphatically belonged to the first class. He cared nothing for position. But he cared immensely for what he believed to be in his country's interest. He was consequently a delightful person to work with. In discussion he always put forward his real opinion, supported by his real reasons. There was never any danger that agreement reached on that basis would be upset for personal and private considerations. It was a bad day for the League when, some months later, the collaboration between Wilson and House ceased. But for that, the League might have been successfully steered through the American Senate and the course of World history might have been very different.

The conferences with House and Lansing, though they showed that they and especially House were more or less in agreement with the British point of view, yet led to very little progress. Nothing could be done without the concurrence of the President and he was busied with other matters. Accordingly I went to see Monsieur Bourgeois, who had been appointed by the French Government to deal with League questions, with the assistance of Monsieur Larnaude. I found that there was a French scheme for the League, much more elaborate than ours. As will be seen, the document on which the Paris discussions proceeded was predominantly Anglo-American. The French accepted this mode of procedure. But on one point M. Bourgeois was irreconcilable. He would have liked the Covenant to provide for an international force. But he insisted that at least there should be an International General Staff to foresee and prepare for (*prévoir et préparer*) military action in support of the Covenant. I believe that even as early as my first interview with M. Bourgeois he raised this point. He certainly did so on every available subsequent opportunity, though he was never able to persuade either the Americans or the British that his proposal was then technically or politically possible.

M. Bourgeois was at this time an elderly gentleman with unsatisfactory health. His eyesight was bad and he was extraordinarily sensitive to cold. I have a vision of him attending a Committee at my room in the Majestic Hotel which was reasonably warm. He, however, found it so cold that he borrowed a fur rug of mine which he wrapped round himself, with the red cloth lining outward, so completely that he looked like a gigantic red caterpillar! Apart from this peculiarity, he was a courteous and able colleague with a great power of pouring out a stream of French reasoning, admirably phrased, in an even delivery without special emphasis. He told me that he had once been making a speech and that, in the course of it, he went to sleep. When he awoke a few minutes later he found that he had continued his speech without any interruption.

One incident which happened about this time is worth recording. Soon after I arrived in Paris, Marshal Foch and General Weygand came to see me at the Majestic to urge that France should be given the Rhine as a frontier — a proposal which would have involved a large transfer of Germans to French sovereignty. I, of course, replied that I had no concern with the territorial arrangements to be made, but would convey their suggestion to my Government, which I did, explaining that I was not myself in its favour.

The whole of the British Delegation, with the exception of Mr. Lloyd George and the Foreign Secretary, Mr. Balfour and their personal staff, was lodged in the Hotel Majestic, which had been hired for the purpose. Great care was taken to secure secrecy. Every official and servant in the place was British, including, unfortunately, the kitchen staff. The only exception was the lift-man, who was French — why, I never understood. In other ways the building was comfortable enough. I had an excellent bedroom and sitting room, as well as an office in the neighbouring Astoria.

It was convenient to have the whole British staff so easily available for consultation. But on the other hand, the perpetual Conference atmosphere became rather exhausting. Casual visitors — and there were many of them — were a great relief, though even they expected to talk Conference shop, naturally enough.

The Conference opened on January 12th, 1919. This

book is not a history of it, and I shall say little or nothing about the territorial and financial provisions of the Treaties which it elaborated. The machinery of the Conference consisted of the Plenary Assembly of the Allied and Associated Powers, and a number of Committees or Commissions to which different questions were referred, of which one was the League of Nations Commission, to be described presently. There was, besides, a kind of General Purposes Committee consisting of the two Chief Delegates of France, the British Empire, Italy, Japan and the United States. This was usually referred to as the Council of Ten and over it, as over the Plenary Conference, Monsieur Clemenceau presided with drastic firmness. There was also a Secretariat, the present Lord Hankey and a French colleague being its Chiefs.

As early as possible we got together a Committee consisting of British experts to advise on the terms of the Covenant. Apart from General Smuts and myself, Sir Cecil Hurst, the Legal Adviser of the Foreign Office and now one of the Judges of the International Court at the Hague, was the most important member, and there were besides representatives of the Fighting Services and other Government Departments. My personal Secretarial staff consisted of Captain Walters, afterwards one of the League Secretariat, Mr. James Butler, now a Fellow of Trinity College, Cambridge, Mr. Philip Noel Baker, now Member for Derby, and Viscount Cranborne (unpaid).

After we had been in Paris for some days I suggested to Mr. Lloyd George that it would be a good plan if the Conference were to pass a resolution in favour of the League. He agreed, and at his request I made a draft which he presented to the Council of Ten. With some slight alterations it was accepted by them on January 22nd and this was confirmed at a full meeting of the Conference on January 25th. It was in the following words: —

1. It is essential to the maintenance of the world

66

settlement, which the Associated Nations are now met to establish, that a League of Nations be created to promote international co-operation, to insure the fulfillment of accepted international obligations and to provide safeguards against war.

2. This League should be created as an integral part of the general Treaty of Peace, and should be open to every civilized nation which can be relied on to promote its objects.

3. The members of the League should periodically meet in international conference, and should have a permanent organization and secretariat to carry on the business of the League in the intervals between the conferences.

The Conference therefore appoints a Committee representative of the Associated Governments to work out the details of the constitution and functions of the League.

I should like to record here my great personal obligations to Mr. Lloyd George throughout the Conference. He and Lord Balfour occupied two flats in a building in the Rue Nitot, very near to the Hotel Majestic. The Prime Minister was good enough to express a wish to keep in close touch with me, and told me that if I ever wanted to see him I was to propose myself to breakfast. Of this very kind invitation I often availed myself. Those breakfasts are among the most delightful recollections of my life. Among his many very remarkable qualities, I incline to think that his marvellous vitality is the most exceptional. Whatever was going on at the Conference, however hard at work and harried by the gravest responsibilities of his position, Mr. Lloyd George was certain to be at the top of his form — full of chaff intermingled with shrewd though never ill-natured comments on those with whom he was working. His mind had one peculiarity. It was like a search-light turned to different subjects on different days. Sometimes it might be on the League of Nations, or the negotiations with this or that Power. Whatever it was, that question and that question only was brilliantly illuminated. Attempts to discuss anything else were not encouraged and were rarely successful. But to me personally he was always considerate. I only remember one occasion on which we disagreed about League matters, and that was over some question of American naval policy rather than over the League itself. Apart from that, following what I think was his usual practice, having entrusted General Smuts and me with the League negotiations, he left the details very much in our hands. So long as he did not seriously differ from what we were doing, he left us to our own devices. If he had seriously differed he would not have hesitated to remove either or both of us. That is, surely, the right attitude for a Prime Minister to adopt. As another Prime Minister used to say: — 'It is no use jogging the elbow of the man who is driving'.

Meanwhile, President Wilson and his Delegation were working at an American draft of the Covenant. As appears from the invaluable volumes of Mr. David Hunter Miller, the President made several Drafts, and on Sunday evening, January 26th — the day after the Conference had accepted the League Resolution — he sent for General Smuts and me to his apartment and expounded his proposals. He was living at that time in rather a grand house near the Parc Monceau, and he kept us for some hours going through his draft. This was the first time I had had any talk with him, and the first impression was not altogether favourable. He struck me as being rather dogmatic and yet not having a very clear idea of what was really needed. The draft was verbose and contained some propositions which appeared obscure and irrelevant. But this was only the first impression before I had realized his great qualities of courage and eloquence and his profound desire to establish peace on a firm and lasting basis. One observation remains which illuminates his character. He told us that he wanted to call the document the Covenant 'because', he said, 'I am an old Presbyterian'. That was undoubtedly the spirit in which he approached the question and, perhaps, explains some of his impatience with what he conceived to be the political partisanship with which the League was attacked in the United States.

As we went away I made some criticisms to General Smuts of the President's draft. The General agreed, but declared that, nevertheless, we must work on it as our basis. Accordingly after some discussion it was settled that the legal advisers of the two delegations, that is to say, Mr. David Hunter Miller for the Americans, and Sir Cecil Hurst for the British, should go through the draft and put it into acceptable form. This they did, working in the closest co-operation and with untiring industry in order to get the draft ready for the first meeting of the Commission which had been appointed by the Conference to prepare the articles of the Treaty which were to deal with the League of Nations. Considerable changes were made in the form of the President's draft which was assimilated to our British draft. But the substance was for the most part unaltered. The work was finished and submitted to the American Delegation and then, on the morning of the first meeting of the Commission I received a message that, on further consideration, the President preferred his own draft and was going to present it to the Commission, scrapping the Hurst-Miller draft altogether. I was much agitated, partly because there were things in the President's draft which would have been very difficult for the British to accept, and partly because I feared — quite groundlessly, as it turned out — that the President regarded himself as a kind of dictator. I accordingly hurried to the Hotel Crillon, which was the American Headquarters, and then learnt that the President was quite ready to sink his own preference and take the Hurst-Miller draft. I recall the incident because it illustrates the kind of aloofness which sometimes made the President make proposals out of tune, as it were, with the thoughts and intentions of his fellow-negotiators, coupled with his readiness to meet their views as soon as he realized what they were.

I have already recorded the passing by the Plenary Conference of a Resolution in favour of a League of Nations, and it was on the basis of that Resolution that the Committee to settle the detailed scheme of the League was appointed. It consisted of two delegates from each of the five Great Powers, and one each from ten of the others, so that about half the Powers represented at the Conference were concerned in drafting the Covenant. President Wilson was in the Chair, assisted by Colonel House as the other American delegate. On their right sat, usually, the French and Italian delegates, MM. Bourgeois and Larnaude, and Signor Orlando — then Prime Minister of Italy — and Scialoja, who remained till his death a convinced supporter of the League. On the left of the Chair came the British Empire, represented by General Smuts and myself, and Japan, represented by Baron Makino and Viscount Chinda. Among the other States, the most prominent were Mr. Venizelos of Greece and Mr. Hymans of Belgium. We held, in all, fifteen sessions, interrupted by President Wilson's visit to America in February. He in fact presided at every meeting but one of the Commission. He left a good deal of the detailed work to me; but was always ready with his great eloquence and authority to intervene if any difficulties arose. Throughout, the British and American delegations worked in complete harmony.

None of the ex-enemy or neutral powers were members of the Commission, since they were not members of the Conference. This was, in my view, a great pity, particularly as to the ex-enemy Powers. But in the atmosphere of the Conference it was perhaps inevitable. As far as the neutral Powers were concerned, they attended a meeting presided over by myself to discuss the Covenant before it had been finally agreed upon by the Commission, and their views were duly considered. The only opportunity for the ex-enemy Powers to state their opinion on the Covenant was when it was presented to them with the rest of the Treaty. It was this procedure which enabled the Germans to say that the Treaty, including the Covenant, was the result of dictation and not discussion. It was a grave error and the excuse

LEAGUE OF NATIONS COMMISSION OF THE PARIS CONFERENCE

Including, in the back row: Colonel House, General Smuts, President Wilson, Mons. Hymans, Mr. Wellington Koo, *and in the front row:* Baron Makino, Mons. Bourgeois, Lord Cecil, Signor Orlando, and Mons. Venizelos

that it was vital to get the Treaty settled rapidly never seemed to me adequate. The atmosphere of *Vae victis* is not a good one in which to frame a treaty of lasting peace. But as far as the terms of the Covenant are concerned, I do not think that they contained anything hostile to the interests of Germany. Indeed, the decision by the Commission to fix the seat of the League at Geneva rather than Brussels was due entirely to the desire to dissociate it as far as possible from the passions of the war. The delay in admitting the ex-enemy Powers to the League — another great error — had nothing to do with the Commission. Nor was it in any sense responsible for the allocation of Mandates, which was done not by the Commission or by the League, but by the Allied and Associated Powers themselves. Finally, it should be remembered that of the three Great Powers that have broken away from the League, two were among the 'victorious' Powers and had their full share of responsibility for all the provisions of the Treaty of Paris. Indeed, some of the least defensible articles of those treaties, as for instance the transfer of the Tyrol to Italy, were agreed to at their express request.

The first meeting, on February 3rd, took place at the Hotel Crillon, like all the subsequent meetings. Though there were differences of opinion, our proceedings were generally harmonious. Indeed, I do not remember any 'incidents' except one, when I, through ignorance of the *nuances* of the French language, described a contention by M. Bourgeois as *absurde* and had to withdraw and apologize! On another occasion, I declined to agree to the adjournment of an important Committee so as to enable M. Larnaude to attend a *sauterie* given in honour of his daughter. He was grieved, but forgave me.

I shall not attempt to give a detailed account of our discussions. It will be enough to trace the general lines on which they proceeded. And first the historical and political limits of what seemed possible should be noted. Nothing can be more certain than that any attempt to erect a super-State would have failed. It was for that reason that it was insisted that in accordance with the ordinary rule in International Conferences no binding decision on any question of substance must be taken except unanimously.[1] Questions of procedure were allowed to be decided by majority, but nothing else. On the whole this provision has not worked badly. In very few cases has it caused even serious delay, and those mainly in the matter of internal management such as the composition of the Council or the allotment of expenditure among the Members of the League. Any tendency to mere obstruction has been controlled by the pressure of publicity — no doubt one of the most important elements in League procedure, as will appear later on.

I do not, therefore, regard the so-called unanimity rule as a blot upon League procedure. At the worst it may have made the Council and Assembly cautious in discussing radical proposals, but that, I am inclined to think, is, in international affairs, a good thing. Anyhow, whether the rule is good or bad, none other was possible at Paris. The Great Powers were obsessed with the wholly unreal danger that the small Powers might band together and vote them down. The smaller countries were more reasonably afraid that their stronger neighbours would easily persuade a majority to give them whatever they wished, irrespective of the protests of the weaker States.

The decision against majority domination, necessary and perhaps beneficial as it was, no doubt diminished the executive scope of the League. It made it impossible, for instance, to re-draw the map of Europe. But it would have been unreasonable to expect those men who, in the other Commissions, were settling what they believed would be an enduring peace, to be keen to set up machinery to review their handiwork. As will be seen, an article was inserted enabling the League to reconsider obsolete treaties or other dangerous international conditions, but the machinery was

---

[1] But in dealing with disputes under Art. 15 of the Covenant the votes of the parties to the dispute are not counted. See page 94.

perhaps too conservative to be effective. Little use has, in fact, been made of it.

In spite of these difficulties, the League Commission was determined not to be satisfied with a document expressing no more than a vague aspiration for peace. We met under the shadow of the Great War. We had all been through it in one way or another. We knew the waste and destruction it had caused, the suffering of the men and the anguish of the women. While we were sitting there, something like chaos was reigning in Austria, in Hungary, in Germany and in Poland. Revolutions had taken place in many countries and were threatened in others. The chances that the Peace Treaties would be far-seeing and merciful were remote. To create some barrier against future war rightly seemed the most important work for the Conference and that work the President and some others of us believed could only be accomplished by the creation of an effective League of Nations.

If, then, the creation of a super-State was out of the question, what, short of that, could be done which might prevent war? We knew that at the conclusion of other wars clauses had been inserted in the Peace Treaties declaring that for the future the High Contracting Parties intended to abjure enmity and violence. The Holy Alliance, as already stated, at the end of the Napoleonic wars, after setting out the most unimpeachable maxims of international morality, proclaimed that the signatories, including almost all the belligerents, would govern their foreign policy by those principles. The result was nil. Something more practical than that was essential. Naturally the events preceding the outbreak of war in 1914 were examined. Diagnosis must come before treatment. We noted that Sir Edward Grey had striven his utmost to induce Austria and Serbia to bring their quarrel over the murder of the Archduke and Archduchess at Serajevo before an international Conference, and we knew that Grey believed that, if that could have been done, war might have been averted. So everyone agreed to the British proposal which became Articles 10 to 15 requiring that, before resorting to war, international disputants should try every means, whether by negotiation, arbitration or mediation, to settle their quarrel. Pacific action of this kind was to be completed within six months of laying the dispute before the League, and no war was to take place for three months after a decision had been reached. If the matter was recognized by the parties to be suitable for arbitration, that is, if it turned on a question of international law, or the interpretation of a treaty or some controversy of fact or as to the amount of damages suffered, then it was to go to arbitration and the parties were to be bound by the decision. If the dispute did not go to arbitration, then it was to be brought before the Council of the League who, after considering it were to make public their report thereon. If the report was unanimous, then no State was to go to war with any State because it had carried out the report. If, on the other hand, the report was not unanimous the members of the League might each decide for themselves what action if any they ought to take. It will be seen that there is no provision for the enforcement of any decision by the Council, except so far as the provision goes which lays it down that no State is to be attacked because it carries out the Council's unanimous decision. That was the deliberate policy of the framers of the Covenant. They desired to enforce on the parties a delay of some months before any war took place, believing that during that period some pacific solution would be found. But they did not think that it would be accepted by the nations if there was an attempt to compel them to agree to a solution dictated by the Council. In coming to this conclusion they had in view the state of feeling in several countries, including Britain and America. Even so, the Covenant was regarded by the people of America as both too great an interference with their sovereignty and as likely to involve them too much in international disputes, and I remember the then Duke of Northumberland writing that the effect of the Covenant was to subordinate British sovereignty to M.

Bourgeois! Yet all that the Covenant proposed was that the members of the League, before going to war, should try all pacific means of settling the quarrel. Those who now criticize the Covenant as ineffectual and propose much greater sacrifices of national sovereignty may be invited to consider carefully how the exceedingly moderate proposals of our Commission were actually received.

As a matter of fact, these elaborate provisions under Article 15 for investigation, publicity and delay have never come into play. In all the cases in which the League either did interfere to prevent war or was asked to interfere and did not do so, the aggressor nation acted or threatened to act in open disregard of the League and its machinery.

It will be observed that Articles 10 to 15 of the Covenant which I have described do not indicate what is to be done if, in breach of their obligations, either of the parties to the dispute resort to war. That is dealt with by Article 16, which in effect, provides that each member of the League is bound to take its part in imposing on the recalcitrant Power such diplomatic and economic pressure as is within its power. It is only if these fail to secure peace that any question of military action arises. In that case, the Council is to advise what military effort each member of the League is to make 'to protect the covenants of the League'. Doubts have been raised as to what are the duties of members of the League under this Article. To me it is clear that each member of the League is separately bound to take action, independently of any decision of the Council though, in practice, it is convenient that the Council should express its opinion as to what ought to be done so as to secure common action. Further, it is equally clear that, though the obligation rests separately on each member of the League, it is an obligation to take joint and not separate action. That is the meaning and purpose of the whole Covenant. It is an attempt to combine the members of the League in an effort to achieve peace and security by means of international co-operation. Article 16 is part of the machinery with that object and, in accordance with the ordinary rules of construction, its wording must be interpreted by reference to the general purpose of the document. Any other construction would lead to an absurdity, for it would require even the weakest members of the League to take action against the strongest, though no other member of the League was prepared to do anything. On the other hand, it does not mean that no member of the League is bound to do anything unless all the members of the League or, as some people even have suggested, all civilized nations, are ready to act. Such an interpretation would also lead to an equal absurdity since the defection of even the smallest State would free all the others from their obligations. What, then, are the limits of the obligation of each State under this Article? Surely here again the answer is to be sought by considering the purpose of the Covenant. The object was not to punish the wrong-doing State, still less to oblige every State to make a demonstration of its hatred of aggression. The object was simply to stop war and, consequently, the duty of the members of the League under this Article is to do everything within their power which they think will effect that result. For that reason it is desirable that the Council should meet as soon as possible after the aggression has taken place, so as to advise what part each country should play in preventing or stopping the aggression. This becomes clearer if Articles 10 and 11 are considered. Article 10 lays down the general proposition that it is the duty of the members of the League to respect and preserve as against external aggression (so that it does not apply to internal commotions such as the Spanish war was at its commencement) the territorial integrity and existing political independence of all members of the League; and it places upon the Council of the League the duty of advising how this is to be done.[1]

On the other Articles I have been considering very little discussion took place in the Commission. The general principle of sanctions was unanimously accepted from the

[1] This matter is further discussed at pp. 125 *et seq.*

outset. But Article 10 led to considerable discussion. I, for one, objected to it on the ground that it seemed to crystallize for all time the actual position which then existed. Eventually it was agreed to, subject to a provision for the pacific modification of the *status quo*, which became Article 19 of the Covenant. It is right that if resort to war is forbidden, other means should be provided for correcting international injustice.

Article 11, which has been the most useful of all the anti-war provisions of the Covenant, deals not with the stopping of aggression but its prevention. It lays down the principle that any war or threat of war, wherever it may take place, is a matter of concern to all members of the League. That is a new principle and one of very great importance. The Article goes on to make it the duty of the Council of the League, in such an emergency, to take any action necessary to safeguard peace. This is founded on the vital principle that peace is indivisible. To us, in Paris in 1919, this seemed axiomatic. We had just been through a war, the result of a political murder in a Balkan State, which had desolated Europe and whose effect had been felt in almost every part of America, Africa, Asia and Australia. If such a catastrophe was to be avoided in the future, every war, wherever it occurred or threatened to occur, must be nipped in the bud. Article 11 went further. It gave to each member of the League the 'friendly right' to bring to the notice of the League any circumstance which threatened to disturb international peace. Not enough use has been made of this provision, which the League owes to President Wilson's initiative. It seems a complete answer to those who say that the Covenant contains no power to deal with undesirable international conditions.

Article 11 was accepted unanimously and without debate. The only other Article dealing with what may be called the direct prevention of war is Article 17. It aims at extending the powers of the League to disputes leading or likely to lead to war in which one or more of the Powers concerned are not members of the League. The provisions of this Article have scarcely been used nor are they, in existing conditions, very likely to be used. It may, therefore, be enough to say that the machinery proposed is to offer to the disputing States temporary membership of the League. There is no suggestion in Article 17 that Articles 10 and 11 should be applied to States outside the League. But it would seem that Article 11 by its own terms applies to all countries, whether members of the League or not.

So much for what I have called the direct prevention of war under the Covenant. This is the kernel of the whole scheme. The League was brought into existence as an alliance to stop war, open to all civilized states. Every provision of the Covenant is subsidiary to this purpose and if the means of fulfilling it disappear, the whole basis of the Covenant is destroyed. That is my answer to those well-meaning persons who think that they can preserve the League while taking from it all means of preventing war. It is the old story of Hamlet without the Prince of Denmark.

I have already explained how the War Cabinet in England insisted on the insertion in the scheme for a League of Nations of a provision for the general reduction and limitation of armaments. With that object, Articles 8 and 9 were inserted in the Covenant — the first Articles after those dealing with the constitution and machinery of the League. They naturally were carefully considered by our naval and military advisers. The British Committee examined and approved the wording of the proposal before it was adopted by the Commission; and the Commission itself gave considerable time to its discussion. It was at this point that Bourgeois pressed most strongly for the creation of an international General Staff. He received little support and the British and American delegations were convinced that the practical and political difficulties in its way were overwhelming.

Article 9, which provides for the creation of a permanent Commission to advise the Council of the League on military, naval and air questions, was in part a concession to Bourgeois' views. It was, in practice, a complete failure. It consisted of military, naval and air experts who had to do what their professional superiors at home desired, and that was almost invariably that they should do nothing themselves and if possible prevent anyone else from doing anything. The most legitimate of the German grievances against the Paris Peace was largely the result of this attitude. The Allies had pledged themselves absolutely to the international reduction of armaments as soon as Germany had disarmed; yet for months and years after they had formally acknowledged that Germany had fulfilled that obligation, they took no effective step to follow suit. It was the only case of importance in which the Allies failed to implement their contractual obligation and gave Germany at least a plausible pretext for disregarding other provisions of the Treaty.

Article 8 has three substantive provisions. By the first, the Council is directed to formulate plans for the reduction of armaments, for the consideration and action of the several Governments. This is a general international obligation. It does not require any Government to take action except as part of a general plan. The claim, therefore, sometimes made in this country that British reduction of armaments between 1920 and 1932 was in execution of Article 8 is a complete misapprehension. The whole purpose of the Article was to lessen the inclination to war, and that could only be done by general action. The reduction by one Power only, especially a pacific Power, of her military preparations was of no use as a measure for peace. Indeed, it might and probably did have the opposite effect.

The Article also embodies an undertaking that the members of the League will interchange full and frank information as to their actual and potential armaments. No serious attempt has been made to make this undertaking effective, beyond communicating to the League information that was already public property. Thirdly, by the Article, the Members of the League agree that the manufacture by private enterprise of munitions and implements of war is open to grave objections and the Council is charged with the duty of advising how the evil effects attendant upon such manufacture can be prevented. The Council has not given any such advice, and on this point the British Government has been more actively remiss than its collegues. It is, perhaps, worth while to note that, though in this and other Articles a distinction is made between the Council of the League and the Governments who are members of it, for convenience of drafting, there is obviously no real distinction of that kind. The League consists of Nations represented by their Governments, and can take no action apart from them. If the League has failed in some respects, it is because the Governments or some of them actively or passively desired that it should fail.

The remaining Articles of the Covenant, apart from those which establish the Constitution and Procedure of the League, deal chiefly with international co-operation. In Article 23 are set out a number of subjects of international importance on which the League is to take action. They include conditions of labour, treatment of natives, the traffic in women and children, the sale of noxious drugs, communications, and health. On all these matters much has been done and, by general consent, the work is admitted to have been excellent. It is not too much to say that by the social activities of the League and the parallel industrial work of the International Labour Office, many millions of human beings have received, directly and indirectly, substantial benefits. Critics of the League do not always remember this, or if they do they suggest that it would be well if the League confined itself to such subjects. For reasons already given I believe that the last suggestion is impracticable. The whole activities of the League will stand or fall together.

Discussions in the Commission on these points were not very important except for an attempt to enlarge their scope by bringing in questions of religious and racial equality. These were eventually excluded on the ground that their discussion would be too controversial in the international conditions which then prevailed. Throughout our deliberations we were anxious only to attempt the minimum that was necessary for the preservation of peace, leaving further developments to be made as and when they became possible. I am still of opinion that this was a wise course.

There was, however, one subject which, though it went beyond this standard, we could not avoid. In the course of the war, subject territories had been conquered from Germany and Turkey. It was decided outside our Commission by the main Peace Conference that these territories should not be returned to their former owners. On the other hand, plain annexation was not desired. It was therefore proposed that they should be assigned to certain countries to be administered by them in trust for the well-being and development of the inhabitants in the first place and, in the second, so as to secure equal opportunity for the trade and commerce of the members of the League including naturally the administering country. This is the Mandates system, originally proposed, though for a different purpose, by General Smuts. The Article dealing with it is Article 22. It was not drafted by the League Commission but by the Council of Ten, representing the five principal Powers at the Conference. I have always understood that Lord Lothian — then, Mr. Philip Kerr — was the principal draughtsman, which perhaps accounts for the literary flavour which distinguishes it from the other Articles of the Covenant. It provides for three types of Mandates — Class A, applying to territories which had belonged to Turkey, gave independence subject to guidance by the mandatory Power. The ex-German colonies were placed in Class B and Class C, in which the mandatories have powers more nearly approximating to sovereignty. In each case the League was given the supervision of the mandates through a special Committee. On the whole the system has worked well, though the League has no coercive power beyond publicity.

Article 22 led to little discussion in the League Commission. We accepted it as sent down to us from the higher authority, and inserted it in its appropriate place. Nor had the League, or the League Commission anything to do with the allotment of the Mandates, which as I have said was made at a meeting of the principal Allied and Associated Powers held at the Hotel Trianon, on May 7th, 1919.

There remains to be considered the Constitution and Procedure of the League as enacted in the Covenant. By Article 1 the original members of the League were divided into two categories. First, there were the signatories named in the annex to the Covenant. These were the Allied and Associated Powers, one of which, the United States, declined, after an embittered party fight, to ratify the Treaties of which the Covenant was part. As the discussion of the Covenant proceeded at Paris, it became known that considerable opposition to it was developing in America. At first we were assured that the movement was not important, and throughout President Wilson treated the Senatorial critics of the League with indignant contempt. On February the 14th he went back to Washington for a month, and while there interviewed the recalcitrant Senators without mollifying them. Indeed, to transatlantic observers his methods of controversy did not seem to err on the side of conciliation. No doubt he resented what seemed to him a wicked attack on a great effort for world peace, carried on for party purposes and built up on the ill-informed prejudice of his fellow-countrymen. Whether this was the true view of the position it is not for an Englishman to judge. There can be no doubt of the President's bitterness on the subject. On his return to Paris, he invited Colonel House and myself to dinner to discuss the American situation and especially certain suggestions of changes in the Covenant which our friends in the States, led by the veteran Senator Elihu Root, thought might mitigate opposition. The most important of them was the provision which makes it clear that the validity of the Monroe Doctrine is not affected by the Covenant. The dinner was very agreeable, the President exerting himself to entertain us by telling a number of stories, which he did very well. After dinner, we three retired to another room to consider the American amendments. To most of them it seemed to House and me there was little objection, and we were quite ready to go almost any distance to secure the two-thirds majority in the Senate necessary for ratification. As each amendment came to be considered, if House or I recommended it as an improvement to the Covenant, the President was quite ready to accept it. But if either of us suggested that it would be a reasonable concession to Senatorial feelings, the President was up in arms in a moment and, in order to get his agreement, we had hastily to explain that on its merits it was unobjectionable.

It may be that a more conciliatory attitude on his part would have saved the Treaty. In fact a majority of the Senate voted for its ratification, but not a two-thirds majority. so that the Treaty was defeated. It is only fair to add that the hostile verdict was confirmed by a large majority of the voters in the Presidential Election of 1920. I have always believed that the President despised the Senatorial opposition, being confident that with his personality and great oratorical powers he would be able to get sufficient popular support to crush Senator Lodge and the other objectors. Whether this anticipation was right or not will never be known. The President arranged to make a personal campaign throughout the country on behalf of the Treaty. But it had scarcely begun when he was stricken by illness which entirely disabled him. For many months he was completely laid aside, and during that period Mr. Cox, the Democratic and League candidate for the Presidency, was heavily defeated by Mr. Harding. Mr. Wilson never recovered. I visited America in 1923, in order to explain the League as I understood it to American opinion. In the course of my journey I went to Washington. I called on Mr. Wilson. He was sitting in his drawing room, paralysed, though quite himself to talk to, and he asked me how I had been getting on. I spoke gratefully of the warmth with which I had been received and expressed the hope that he did not think I was doing any harm. He replied courteously, and then added: 'We are winning! Don't make any concessions!' A marvellous exhibition of undaunted courage from one who had not only suffered a severe electoral defeat but was physically incapable of any attempt to retrieve it! I never saw him again. He was a man of great ability, a remarkable orator, and above all of unflinching determination in carrying through any enterprise to which he had set his hand. That is perhaps the rarest and certainly the most important of all qualities for a political leader.

The second category of original members of the League consisted of countries which had not been belligerents in the War and therefore were not signatories of the Treaty but were nevertheless 'invited to accede to the Covenant'. There were thirteen of them and they all accepted the invitation. Six of them were European countries — the three Scandinavian countries, Holland, Switzerland and Spain. The other seven consisted of six Latin-American States and Persia. The first to accept was Spain. Her Ambassador in Paris, Senor Quinones de Leon, was her representative at the Geneva Council and Assembly for many years — a keen and convinced supporter of the League. He was an accomplished diplomat of great charm, invaluable in adjusting personal and other differences among the representatives of Members of the League.

Switzerland had considerable hesitations as to her action. She valued her neutrality very greatly and was exceedingly anxious lest she should compromise it even for the sake of peace. Eventually a formula was found and she joined — a decision which was decisively confirmed on a referendum to her electors.

The three Scandidavian countries and Holland also had doubts about some of the provisions in the Covenant. They felt a reluctance to accept wholesale a document in the drafting of which they had had no share. To meet this very natural feeling meetings of the so-called 'Neutrals' took place which I attended on behalf of our Commission to explain the Covenant and receive criticisms of it, which I duly conveyed to the Commission. These meetings were held during the interval in the session of the Commission caused by

President Wilson's visit to the United States during February and March.

As I have pointed out, neither Germany not any of her Allies were original members of the League. Let me repeat that this was a grave error, the chief responsibility for which rests on the French Government. I, among others, protested without avail. To the French and Belgians, who had suffered a German occupation of their country for four years with the inevitable humiliation and injustice which that involves, the idea that the Germans should be forthwith asked to sit round a table and discuss world affairs on terms of mutual esteem was utterly repugnant. It was natural enough. Probably if the southern counties of England had passed under German rule in the same way as the northern parts of France, we should have reacted very much as did the French. Nevertheless, it was a great misfortune to the League. It helped to create the impression that the League was dominated by France and England and was indeed a mere continuance of their War Alliance. Nor were affairs much improved by the admission of Austria and Bulgaria in 1920 and Hungary in 1923, since Germany remained excluded till 1925, after the Locarno Treaty.

In the first three or four years of the League, a number of countries were admitted to the League, and in recent years some have resigned. These events will be dealt with later. But on one other matter connected with membership of the League something must be said, since it was much used by the opponents of the League in America. During the war, the British self-governing Dominions and India played a great part. They fought with great gallantry, both in France and Turkey, and were represented on the Imperial War Cabinet which met during the War. Indeed, General Smuts became one of the chief members of the ordinary War Cabinet. It was accordingly decided that they should send delegates to the Peace Conference and should sign the Peace Treaties, and they thus became original Members of the League. There were five of them — Canada, Australia, New Zealand, South Africa and India, and a great outcry was raised in the United States on the ground that this gave the British Empire six votes. It was pointed out that since all important decisions of the League, in accordance with the usual international rule, had to be unanimous, this was of no importance. Moreover, the self-governing Dominions were in no way controlled or controllable by the Mother country. In actual fact, the Dominions have often taken a line of their own at Geneva, though on great questions of international policy the States forming part of the Empire have generally though not always thought alike. The position of the Dominions has certainly been quite innocuous from the point of view of other nations, and from our Imperial point of view it has been of the utmost value. Everyone knows the difficulties which beset the foreign policy of the Empire. It is carried on mainly from London and, as far as foreign nations are concerned, they are entitled to regard the Empire as one entity. If a European war takes place in which we are engaged, the position of a self-governing Dominion is complicated. From her point of view she is entitled to remain neutral, and in the United Kingdom we have assented to this doctrine. But it does not bind foreigners and they could, if they chose, treat any part of the Empire as enemy territory and its citizens as enemy individuals. Conversely, if one of the Dominions became involved in a foreign war, we should no doubt treat their quarrel as ours. This situation makes it essential that the Dominions should be kept fully informed and, if possible, consulted on all foreign questions — not always a very easy matter with an Empire scattered over the face of the globe, in spite of modern means of communication. Indeed, nothing can adequately take the place of direct personal discussion in such matters. Yet any suggestion of anything like an Imperial Cabinet meeting continuously in London has always been decisively rejected by the Overseas Governments on the ground that it is inconsistent with their independence. Such an organization as the League is open to no such objections. It provides a meeting-place for delegates from the Dominions and the United Kingdom at which all questions can be freely discussed and conclusions arrived at on the footing that the Dominions are in exactly the same position as any other Sovereign State. Nor has this ever led to the slightest Imperial difficulty. On most questions, as I have said, the representatives of the Empire have found themselves in full agreement. Their way of thinking is usually the same. On the few occasions when important differences of opinion have taken place they have either been adjusted after discussion or left to time to find a solution. If only some means could be devised to make the League machinery and atmosphere continuous, the Imperial complications of our foreign policy would be at an end. It should be noted that what I have said applies only to an inter-State organization. If the League were transformed into a Federal Union, deciding by majority, it is evident that other problems would arise.

One word as to India. Her sacrifices during the war were great and valuable. She was therefore very rightly given the same position as a 'self-governing State, Dominion or Colony' to quote the words of Article 1 of the Covenant. But in fact she was at that time controlled through the India Office by the United Kingdom Parliament, and in the last resort would have been bound to vote and act at Geneva in accordance with the views of the English Cabinet. This anomaly was recognized and discussed in our Commission. But no serious objection was taken to it.

Thus at the start there were forty-two States Members of the League, which did not include Germany, Russia, the United States, Austria, Bulgaria and Hungary. By 1928 Germany, Austria, Bulgaria and Hungary had joined, and soon afterwards Russia came in. The United States which for some years was almost definitely hostile to the League has latterly drawn much nearer to it. She served on many of its most important Committees and has joined the International Labour Office. I believe it may be assumed that the U.S.A. would be very unlikely to take an unfriendly attitude towards any League action for peace or international co-operation. Her spokesmen have recently expressed themselves very cordially about it. On the other hand, the adhesion of Russia[1] has been perhaps more than balanced by the resignation of Germany, Italy and Japan, though Italy and Germany were never very whole-hearted members of the League, and Japan took little part in European affairs. On the whole, the League has lost ground in South America, though it is an open question whether the Latin-American States ever added much strength to it. As the Pan-American League grows stronger it is not improbable that its members will attach less importance to the Geneva institution unless, indeed, as time goes on some express connection between the two institutions should develop. That certainly would be an excellent thing for World Peace.

The Covenant provides in its second Article that the executive organs of the League are to be the Assembly, the Council and the Secretariat. The Assembly meets regularly in peace time once a year in September, for about three or four weeks. The Council meets now regularly three times a year. Both bodies have had from time to time special meetings. Each body is entitled to deal with any international question by its own authority. There is in form no appeal from the Council to the Assembly. But cases of importance, if they come before the Council, are often referred by it to the Assembly, especially if any members of the League desire that this should be done. The president of the Assembly is elected each year by that body. The members of the Council preside over it in rotation.

The Council consists of what may be called the Great Powers, as Permanent Members, and originally four but later nine other members who are elected by the Assembly and hold office for three years and are then ineligible for a period unless the Assembly otherwise decides, so as to secure

---

[1] Since this was written Russia has ceased to be a member of the League.

a rotation among the Members of the League. These arrangements were the occasion of considerable discussion before they were settled. It is noteworthy that differences of opinion as to such matters have created much warmer feelings and have been more difficult to settle than far more important questions involving, it may be, the peace of the world. It is, perhaps, natural that grave matters as to which weighty considerations exist should be decided more easily by reasonable men sitting together and all desiring to find a solution which will make for enduring peace, than questions of personal or national *amour propre* about which reasons properly so-called may not exist. Certainly this has been the experience at Geneva. I do not recollect a single case where, for instance, a question as to which country was the aggressor in actual hostilities has given rise to serious doubt. But competition for seats on the Council or even for Chairmanship of Committees has sometimes led to acrid discussion and heartburning.

Essentially the Assembly and Council are forms of International Conference differing chiefly from the ordinary type of such gatherings because they are not summoned to deal with a particular issue but have a continuing existence with periodical meetings. One advantage of this plan is that if agreement is not reached at one session, its further consideration can be adjourned to the next; whereas an International Conference of the normal type, if it adjourns, usually dies.

The other organ of the League, the Secretariat, is more novel. It has been called an International Civil Service and is the first of its kind in history. The first Secretary General, its chief officer, was appointed by Article 6 of the Covenant, at my suggestion. There had been an idea of making the office an almost independent institution, its occupant being called Chancellor. The eminent Greek Statesman, M. Venizelos, was, I believe, sounded as to his willingness to take the post. He refused, and for that and other reasons the nature of the post was modified and was assimilated to that of the Permanent and non-political Under-Secretary of a British

Government Office. It could not be quite the same because there was not and could not be a Secretary of State. The Secretary General's chief is the League itself, speaking through the mouth of the Assembly or, more usually, the Council. He directs the other members of the Secretariat, who are appointed on his nomination by the Council; he prepares, with his assistants, the work of the Assembly, the Council and their Committees, and usually drafts their reports and resolutions; he makes suggestions for overcoming difficulties if they occur, and his advice is at the service of the Organs of the League or the Members of which they are composed. It is obvious that a Secretary General of ability, tact and judgement will have a great say in the policy of the League. It is, however, of the utmost importance that it should not be allowed to drift altogether into his hands. If it does, there may be an exaggerated tendency to seek the line of least resistance which will often mean the postponement of a crisis which might have been solved by firm handling, to an occasion when time and change have made it insoluble.

The First General Secretary, Sir Eric Drummond, now Lord Perth, had very remarkable qualities of mind and temperament required for his office, especially in dealing with questions of international policy. He was a model of tact, exceedingly resourceful in difficulties, absolutely fair and impartial, and with a rapidity of apprehension which I have rarely seen equalled. He was no orator to a meeting, but in committee he could express his view, when asked to do so, most persuasively. Above all, he acquired the confidence of all nationalities. They were certain that his judgement, usually excellent, would be quite unaffected by national prejudice. More than once when differences of view have arisen between the British and some foreign delegate, I have seen the latter ask Sir Eric what he thought, and accept his advice, whatever it was, without question. No term of office was fixed for him in the Covenant, and it was therefore left to Sir Eric, practically, to say when he thought he ought to go. As that time approached it was very striking and, to a fellow Briton, very gratifying that it was the foreign members of the Secretariat who felt most deeply the danger to the League of Sir Eric's approaching departure.

The other members of the Secretariat have been drawn from different nationalities, the object being to give to each State an adequate part in the League administration, subject to the overruling consideration of personal competence to fill the various posts.[1] On the whole, the institution has worked well. Many of those selected were of outstanding ability and devotion to the League. In several cases they accepted salaries lower than their market value so that when they left, as time went on, it was to their pecuniary advantage. Generally speaking, the Secretariat appreciated that they were international officers and did their best to act with complete impartiality. Latterly there were some exceptions to this rule. The German and Italian Governments, especially the Italian, regarded their nationals in the Secretariat as Government emissaries, taking their orders from Rome and Berlin. The result was that they had very little personal influence. In view of the kind of charges that are often made against France, it is right to say that the French members of the Secretariat were usually both impartial and efficient.

One department of the Secretariat, that of the Interpreters, was remarkably successful. With very few exceptions they shewed devotion and skill in a high degree. One of them whose assistance I often had in the early days of the League, M. Privat by name, could not only reproduce accurately and without delay in French an English speech, but could throw it into the form which a Frenchman would have adopted if he had been the speaker.

Much of the work of the Secretariat was concerned with internal organization. The general work of the League was dealt with by the Council and Assembly and their permanent and special Committees. The debates in the

---

[1] See for detail of organization, *The Society of Nations*, by Felix Morley, published by Faber & Faber.

Council and Assembly were often of the highest importance. They might have been even more so if the Great
Powers had fully used the opportunity thus given to them to
expound to the world their policy on the urgent questions
of the day. Unfortunately, the tendency was to say as little
as possible in public, owing, partly, to the old and mainly
bad tradition of secret diplomacy and partly to the shrinking
from taking definite decisions — the besetting sin of democratic
statesmen. It is surely the case that the sooner and more
clearly the intentions of each important Power are laid before
the world, the less chance there is of those misunderstandings
which are among the chief causes of international unrest.
I know it is said that if an unwise statement is made in public
it is not easy for later and more prudent counsels to prevail,
whereas a mistake in private can be readily rectified. There
is some truth in that in the case of really private *tête-à-tête*
conversations. But if the discussion takes place in anything
in the nature of a committee it is very much less true. To
withdraw from a position taken up in committee is not much
less humiliating than if it had been adopted in open debate.
And so far as the contention has any value, it cuts both ways.
A statesman will be less prone to take an unreasonable
attitude before the world than before colleagues for whose
individual opinion he probably cares very little. Finally, the
proceedings of an international Committee are never really
private. They are almost always reported. But instead of
there being one accurate report made by shorthand-writers
— or, nowadays, directly broadcast — there are a number of
tendencious reports put out by zealous nationals in order to
persuade the citizens of each country that their representatives'
views triumphed. No doubt it is more gratifying to certain
temperaments to sit in secret conclave, with other distinguished
individuals, at which the future of the world is settled, than
to take part in a public debate where world opinion is the
judge of who is reasonable or the reverse. But it is my
profound conviction that, though in certain cases really
private conversations may be useful, publicity is an

immensely powerful guarantee against injustice and misunderstanding.

I am aware that diplomatic opinion is largely against me on this point, partly because a profession tends to believe in the wisdom of its traditional methods, and partly because diplomats are not practised in public speaking and consequently dislike it. All the same, I maintain that one of the great merits of the Geneva system was its publicity, that it was possible to say things openly in the Assembly which it was very desirable to say and which could not have been said under old diplomatic conditions, that frequently agreement has been reached under pressure of publicity which could not have been reached otherwise, that when the Council sat in private it very often failed to reach any conclusion, and that I cannot myself recollect any occasion in which publicity did or would have done harm except where the fitness of some individual for an appointment or the like was to be discussed.

Perhaps the most important part of the work of the League is done in Committees. There are, or used to be, six Committees appointed by the Assembly at the beginning of each session to deal with the various questions that are included in the Annual Report presented by the Secretary-General. They used to be divided into the following categories: Legal, Social, Disarmament, Finance, Humanitarian and Political. If any question was raised not contained in the Report, and the Assembly agreed to entertain it, it was referred to the appropriate Committee before it was further discussed. The Committees sat in public — set speeches being for the most part discouraged — and stated their conclusions in Reports which were conveyed to the Assembly by *Rapporteurs* who explained their terms. All decisions in Assembly or Council, except on questions of procedure, have to be unanimous, as has been said, but that does not apply to Committees since the Resolutions have no force unless approved by the Assembly. The unanimity rule is the result of the doctrine that it is contrary to the sovereignty of any

State for it to be overruled by other States. But at the first Session of the Assembly, Monsieur Hymans, who had been chosen as President, decided that, if a Resolution was carried by a majority in the Assembly, it could operate as a recommendation (*voeu*) though not as a decision. In most cases since the League has no coercive power, except to prevent a resort to war, the practical difference between a recommendation and a decision is not very great. I believe that no similar ruling has been given in the Council, but I have little doubt that if the question were formally raised there a similar rule would be established.

In practice the disadvantages of the unanimity rule have not been so great as critics of the League often allege, as I have already said. No doubt it sounds as if an Assembly of some fifty nations, or even a Council of ten to fifteen, would rarely reach a unanimous decision. But it must be remembered that a very large part of the work of the League is non-contentious, that all of it that comes before the Assembly is first thrashed out in Committee by representatives of Nations who desire the success of the League (or otherwise they would not be there) and that on any question between two States likely to lead to a rupture, which is brought before the League under Article 15, the votes of the parties to the dispute are not counted in computing whether a decision has been unanimous. It is true that it is doubtful whether this exception applies to proceedings under Article 11, designed to prevent war. But even so, the number of cases in which a decision has been prevented by failure to obtain unanimity is not great. Indeed, I do not think any such case has occurred in any coercive action by the League. The effect of the rule in preventing proposals being made or pressed has no doubt been much greater. The failure, for instance, to improve the action of the League in relation to minorities has been partly the consequence of the impression that no proposals of that kind could obtain unanimity, and there have been other cases of the same kind. On the other hand, the rule has made those who were anxious for a change careful to draft their proposals in as inoffensive a way as possible, surely a good thing in itself. This, coupled with the necessity for opponents to be ready to face publicity, has prevented the unanimity rule from seriously hampering the League's work.[1]

In addition to the Assembly Committees, there are a number of other committees which have sessions all the year round. Some of these are standing Committees to deal with general subjects such as Finance, or Communications, or Narcotic Drugs. These consist of persons chosen for their special competence and though they come from different countries and have often been selected after consultation with the Governments of those countries, they are not in any sense representatives of Governments. They can therefore give their opinion freely on the merits of the questions brought before them. There are other special committees appointed to deal with particular political questions. There was one on which I sat, charged with the duty of making recommendations for the better government of Liberia, and there have been many others. These usually consist of representatives of Governments who are bound by their instructions and consequently do not often make far-reaching proposals. Sometimes a Committee contains members who do and others who do not represent Governments. There was one which sat for a long time on the Disarmament question, which rejoiced in the strange title of the Temporary Mixed Commission for Disarmament. It did excellent work. But its Government members were uncomfortable and eventually persuaded their home authorities to destroy it before it reached final decisions. As a general rule all officials, military and civil, dislike change. I have often heard it said that the great Disarmament Conference which met in 1932 was brought to nought by experts. In a sense that is true, but it was partly because the experts were officials. I do not mean

---

[1] It will be remembered that the Disarmament Conference, which perhaps was hindered by the need for unanimity, was not part of the League machinery.

that officials are not admirable people and of the greatest value. But they are not usually good directors of policy. That is the work of Ministers directly responsible to the sovereign authority of their country, be it democratic or not. The Ministers should of course consult their officials and duly consider all the dangers and difficulties which will be pointed out to them. But in the end they and not the officials should decide. The officials should be, as the Americans say, always on tap and never on top.

Of the other constitutional provisions of the Covenant, two only need be noticed. By Article 18 all Treaties have to be registered and published. The object was to strike a blow at secret diplomacy. I am afraid it has only been partially successful even among members of the League. Still, the principle is right and when the present reaction against international civilization has spent itself, Article 18 may help to make statesmen see that all these underhand tricks of secrecy and the like are futile and pernicious.

Article 19 is of greater importance. It is the first attempt to create machinery for changing obsolete and dangerous international arrangements. By it, the Assembly is empowered to advise the reconsideration of Treaties which have become inapplicable and international conditions whose continuance might endanger the peace of the world. Very early in the proceedings at Paris I had urged that the permanence of treaties might become in the future as in the past a danger to peace, and that the Covenant should contain provisions for their modification. When Article 10 was under consideration, which guarantees as against external aggression the territorial integrity and existing political independence of all members of the League, I again pressed that this Article should be made subject to provision for pacific change. Various proposals were discussed, and eventually Article 19 emerged as the furthest to which we could go. Even so, scarcely any use has been made of it. It is said that nothing can be done under its terms without unanimity. But the Assembly could make recommendations for change, under the Hymans ruling, by majority, and if the majority approached unanimity, the international effect would be great. Suggestions have been made for increasing the effectiveness of the Article, and these will be examined later on. But it is well to state here that the difficulty is to arrange for the change of treaties without doing more harm than good. The existence of undesirable treaty arrangements may do great harm. But to encourage every discontented section of every State to ask for revision of any treaty to which they object, may produce a greater atmosphere of unrest than the existence of the treaty could. That, at any rate, was the strong view of my colleagues on the Commission and it was with some reluctance that they agreed to what now seem to some the excessively conservative terms of Article 19.

When the first draft of the Covenant was complete it was, on February 14th, 1919, laid before the Plenary Conference by President Wilson. No decision was asked for; criticism and suggestion were invited. The President, after reading the Covenant, made some observations about certain of its provisions and about the spirit of the discussions in the Commission. He insisted that the instrument depended chiefly upon 'the moral force of the public opinion of the world and the cleansing and clarifiying influence of publicity'. And he added that armed force was in the background and that 'if moral force of the the world will not suffice, the physical force of the world shall'. In a splendid phrase he defended the simplicity of the Covenant, declaring that 'A living thing is born' which must grow and develop in accordance with the law of life; and described it not only as 'a definite guarantee of peace' but as 'a great and humane enterprise' — and the last it certainly was. I followed, on behalf of the British Empire. After stating that our purpose had been 'to devise some really effective means of preserving the peace of the world consistently with the least possible interference with national sovereignty', I said that we did not seek to produce a building finished and complete in all

G
97

respects but only to lay a sound foundation on which such a building might be erected. 'If', I went on, 'it is merely a repetition of the old experiments of Alliance, if we are merely to have a new version of the Holy Alliance, designed for however good a purpose, our attempt is doomed to failure. Nor must it be merely an unpractical effort in international dialectics. It must be a practical thing, instinct with a genuine purpose to achieve the main objects we have in view.'

In both of the speeches from which I have quoted will be found references to the International Labour Office, and Mr. George Barnes who also spoke for British labour, dealt incidentally with that subject. The I.L.O. was established by an entirely distinct document, the work of a different Commission. It was not part of the League but had a separate constitution in which not only the Governments of the different countries but the Employers and Workmen also had their part. It owed much at its start to the broad common sense, the excellent judgement and the complete disinterestedness of Mr. Barnes. Indeed it is owing to his excessive modesty that he has perhaps not received all the credit that is his due. The I.L.O. was also fortunate in its first Director — Monsieur Albert Thomas, a man of extraordinary energy and eloquence. He had very pronounced opinions and since he called himself a Socialist he was generally believed in London to be extreme, which was far from being the case. He did desire very genuinely the welfare of the working class and when his plans were resisted he never lacked courage in their defence. The result was some difference of opinion with the employers. But I believe that before his untimely death he had very largely conquered their respect and they ceased to attribute to cunning what was in fact the result of clear-sightedness and courage.

Though the I.L.O. was separate from the League, it too was established at Geneva and its expenses formed part of the League Budget. My personal knowledge of its working was not great and I shall not therefore attempt a detailed description of it. It has had a useful career and the annual review of its activities, by Monsieur Albert Thomas and afterwards by Mr. Harold Butler, were among the high lights of Geneva.

Directly after the Plenary Conference of February 14th, President Wilson left for America and did not return until a month later. There was thus a gap between the ten first sessions of the Commission and five later ones. During the interval the meetings with the Neutrals[1] took place which I have already mentioned. Meanwhile, the President had been engaged in his discussion of the Covenant with Senator Lodge and his friends, and we received in Paris a number of comments and criticisms from various sources in addition to those made by the neutrals. On the whole the atmosphere was friendly, apart from the rumblings of the approaching storm in America.

Except for a provision directly saving the Monroe Doctrine from any possible injury by the Covenant, and a recognition of the equality of men and women as far as the League was concerned, no very substantial change was made in the terms of the Covenant during the concluding meetings of the Commission. On April 28th it was presented to the Plenary Conference by the President, and adopted by it. Geneva was established as the Seat of the League, Sir Eric Drummond was appointed its first Secretary General, and Belgium, Brazil, Greece and Spain were named as the first non-permanent members of the Council to hold office till the Assembly arranged for others. Monsieur Bourgeois then not for the first time urged the appointment of a Commission to prepare plans for the military and naval forces needed to carry out the obligations of the Covenant, but did not press for a decision on the point after an intervention by Monsieur Pichon, then French Minister of Foreign Affairs. Monsieur Pichon went on to give a little comic relief to the

---

[1] The Neutrals' meetings took place after the President's return but before the Eleventh Session of the Commission.

situation by proposing that Monaco should be a member of the League. His nose was sharply bitten off by Monsieur Clemenceau in the Chair, and the proposals of President Wilson were accepted.

Shortly afterwards I received the following letter from President Wilson: —

Paris, 2 May, 1919.

My dear Lord Robert,

The enclosed message from Washington from our Acting Secretary of State raises an important question upon which I would be very much instructed by your opinion, if you would be kind enough to give it.

In the hurry of the breaking up of the session the other day, I did not have an opportunity to congratulate you as you deserved to be congratulated, on the successful termination of the labors of the Commission on the League of Nations. I feel, as I am sure all the other members of the commission feel, that the laboring oar fell to you and that it is chiefly due to you that the Covenant has come out of the confusion of debate in its original integrity. May I not express my own personal admiration of the work you did and my own sense of obligation?

Cordially and sincerely yours,

WOODROW WILSON.

Lord Robert Cecil,
Hotel Majestic.

CHAPTER III

EARLY YEARS

(A) 1920

I FLEW back to London, not without trepidation since flying was still in its infancy as a means of civil locomotion, and resumed my work in Parliament. I received more than one suggestion that, as the Welsh Church question was out of the way, I should rejoin the Government, but I declined since my only real interest in politics had become the League of Nations and I believed that I could do more to help it outside the Government as it then was than inside it. The House of Commons contained an overwhelming majority of Conservative Members mainly of the commercial class. The Liberal Party was shattered by the quarrel between Mr. Asquith and Mr. Lloyd George, so that such opposition as existed was predominantly Labour. An experienced observer said that when he looked at the right of the Speaker's chair he thought he was attending a Chamber of Commerce. When he looked at the left he thought it was a Trade Union Congress. All or almost all the House professed support of the League; very, very few knew anything about it. Some of the Conservatives in their hearts disliked it, many disbelieved in it. Even the Labour Members were at that time doubtful. The Liberals in the opposition were its best friends and they were powerless. If I had rejoined the Government I should have necessarily been bound by Government views and I was not quite sure what position it would have been possible for me to adopt. Looking back, I think my decision was right. Subsequent events showed that I was out of touch with Conservative thought, the Liberals with whom I was most in agreement, especially with Lord Grey, were down and out, and I was not then prepared to become a member of the Labour Party.

The political situation was abnormal. The House of Commons was, as I have said, overwhelmingly Conservative. But the Prime Minister was a Radical who, before the war, had been regarded by Conservative opinion as a very dangerous politician. As long as the war lasted everything was subordinated to the necessity for victory and on that point no criticism could be made against Mr. Lloyd George. He was a remarkable War Minister and it was generally acknowledged that he had contributed largely to its successful issue. But once it was over differences of temperament and opinion between him and his Conservative followers began to show themselves. During 1919 and 1920 the Government were in no danger of serious Parliamentary defeat. The majority was too large for that; but it was not fundamentally solid. In the country, the political position was even more insecure. The old land-owning Conservative leaders had lost much of their position. I have already pointed out that the Tariff Reform movements had accelerated the substitution of the commercial for the land-owning class, and the war carried this tendency further. Speaking generally, landowners gained nothing and lost a great deal, both in person and in property, by the war. On the other hand, a good deal of money had been made in commerce with the inevitable result that those who had profited in this way also strengthened their political position. The new rich, as it was said, had taken the place of the new poor. But in certain sections of the people the change was not fully or gladly accepted. Then there was a fairly widespread feeling that what was rightly regarded as the great evil of the war had been due to the errors and incapacity of the governing classes. In foreign affairs the great mass of the people were no longer disposed to accept without question decisions of the Front Benches. In addition to these special considerations, there was the general restlessness following the excitement of war, and the dissatisfaction with the hardships which the period of reconstruction necessarily brought with it. The result was a good deal of political and industrial unrest. There were many strikes, the position in Ireland was deplorable and even in England there was an appreciable amount of revolutionary feeling. I visited my constituency in Hertfordshire in the late summer of 1919. It was harvest time and I thought that instead of trying to have meetings which would not have been welcomed, I would try to see and talk to the labourers in the fields. Accordingly, I went about from farm to farm, arranging with the farmers that I should see their labourers without their presence. One thing became very clear. The farmers were far less popular than they believed themselves to be. At one village the people had collected in a schoolroom without any of their employers being there. In opening the discussion I said: 'Of course there are good employers and bad employers'. I was instantly interrupted by someone saying, with general applause: 'Not here! they're all bad!' Another time a young road-mender of most placid appearance gave me a shock by saying that he was in favour of revolution!

The course of events in Ireland did not improve matters. A series of cruel and cold-blooded murders were occurring all over the South and West of that country, which were dignified by the name of Civil War, waged to obtain the independence of nationalist Ireland. For the most part they were of the ordinary terrorist description — sudden attacks by armed bands on unarmed and peaceful citizens of both sexes. That was bad enough, but the form of repression which gradually grew up was far worse. A special police force was raised which was nicknamed the Black and Tans, and they were encouraged or permitted by the Government to carry out reprisals of the most indefensible character. The climax was perhaps the burning, in 1920, of a great part of the city of Cork in return for one of the terrorist murders of some police. This went on through the end of 1919 and 1920 until a treaty of peace was made in 1921 with the leaders of the terrorists, by which the Home Rule Bill for South Ireland, already before Parliament, was considerably extended. I had become convinced that Home Rule in some form or another was inevitable. But the acts by which it was secured and the attitude of the Government towards them were terrible. Few worse pages can be found in our history, and I much fear that the end is not yet. Concession to violence, national or international, is rarely justifiable or successful. One consequence of this atmosphere of discontent was to make the common people very receptive to the conception of a League of Nations. They were ready and even anxious to hear of some plan by which future wars might be averted.

During the Paris Conference I had joined the League of Nations Union, of which Lord Grey was President, and I became Chairman. It was still in its infancy but there was reason to think it could be greatly increased in strength for the popular interest in the League was enormous. We held a great meeting in the Albert Hall soon after my return from Paris, with Grey in the Chair, at which I tried·to explain the Covenant and what we hoped from it. The meeting has been followed by others in the same place and by very many all over the country. The total number must run into many thousands and the great majority of them have been full and even crowded, though naturally the enthusiasm is less now than it was at the beginning. Still, even so, the interest in the subject is very great. Whenever we have tested the feeling of the country, as we did in the Peace Ballot less than five years ago, it has shown that there are millions of our fellow-countrymen who desire the success of the League and still believe that it can and should be made the 'keystone of our foreign policy'.

One of the great compensations for work in the Union was that it brought me into close relations with two very remarkable men, Lord Grey and Dr. Gilbert Murray. Grey I had known since we were at Oxford together. I had sat with him — or, rather, opposite to him — in the House of Commons since 1905 when I was first elected. He was to me the most persuasive speaker I ever heard — not what is ordinarily described as a great orator. He made no appeal to the emotions, he rarely coined phrases or uttered epigrams.

MR. P. J. NOEL BAKER, M.P.

Indeed, he did not strike one as advocating any cause. But the facts and arguments were so arranged that at the end one conclusion and one only seemed inevitable. There is an old legal story of a traveller from York who had as his fellow-traveller a special juryman who had been sitting on the juries at the Assizes. The juryman was full of admiration for Counsellor Brougham — such a wonderful orator, so brilliant, such a powerful reasoner, such command of language, and so on. At last the other traveller asked him whether the juries had not always given verdicts for his opponent, Counsellor Scarlett. 'Oh, yes!' said the juryman, 'of course we did, for it so happened that his client was always right!' But Grey was much more than a persuasive speaker. He had excellent judgement, great force of character, a genuine patriot with a very high sense of public duty apart from his dislike for official life. His courage in carrying on his work in spite of domestic tragedies and increasing physical difficulties alone entitles him to the gratitude of his country. Nor is it easy to over-estimate the advantage we gained during the early part of the war by having as our Foreign Secretary a man whose high purpose and sincerity were recognized and trusted throughout the world. To me he was uniformly charming and my collaboration with him first in the Foreign Office and afterwards in advocacy of the League are among my most valued memories.

Gilbert Murray is still with us, and I must therefore speak of him with greater restraint. I will only say of him that he is the most self-less man I have ever known, with a most delightful sense of humour and a mastery of style.

We had many other collaborators, only three of whom can be mentioned. There was and is Lord Davies, with his active imagination, his unfailing courage and his great generosity. Then there is my great personal friend, Philip Noel Baker, with almost every intellectual gift that a politician can desire coupled with unsparing devotion to the cause of peace. And finally should be named Dr. Maxwell Garnett who, coming as Secretary of the Union when its fortunes were at a low ebb, was largely instrumental in raising it by his energy and ability to a position of very great influence and political power.

Meanwhile, the Treaty of Versailles had been signed and ratified and the other Treaties followed a few months later, and so closed one chapter in the great world drama. Looking back one can see that the Treaties might have been better. Still, I have often doubted whether the territorial arrangements could have been very much improved. The retrocession of Alsace-Lorraine was inevitable. The Saar compromise worked out all right. There is more doubt about the advisability of some of the smaller readjustments in Western Europe and it is the fashion now to condemn the Czecho-Slovak solution. Still, no one I imagine thinks that it would have been either right or reasonable to have done then what has recently been carried out. It may have been wrong to leave two or three million Germans in the Sudeten Provinces, part of Bohemia and Moravia, as they had always been. It would have been far more indefensible to hand over to conquered Germany the eight or nine millions of Czechs and Slovaks who had heroically fought for their freedom. The best plan, no doubt, would have been to have left the final frontier line to be settled under the League later on. The same observation is perhaps true of the Polish Corridor, though it is difficult to see what other satisfactory outlet to the sea could have been given to Poland. Similarly there is much open to criticism in the allotment of territory to the South Eastern States of Europe. It is easy to make objections to what was done, but it must be admitted that in view of the perplexing intermixture of races in that part of the world no perfect settlement was possible. There would certainly have been very much to be said for adopting at Paris only provisional settlements of these very highly contentious matters, leaving the ultimate adjustment to be made by some such machinery as that which worked so well in the case of the Saar. But that would have been to have asked of the statesmen in Paris a far more convinced support than they felt able to give to the new instrument of international co-operation which was then, for the first time, tentatively brought into existence. Those who have read and pondered on the descriptions of the Conference at Paris so brilliantly given by Mr. Harold Nicolson and others will, I hope, agree that the framers of the Covenant, and still more, the inner Councils of the Conference, might easily have done worse. Nevertheless, we can now see that grave mistakes were made. In the first place, no one now defends the financial provisions of the Treaty. On that point, Mr. Keynes has turned out to be right on all important points in his *Economic Consequences of the Peace*. Next was the failure to allow the Germans an adequate opportunity of discussing and criticizing the terms of peace before they were signed. This was particularly unfortunate in the case of the Covenant, where the co-operation of all nations was almost vital. Finally, and most essential of all, was the exclusion from membership of the League, for months and in some instances for years, of the enemy Powers and especially Germany. She was excluded on the theory that she was a criminal country, not fit to associate with others — a fantastic exaggeration of the principle of national responsibility even if the war-guilt doctrine is fully accepted. For the Government of Germany and the spirit of its people in 1919 were as different as possible from those which existed five years earlier. I remember going to see Monsieur Poincaré a year or two later to beg him to agree to the entry of Germany on the grounds of the general interest. He persisted in treating the League as a kind of international club to which only nations of unblemished reputation should be admitted. It was an inexcusable error and has had grievous results. Nevertheless, there was a considerable section of opinion which later on desired to exclude Russia on similar grounds.

The first meeting the Council of the League was held in Paris on January 16th, 1920. I was not present. I believe Lord Grey, who happened to be in Paris, was asked to attend as a guest of honour. The meeting was mainly formal.

There followed during the spring and summer of that year some nine other meetings of the Council which dealt with current events such as typhus in Eastern Europe and the restoration of war prisoners to their homes. It also took steps for the organization of the machinery of the League in matters of Health, Finance, the Permanent Armaments Commission, the Government of Danzig and the Saar, and the working out of the Mandatory system. A more important matter was the appointment of a Commission of Jurists to draw up a scheme for the establishment of a Permanent Court of International Justice. Finally, it dealt successfully with a dispute between Sweden and Finland over the Aaland Islands and discussed but did not in fact intervene in disputes between Russia (who was not a member of the League then) and Persia, which was settled by agreement, and between Russia and Poland which was not. It was also occupied with the earlier stages of the long and complicated dispute between Poland and Lithuania.

While the Council was taking these initial steps in the League's history, its friends in England were engaged in explaining and defending it in the country and in Parliament. The attitude of the Government towards it was ambiguous. No attempt was made to transfer important international work to it. That was still mainly transacted by a number of special conferences and by a body called the Conference of Ambassadors, at Paris, which was set up to work out the details of the Paris Treaties. At first the League was hardly mentioned in the King's Speeches and little or no attempt was made to co-ordinate our general foreign policy with that pursued by our representatives in the League. I tried to get a circular despatch sent to all our Ambassadors and Ministers at Foreign Courts, calling their attention to the new departure in international policy and instructing them to support it in every way possible. I do not think that any such general instruction has ever been sent. On the contrary, an atmosphere of semi-hostility was allowed to grow up in our Diplomatic Service both at home and abroad. Influential officials in the Foreign

Office did not conceal their suspicion of the League and all its proceedings. It is right to add that Balfour was always a convinced supporter of the League and that, as time went on, the official attitude improved. I am speaking of 1920.

One day, in the summer of that year, the Agent General of South Africa came to see me in the House of Commons and gave me a wholly unexpected invitation from General Smuts, at that time Prime Minister in South Africa, to attend the First Assembly of the League as second South African delegate, the Agent-General, Sir Reginald Blankenberg, being the first. I accepted with alacrity. The South African Government, unlike the Government of the United Kingdom, recognized the state of marriage and paid my wife's expenses as well as mine. So we both went to Geneva, arriving there on November 14th. I had been made aware, from various quarters, that my presence at Geneva representing a Dominion was not agreeable to the official mind. I was urged, after my arrival, by high authority, to abandon my delegacy, being told that the French objected to my representing South Africa. If they did, they carefully concealed that opinion from me. It did happen that occasionally I was unable to accept the French view, and vice versa. But broadly we were the best of friends and during my time at Geneva I had the happiness of collaborating with Bourgeois, Viviani, Paul-Boncour, Hanotaux, de Jouvenel, and, above all, Aristide Briand. I did not resign. To my mind it was entirely a matter for the South African Government, and if they were satisfied to be represented by me no one else had any business to interfere. That I retained the confidence of General Smuts I think I may claim. I had worked with him during the War and, as I have already recounted, he took up the idea of the League warmly and wrote his very effective pamphlet in its defence. Then we sat together on the League Commission in Paris and knew one another's mind thoroughly on all the questions involved. The result was that he never gave me any detailed instructions. Occasionally I cabled to him asking his wishes on some special question, and always received a reply authorizing me to take whatever action seemed to me best. An ideal chief, especially when one knew his profound understanding of what the League meant and his unwavering support of it. I have known few men of such an acute and available mind or having such a power of putting into effective and eloquent language his thought on any subject.

The day after my arrival, Major Anthony Buxton, a member of the League Secretariat, came to welcome me. At the time I was rather discouraged by the attitude of highly-placed personages and was proportionately grateful for Tony Buxton's characteristic kindness. For many years he occupied a unique position at Geneva as a great sportsman and lover of birds and fishes some of which, in another capacity, he so skilfully destroyed! He had a pack of beagles and it was the practice of the more energetic members of the Secretariat to rise at about four in the morning — at least, so I was told, for I never joined them — in order nominally to pursue the hare. It was claimed that two hares were known to exist within hunting distance. One was familiarly known as Jules — I never heard the name of the other if, indeed, he existed. In default of hares, the hunt pursued foxes. But I believe it was a bloodless sport as befitted one associated with the Peace capital of the world. When he was not hunting or fishing or watching birds — all of which took place out of office hours — or doing League work, Tony made a speciality of entertaining foreigners of all sorts who were devoted to him, as indeed were most people. He was in the best sense a great social force for peace and, as I have said, one of the institutions of Geneva.

Some forty-one countries were represented at this first meeting of the Assembly. None of the ex-enemy States were there, though Austria and Bulgaria were admitted during the Session. Even so, most regrettably, Germany was not present. Nor was Russia, whose Government at that time regarded the League as a capitalist institution! Nor, of course, was the United States. Indeed, a Presidential Election had just taken place in which the League Candidate, Governor Cox, had been heavily defeated. Of the successful candidate, President Harding, all that need be said is that he was in almost every respect the antithesis of President Wilson.

The first official act of importance of the Assembly was the election of the Belgian delegate, Monsieur Hymans, as its President. No better choice could have been made. He was distinguished both as a diplomat and as a Minister, since he had been, during the war, his country's representative in London, and he afterwards became her Foreign Minister. He made an admirable President — courteous, dignified and resourceful, as when he ruled that a resolution carried in the Assembly by a majority, though it could not rank as a decision, might yet be regarded as a recommendation.

The Assembly then proceeded to discuss the Report presented to it by the Secretary General on the work done by the Council. On this text any question of Foreign Affairs was in order, since it was either mentioned in the Report, in which case it could clearly be discussed, or else it was not mentioned and then reasons could be given why it ought to have been.

The annual opening debate of the League Assembly should have been a great opportunity for clearing up international misunderstandings. Even in the First Assembly, the number of distinguished statesmen present was considerable and as time went on more of them came. What an audience to which a British Foreign Minister might explain, with conciliatory candour, exactly where his country stood on any burning question of the day, to be followed by similar declarations on the part of the other leading Powers. There were occasions when something of the sort was done as, for instance, the celebrated interchange between Stresemann and Briand. But they were rare, and the bureaucracies set their faces against such indecent frankness! Yet I cannot doubt that such an annual autumn cleaning would have done more to make international relations wholesome than all the semi-private confabulations of distinguished individuals which, as far as I can see, have often led to trouble and have been very rarely productive of good.

In the first Assembly not much of importance was said, most of the speeches being concerned with the principles of the League. At the start there was a silly controversy between the Council and Assembly as to their respective jurisdictions, which prevented most of the chief members of the Council taking part in the opening debate and led to a most unusually perverse attempt, at the end, by Mr. Balfour to prevent the Assembly discussing Mandates. It was fortunately a passing phase, prompted probably by some timorous bureaucrat, and thenceforward, as long as he was able to come to Geneva, Mr. Balfour was equally the friend of Assembly and Council. I only mention it here because this kind of official and national *amour propre* did far more than any international dispute to prevent the League from acquiring that unity of feeling — that *esprit de corps* — without which an institution is apt to be at the mercy of any passing wave of unpopularity.

The controversy was, in fact, easily settled upon the basis that both Council and Assembly were entitled equally to deal with anything affecting the peace of the world, but that neither should butt in if the other were already engaged in considering any particular question. A careful reading of the Covenant shows that in matters of internal organization certain questions are allotted to each of the two bodies.

When the Assembly first met it was quite wanting in the unity to which I have referred. It had no belief in itself. It was harassed by raucous shouts of triumph from the isolationists and anti-Wilsonians in the United States who proclaimed on the first of several occasions that the League was dead. It was known that one of the chief Latin-American States, the Argentine, was going to withdraw from the League. Things looked black and those who had feared that the Assembly would never work seemed to be justified. And then a very remarkable incident occurred. A war was in progress in Armenia, Mustapha Kemal having invaded that country. The question had been before the Council who had not felt able to do anything much. It was accordingly proposed that further steps should be taken by the Assembly to give assistance to the much-enduring Armenians. Instantly the whole atmosphere of the Assembly changed. Here was a call to action not in the interest of this or that Member of the League but to put an end to an indefensible aggression, to strike a blow for the Rule of Law in International Affairs. The answer was immediate. Monsieur Lafontaine, the Socialist delegate from Belgium (the three Belgian delegates represented the three chief Parties in that country, Catholic, Liberal and Socialist) made one motion, I made another, Viviani for France, in a fiery intervention, made a third. Balfour very prudently pointed out the difficulties of action. But the Assembly would not hear of doing nothing: such counsels were not worthy of the League (note the first sign of an embryonic *esprit de corps!*). The Resolutions were amalgamated and passed unanimously and a Committee was appointed to draw up plans for helping Armenia. At that point the need for doing so ceased. Armenia came to an agreement with Soviet Russia by which she became in effect a protectorate of that country and the Turkish invasion stopped. But the Assembly was changed. As Mr. Wilson Harris observed: 'The real achievement of the Assembly was to find itself. It met as a collection of forty-one Delegations. . . . It had welded itself . . . into a single cohesive, self-conscious instrument confident of itself, convinced of having a mission to discharge and resolute to discharge it.'[1] That spirit, the birth of which I have tried to describe, remained and grew year by year till 1931, when the disastrous period of recession began.

Besides this supremely important achievement, the Assembly did a good deal of useful if not very exciting work.

[1] *What They Did at Geneva.* An account of the First Assembly of the League of Nations, by H. Wilson Harris. Published by The Daily News Ltd.

It established its rules of procedure, it admitted six new States including Austria (since deceased!) and Bulgaria, it pushed forward the campaign against typhus in Eastern Europe, it set up technical organizations to deal with Economics and Finance, Transit and Communications, and Health, it began its work on Opium and the White Slave Traffic, it set up the Mandates Commission (one of the most successful of the League activities) and it set going administrative machinery for other purposes. Further, it took three other steps of considerable practical importance. It made a beginning in organizing the election of the Non-Permanent members of the League. This was obviously necessary, but it was not wholly beneficial. It began an era of change which did not close until the number of the Non-Permanent members swelled to nine and Brazil resigned because she was not made a permanent member. More important even than this, the unity of the Council was weakened. The original Council continued unchanged for several years, except for the substitution of China for Greece. This gave a certain stability to its decisions; the members personally knew and trusted one another. The *esprit du Conseil* became a real and important thing. I am convinced that if there had been that *esprit du Conseil* during the Abyssinian affair, the Council might conceivably not have taken action against Italy; but if it had, it would have gone through with it till success had been achieved.

Another thing the first Assembly did was to draft a definite Convention for the Establishment of the Permanent Court of International Justice at the Hague — an institution which has worked almost without a hitch. And finally, it set up the so-called Temporary Mixed Commission for the Reduction of Armaments, which, in spite of official frowns, took by far the most practical steps that have yet been taken for that vital purpose.

The first Assembly of the League of Nations came to an end on December 18th, 1920, and I returned to London. The first part of 1921 was not encouraging in England. There were strikes and unemployment. The financial position was depressing. The condition of Ireland continued to be very bad. Then, in March, Bonar Law, who had been the Leader of the House, resigned from ill-health. In spite of his great ability and powers of speech, his own conscientious temperament made political life very difficult for him. He never could put out of his mind any question even after he had taken action on it. He was for ever casting back and wondering whether he had given a right decision — until he had worn a hole in his nervous system. His resignation was a great loss to his Party and to me personally. It was perhaps partly due to this event that I ceased to sit on the Government side of the House and in consequence was deprived of the Conservative Whip. For a time I acted mainly with the Liberals, with whom I generally found myself in agreement on questions of Foreign Policy. This was easier for me since I had, the previous year, supported the election of Mr. Asquith when he re-entered the House as Member for Paisley. But I did not join the Liberal Party. My hope was that a new Coalition might be formed presided over by Lord Grey. It was to consist of Liberals under Mr. Asquith, the Conservatives who were dissatisfied with Mr. Lloyd George's Government, and some of the moderate members of the Labour Party. Looking back, one can see there never was any chance of success for such a system. In fact, it broke down because Lord Grey refused to come forward unless he was asked to do so by Mr. Asquith, and Mr. Asquith was very far from taking any action of the kind. The truth was that Mr. Asquith, having been in office for many years, during eight of them as Prime Minister, tended to regard a Liberal Government as the normal political condition at Westminster, any other being a temporary interlude which would soon disappear. Traces of this opinion still linger in some of the survivors of his school of Liberalism.

Meanwhile, Ireland went from bad to worse. The newspapers were filled with reports of murder and reprisals of a barbarous character. At last a truce was agreed upon which, after complicated negotiations, resulted in an agreement between Sinn Fein and the Government to give South Ireland the status of a self-governing dominion under the Crown. A good deal of argument took place as to the terms in which allegiance to the King should be acknowledged. But allegiance is an attitude of mind and unless it exists, no form of words will create it.

This settlement was vehemently opposed by a section of Conservative opinion in both Houses. With some hesitation I supported it on the ground that it was too late to resist some concession and that if any was to be made it was better that it should be sufficiently thorough-going to have a chance of real acceptance by Sinn Fein. The minorities against the Government were small. But they represented a much larger feeling in the country, as soon appeared. It was the Irish 'surrender' which sealed the fate of Mr. Lloyd George's Government.

It had been arranged that the Assembly of the League should meet in September of that year. I was again appointed a representative of South Africa. Sir R. Blankenberg was again my leader and we had a delightful colleague in Gilbert Murray. The proceedings at the Assembly marked a further stage in the progress of the League. In the words of Monsieur Hanotaux, it became *bien enraciné*. Many of the representatives of the Member States had been at Geneva the previous year and knew each other. The Council, still led by Balfour and Bourgeois, had had only three meetings during the year, as compared with eleven in the previous year, though they had lasted much longer. It was the best period of the Council, which had fortunately quite abandoned its jealousies of the Assembly, and the two bodies co-operated fully with one

another. It is tragic to look back on the vigour and hopeful-
ness that then animated the League and compare it with the
anaemia to which various causes have brought it to-day.

One change in the representation of the United Kingdom
is worth noting. Mr. George Barnes was succeeded by the
present Lord Rennell. The reason of the change was that
Mr. Barnes claimed a certain amount of liberty of speech
in the Assembly which shocked the bureaucracy in London.
He had made a rather outspoken criticism of another country
in the First Assembly and he was required to undertake not
to do so again. He refused, and Lord Rennell was asked to
come in his place. I regretted the decision of the Government.
No one could have been more charming than Lord Rennell.
He had great diplomatic experience and everyone recognizes
his outstanding ability. All the same, he was not so typically
English as Mr. Barnes. The Assembly of the League at its
best should be more than a meeting of the mouthpieces of
different Governments. As far as voting is concerned, of
course each Delegation votes as instructed by its Government.
Nothing else is possible. The Government is the only international spokesman of the nation. But it is, nevertheless,
nowadays of the highest importance that foreign nations
should realize how the people behind Governments look at
the various questions that arise. It is one of the advantages
of the League system that strict diplomatic proprieties need
not be observed. A national delegate should not only expound
the actual policy of his Government but should also convey
to the intelligent foreigner the point of view of his compatriots on the subject. No one who has heard Dr. Nansen,
or Monsieur Briand, or Monsieur Hymans can have failed
to appreciate how each of those speakers represented a special
national standpoint different from that of the other members
of their delegations and also from that of the average Briton.
As an exponent of the point of view of the average Briton
Mr. Barnes was hard to beat, and if the Government had
really appreciated how much the new system might be made
to help international understanding they would not have

lightly parted with Mr. Barnes. Since then it has become more and more the tendency to make the British Delegate at Geneva a mere sample of the Government of the day.

Another step was taken at this Assembly in the other direction. It became the practice for all the regular Committees of the League to sit in public. I believe that everyone who has had experience of the Committee discussions will agree that they have generally been admirable both in form and substance. The rule of publicity was at first vehemently opposed, especially by the representatives of France and Italy. It was said that it would lead to great waste of time and probably be productive of 'unfortunate incidents'. Neither fear was justified. I will not say that no speaker ever talked too much or that it did not occasionally happen that someone expressed himself too warmly. But no harm was done. The garrulous found that their effectiveness varied inversely with the length of their speeches, and the irritable controlled their tempers. Every discussion was carried on under the criticism of the world, no misrepresentation as to the words used was possible, and the speeches, though not so eloquent as in the full Assembly, kept more strictly to the point.

The numbers of the States who adhered to the League had been increased to some fifty-one when the Assembly met. The three Baltic States, Lithuania, Latvia and Esthonia, were admitted, bringing the number up to fifty-four. Each of the new Members was asked its attitude about minorities and in some form or another they let it be understood that they would act upon the principles of the Minorities Treaties which had been accepted by the new States created by the Treaties of Paris. This had been agreed to in accordance with the doctrine laid down at the Congress of Berlin that, where by Treaty a State was brought into existence or given a large extension of territory, it was reasonable that it should give undertakings to treat fairly its racial, religious or linguistic minorities. Poland, for instance, and Czechoslovakia were bound by these engagements to give to their minorities treatment as good as that which their other subjects enjoyed. This provision was put under the guarantee of the League and machinery was created by which any complaint made by a minority could be investigated by a special committee of the Council. There was also, later, a provision by which the Council could take the opinion, on any disputed question of fact, of the International Court of Justice at the Hague. The subject is an extremely difficult one. It is certainly very desirable to protect minorities not only from such atrocious persecution as the Jews have endured in Germany, but even from such lesser hardships as are liable to affect any racial minority which has not been completely assimilated to the majority. On the other hand, any attempt by an international body to interfere too much in the internal administration of any country not only rouses deep resentment but may easily do more harm than good. The best guarantee of good government for a minority is the existence of complete interracial good-feeling, and if a minority is encouraged to make factious or unreal complaints all hope of creating good feeling must be abandoned. On the whole I believe the minorities work carried on for many years at Geneva did good. It was a protection for the minorities against oppression and afforded to the national government an answer to ignorant or malevolent critics. Dr. Benes, in a speech at this time, expressed this view forcibly, and he used always to tell me that he welcomed any appeal to Geneva by the minorities in his country. They in fact did appeal on several occasions and I believe that in no case did any condemnation of the Czech Government follow.

The Minority question was discussed continually both inside and outside the League. Many criticisms were made of the methods adopted to protect minorities. The procedure was as follows. Any complaint received at Geneva of unfair treatment of a racial, linguistic or religious minority of the citizens of a State bound by the principles of the minorities treaties was in the first place examined to see whether it raised a genuine grievance under the Minority Treaty provisions. If it did, it was said to be receivable and it was then referred to a special Committee of three members of the Council appointed *ad hoc*. The petitioners were given an opportunity to submit any further facts or arguments in support of their petition. All the documents were then sent to the Government concerned for their observations; and the Committee made their recommendations and reported them to the Council. It will be noticed that the petitioners were not informed of the reply to their petition made by their Government. This always seemed to me unjust. It was defended on the ground that it was undesirable to treat a Government as an accused party; but the defence was unconvincing. Further, until the Report reached the Council everything was private, and petitioners were not even told the grounds on which the Committee of the Council had acted. Finally, and this seemed to me the most important point, the Committees of the Council varied with each case. Sometimes they were admirable. At others, their principal object was to get through their business and they tended too much to accept the advice given to them by the League Secretariat which, though in many ways excellent, was, like all official bodies, inclined to pursue the line of least resistance. It would have been far better to have had a permanent quasi-judicial Committee which would have built up a code generally applicable. Still, when all criticisms have been made, I have no doubt that the minority work of the League has been beneficial and that the treatment of the minorities within its scope has been better than that of those outside it.

On many occasions efforts were made in the Assembly to improve minority procedure. But they produced little result. There was a strong feeling in the Governments of the States subject to minority obligations that they were not fairly treated. It was notorious that in some States not so subject the treatment of minorities was as bad as or worse than that obtaining in the Minority States. To every suggestion of reform it was replied that if minority rules were extended to all States there would be a case for making them more effective and consequently more burdensome. But while some States were left free from any control it was indefensible to increase the stringency of the control over others. There was no satisfactory answer to this contention except to extend minority control to all States — which I was never allowed by my Government to advocate.

Perhaps the most important piece of work done at this Assembly was the appointment of the Judges as provided by the Statute establishing the Permanent Court of International Justice at the Hague. The scheme was the work of a committee of Jurists of which the British and American members, Lord Phillimore and Mr. Elihu Root, were perhaps the most distinguished. Previous attempts to set up such a Court had split on the rock of National Sovereignty. On the one hand, every State demanded an equal share in the judiciary; and on the other, even so, many States declined to give to the Court any compulsory jurisdiction over questions affecting their 'honour or vital interests', or even to allow any recommendation that such questions should be submitted to the Court. The jurists met these difficulties by providing that in the selection of the Judges, the Assembly, in which all the States sat who were asked to agree to the establishment of the Court, should have equal rights with the Council, in which the Great Powers had permanent seats. This arrangement satisfied certain South American States and others who rigidly adhered to the doctrine that all Sovereign States are in principle equal! The Assembly and the Council sit in separate rooms and vote independently. If the same candidates are not elected by each body the voting is repeated until agreement is reached. On this footing the first election of Judges was successfully carried out. As to compulsory jurisdiction, the jurists had proposed that the Court should have compulsory power to hear and decide any case which raised only certain questions of law and fact declared to be justiciable, such as the construction of a Treaty, or the assessment of damages, etc. This was, however, too much for the reactionary States Members, including the United Kingdom, and a compromise was agreed upon giving the Court compulsory jurisdiction in cases of that kind if they arose between States which had accepted a special clause conferring that power. This was the Optional Clause, which was not agreed to by us until 1929. I well remember Ministerial discussions before that date as to whether it should be accepted or not, and a negative answer being insisted on because, among other reasons, the Court adopted the Continental rule of evidence instead of our own! As I may not have occasion to return to this subject, let me add that the Court has decided thirty-one cases and given twenty-seven advisory opinions, and that I believe its decisions have in every case been obeyed, generally without serious criticism. In spite of this record and in spite of the efforts of the past and present administrations in the United States, the Senate of that country has steadily rejected the jurisdiction of the Court, though I am glad to say that one of the Judges has always been an American. Those American gentlemen who so rightly denounce the extravagances of the principle of National Sovereignty and believe that it can be cured by the creation of an International Federation would perhaps do well to consider this incident.

Another general question of great importance was discussed at this Assembly. By the Treaties of Peace, Germany and her allies in the Great War had been compelled to carry out a large measure of disarmament. It had at the same time been expressly agreed that, as soon as she had done so, the Entente Powers would follow suit. It is worth while to quote once again the documentary evidence on this point: —

Article 8 of the Treaty of Versailles (and of the Covenant) declares: 'that the reduction of armaments is necessary for the maintenance of Peace' and directs the Council of the League to 'formulate plans' for that purpose. By the Preamble to Part V of the Treaty, 'In order to render possible the initiation of a general limitation of armaments Germany undertakes strictly to observe' the disarmament clauses which applied to her. Most important of all, when the Treaty was presented to the German delegates for signature, they wrote to Monsieur Clemenceau as President of the Peace Conference: — 'Germany is prepared to agree to' her proposed disarmament 'provided this is a beginning of a general reduction of armaments'. To which Monsieur Clemenceau replied: — 'The Allied and Associated Powers wish to make it clear that their requirements in regard to German armaments were not made solely with the object of rendering it impossible for her to resume her policy of military aggression. They are also the first step towards that general reduction and limitation of armaments which they seek to bring about as one of the most fruitful preventatives of war and which it will be one of the first duties of the League of Nations to promote.'

There has been a good deal of logic-chopping as to whether these undertakings were independent of one another or not. The discussion is futile. Whatever conclusion might be reached, from a careful examination of the wording of the two promises, there never was any serious doubt as a matter of common sense that the Germans would, on these pledges, expect their late opponents to disarm as soon as Germany had done so, and if they did not, Germany would certainly regard herself as free to re-arm. Some of us therefore continuously pressed the League to carry out the obligations of Article 8 of the Covenant which requires the Council to formulate plans for the reduction of armaments. The French Government actively and the British Government passively resisted this view. They contended that it was too early to ask for the reduction of the armaments of the victorious Powers, Europe was too much disturbed, and so on. In 1921 no doubt German disarmament was not complete. The Allied Commission of Control which had been appointed to supervise the operation had not then reported. But that, in my view, did not affect the obligation of the League to formulate a scheme for general disarmament. Though France and, to a lesser extent, the United Kingdom obstructed action, they did not venture to oppose it altogether. The Temporary Mixed Commission for Disarmament had been appointed in 1920, and in 1921 the subject was vigorously discussed in the Disarmament Committee of the Assembly. The result was a strongly worded report urging the formulation by the T.M.C. of a definite scheme for disarmament, pressing for effective steps dealing with the Traffic in Arms, and asking that a section of the Secretariat should be created to deal with Disarmament questions. This report was presented to the Assembly by myself as Rapporteur and unanimously adopted by it. The Disarmament Section of the Secretariat was created and seven new members were added to the T.M.C., of whom I was one. From this time forward until the breakdown of the great Disarmanemt Conference in 1934, the League, especially through the T.M.C., continually pressed the necessity of Disarmament.

As I have already explained, in addition to the regular Assembly Committees, there are two types of special Committees appointed by the League. One consists of direct representatives of Governments, and no one else. Generally speaking, such a Committee is only useful in strictly non-contentious matters. For if any contention arises the members of the Committee are bound as a rule to say no more than that they will report the matter to their Governments. I sat on one such Committee to deal with refugees, and we did no good at all. Another instance is the Military Commission appointed under Article 9 of the Covenant which has only been useful as an instrument by which France and England have been able to delay disarmament.

The other type of Committee consists in part or altogether of members appointed by the Council of the League for their interest in the subject to be considered. The Committee can, acting by majority if necessary, draw up schemes which then go to the Council and Assembly for their approval or rejection. This has to be done in public and if the schemes are what public opinion wants Governments are cautious about open repudiation of them. Some of the members of the T.M.C. were Government nominees. But it also had independent members who usually were able to get their way. It was consequently very unpopular with the bureaucracies. But, had its recommendations been adopted Europe might have settled down to peace.

If general reduction of armaments is one precaution against war proposed by the Covenant, another is what it is now the fashion to call collective security. It is important to realize what is the true position of this matter under the Covenant. As I have already pointed out, the force relied upon in the Covenant for all purposes except one is instructed public opinion. The sole exception is that, where any State resorts to war in violation of the provisions of the Covenant, then all the other members of the League are to go to the assistance of the country attacked. In carrying out this principle certain questions arise, the main one being — Is this a joint obligation, only binding if all the States other than the aggressor are prepared to act; or is it binding immediately the aggression takes place, on each member of the League separately? If the first interpretation is adopted the refusal to act of a single minor country releases all others from their obligation. On the other hand, if each country is bound to take action against an aggressor whatever the other States decide to do, it may put an unbearable burden on a loyal member of the League. The problem was considered by the Second Assembly, which at the same time dealt by resolution with a number of details connected with it. The solution adopted was, in effect, that the obligation to go to the assistance of a victim of aggression did indeed rest on each member of the League individually. But since the object and the only object was to stop aggression, a member of the League was only bound to take such action as would secure that result. It was accordingly agreed that it was the duty of the Council to consider any military attack and to give an opinion as to whether it was a resort to war in breach of the Covenant.

If the Council decided that a breach had taken place, then their opinion, whether arrived at by majority or unanimously, should be communicated to the members of the League with a suggestion as to the measures which should be taken against the aggressor and the date on which they should begin. A list was drawn up of the various forms of pressure that might be employed, beginning with the withdrawal of diplomatic envoys, and ending with a complete blockade. All this would be, strictly speaking, merely a suggestion by the Council, since under Article 16 of the Covenant it was the right and duty of each member of the League to decide what course it should take in the circumstances. Evidently if the Council unanimously, or even by a majority, apart from the parties to the dispute, expressed the opinion that one of the parties had been guilty of aggression, most members of the League would feel bound to take any action that would be effective in preventing or stopping such a breach of the peace. Further, if political or economic pressure was not sufficient, it was, as expressly provided by Article 16, for the Council to recommend to League members any military measures that might be necessary. Finally, a clause was added enabling the Council to relieve States who were in a difficult position from taking active steps to exercise pressure. It was intended that all this should be introduced into the Covenant by appropriate amendments, and in the meantime it was agreed by all the members present that they would regard these proposals as 'rules for their guidance' until the amendments had been made, which can only be done by a vote of the majority of the Assembly in which the representatives of all the members of the Council have concurred. In fact, the amendments have not been made and the 'rules for guidance' remain. Under these rules the position is reasonably clear. Every member of the League is bound to take whatever effective action is open to it in order to stop aggression. What will be effective depends largely on how great is the strength which the peace-loving Powers can command. Hence the importance of the Council's recommendation both for economic and military proceedings. A good many erroneous criticisms of collective security under the League would not have been made if there had been clearer understanding of what the system set up by the Covenant really was.

Except in the case of the attack by Italy on Abyssinia the economic weapon of the League has never been actually employed. But in the fairly numerous cases in which the League has successfully interfered to settle international differences or stop aggression, these latent powers have exercised a more or less direct influence on the result of the controversies. Elsewhere I have discussed the subject in detail and I need only mention very briefly here the international controversies dealt with by the League up till the end of 1921.

The first was the Aaland Islands dispute between Finland and Sweden. That was not a case of a resort to war or even of a threat of that kind. It was a dispute between the two countries as to the ownership of the islands, in which the League was invoked not under Articles 10 — 16, but under its general powers to pass upon any matter affecting the peace of the world. Subject to certain conditions, the Islands were awarded to Finland. It was a complicated question and, after full examination by the League, was successfully closed by agreement between the Powers interested.

The dispute between Poland and Lithuania was far more difficult. It arose between two new States created by the Treaties of Peace. Unfortunately it had been impossible to settle the actual boundary between the two when Peace was signed, and that was left to a kind of Committee of the Allied Great Powers called the Conference of Ambassadors. The result was a violent controversy complicated by a war between Russia and Poland in which Russia occupied the territory in dispute, from which, under pressure from Poland, she withdrew after assigning it to Lithuania. In these circumstances Poland appealed to the League, not alleging a resort to war by Lithuania, but asking for the good offices of the League to settle the quarrel. For months and even years the League tried, through Monsieur Hymans, the eminent Belgian delegate, to find a solution, but without success. Indeed, I do not think either of the parties were content with any of his suggestions. They both belonged to the 'all-or-nothing' type of controversialists to whom compromise is almost worse than defeat. At one time a certain Polish General Zeligowski occupied Vilna, the principal town of the district in question. He was disowned by the Polish Government, though they later adopted his action. It was of him that Mr. Balfour, in a public meeting of the Council, said: 'This ambiguous General of uncertain allegiance remains in occupation of the disputed territory'. But the inhabitants of Vilna seemed to prefer Poland to Lithuania and when the Conference of Ambassadors finally came to a decision on the boundary they gave Vilna to Poland — a decision against which Lithuania did not cease to protest. So that all that could be claimed of the mediatory efforts of the League was that open warfare had been avoided. It was a melancholy demonstration, since repeatedly renewed, that mediatorial efforts without force behind them are ineffective.

The dispute between Yugoslavia and Albania, which was also before the League at this time, forms an instructive contrast. Albania was admitted a member of the League in 1921. She had become an independent State just before the war, but her frontiers had not been properly delimited. Nor had this omission been rectified after the war by the Conference of Ambassadors. The result was perpetual skirmishing with Yugoslavia on the north. That was the position at the time of the Assembly of 1921. Evidently the first thing was to get the frontiers settled and the League strongly pressed for that. Italy was obstructive, but she was overruled and at last the Ambassadors acted. At their request a Commission was appointed by the League to report on the position. Thereupon, early in November, Yugoslavia invaded Albania and the British Government called for a Special Session of the Council to consider what steps should be taken under Article 16 if the Yugoslavians did not carry out their obligations under the Covenant. The Council met on November 16th, and simultaneously the Ambassadors decided to constitute a demarcation zone within which the frontier was to be delimited and from which all troops should be withdrawn. The summoning of the Council caused a heavy fall in Yugoslavian credit and Yugoslavia promised to accept the frontier when settled by the Ambassadors and to withdraw her troops. The frontier was delimited and complete friendliness was restored between the two countries. Well might Lord Balfour claim that: — 'No statesman, nation, organization or machinery in the world could have done what the League of Nations had done in this matter'. Without the hint of sanctions under Article 16 this result would not have been reached.

The only other international dispute of importance before the Assembly in 1921 was between Bolivia and Chile. It arose out of an old Treaty of 1879 which, as the result of a war, gave certain territories to Chile. Bolivia now appealed to the League under Article 19 of the Covenant for the revision of the Treaty. Chile contested the right of Bolivia to raise the matter and the question of law was referred to a Committee of Jurists. They advised that, in the form employed by Bolivia, the matter could not be raised. She had asked that the Treaty might be revised. The most she was entitled to do was to ask the Assembly to recommend its reconsideration, and that only if it was obsolete or a danger to peace. I was not satisfied with the decision. I had tried at Paris to get a revision clause much more stringent than that adopted, and had failed. But the sentiment of the Assembly, as of the Peace Conference, was overwhelmingly against me. The feeling at that time, before the era of dictatorships, was that peace depended on the sanctity of Treaties and that anything which suggested that they were subject to change was dangerous. It was a short-sighted view.

Beyond these contentious matters, the Assembly did a lot of useful work. The first attempt to rescue Austria from financial ruin was made. But as this attempt was abortive

I will say no more about it here. I have not space to describe in detail the Assembly's many other activities. The administration of the Saar district and of Danzig, both put under the guarantee of the League, was reviewed. The Saar, after a period of unrest due, perhaps, to the excessive administrative zeal of the first chairman of the Governing Body, settled down and for some ten years showed that with intelligence and goodwill international government could be made to work. Danzig was never so successful, partly because the machinery adopted was not very suitable, but mainly because neither the Poles nor Germans were prepared wholeheartedly to co-operate with one another.

It was at this Assembly that the League first acquired effective supervision of Mandated territories, which has continued with unbroken success ever since. Then there was the Report of the Transit Conference which sat for five weeks at Barcelona and produced a number of proposals for improving the means of international communication. There were a number of valuable but very technical recommendations by the authoritative Financial and Economic Committees of the League; the beginning of the admirable work of the Health Committee; the appointment of the Opium Committee, which has since done work of incalculable value throughout the world; and the vigorous action of another body, the Committee for fighting the infamous traffic in women and children, which has achieved remarkable results. So that the suggestion that the League neglected non-contentious work was then and has always remained untrue.

Two other subjects must be mentioned. The Committee for the Reduction of Armaments was getting under weigh. It began its long struggle for controlling the traffic in arms which, on the whole, has been defeated by the armament interests working through nationalistic fears and prejudices and the immobility of the military mind. Still, something has been done. As to reduction and limitation of armaments generally, only preliminary steps were taken.

Lastly, the Assembly received the Report of the great

DR. FRIDTJOF NANSEN

achievements of their Commissioner, Dr. Nansen, in connection with the restoration to their homes of prisoners of war who had remained in belligerent countries. He was able, by his self-sacrificing energy, to secure the repatriation of no fewer than 427,000 prisoners at a cost of less than a pound a head, of which I am proud to say that the United Kingdom contributed more than half. He was also, at this Assembly, appointed High Commissioner to deal with Russian refugees — an even more difficult task. It was during this Session that I came to know Dr. Nansen really well. I had met him and begun to co-operate with him at the First Assembly. Henceforward we worked closely together in all League matters. By profession he was a scientist interested in a number of subjects and especially in the investigation of ocean currents. He had, as everyone knows, accomplished great things as an Arctic explorer. Since then he had served his country diplomatically both before and during the war. His personal position in Norway was immense and he might have had any public office he liked. But he preferred to work for peace and other great humanitarian causes. He became a Norwegian Delegate to the League and was prepared for any action in support of its principles. Once, when we were talking over some question that had arisen and agreeing to advocate a particular solution, I said: 'If we do that we may have to fight both France and England'. 'Of course', said Nansen, with cheerful conviction! He was totally without any affectation, enjoying a sail on the lake, or very elementary lawn-tennis, or dancing at a restaurant with the enthusiasm of an undergraduate! When he spoke in the Assembly it was with the authority of his character and achievements, and all those who really believed in the League and wished it success were delighted to follow him. Others were more critical. But that made no difference to him. He was almost the only man I have ever met who deserved to be called heroic. With his splendid athletic figure, his clear blue eyes, his delightful chuckling laugh and his selfless devotion to the causes in which he believed, he was in a class by himself.

It was a bad day for Peace, Humanity and the League when he died at a comparatively early age. He has left no successor.

At the conclusion of the Assembly in December, I returned to London. The political situation was difficult. Unemployment was rising and the measures for dealing with it proposed by the Government were thought inadequate. Then there was the Irish Treaty to which I have already referred, which was signed in December of that year. There was also the American invitation to a Disarmament Conference at Washington, which the Government had quite rightly accepted. It was perhaps characteristic of their attitude towards the League that the Prime Minister, Mr. Lloyd George, at the Guildhall Banquet, declared that he placed all his hopes for the salvation of the world on the Washington Conference. The only hope of safety, he said, was in Disarmament. But he said nothing to encourage the efforts in that direction then being made at Geneva.

(c) 1 9 2 2

In the following year, 1922, the situation both at home and abroad remained grave. Ireland was still disturbed, though it gradually improved as the Government of the Free State gathered strength. There was trouble too in India, leading to the resignation of the Secretary of State. Moreover, there were many signs that the Coalition Government under Mr. Lloyd George was crumbling. Repeated divisions in both Houses showed that a number of Conservatives were opposed to a Government led by a Liberal Prime Minister, while the Labour and Liberal opposition were as hostile as ever. The result was that after some months of Parliamentary unrest a resolution was passed on October 19th at a meeting of the Conservative Party withdrawing Conservative support from Mr. Lloyd George. The Government resigned, a General Election followed which returned a Conservative majority, with a large increase in the Labour Members, and a considerable decrease in the National or Lloyd George Liberals. I was again returned as Conservative Member for Hitchin and took my seat on the Conservative side of the House. I had been asked to come out in support of the Independent Liberals. But as Mr. Asquith remained their leader and all hope of a coalition under Lord Grey had vanished, I was unable to respond.

It was noticeable that all the political leaders pledged themselves to the support of the League — Mr. Lloyd George and Lord Grey being particularly outspoken. Mr. Bonar Law, too, the new Prime Minister, declared himself in favour of wholehearted and practical support of the League.

In Foreign Affairs, the plan of Conferences of the victorious Powers in the War had been continued. There was one at Cannes which in the winter of 1922 led to the downfall of Monsieur Briand, at that time French Prime Minister. One of the charges made against him being that he had played golf with Mr. Lloyd George! He was succeeded by Monsieur Poincaré, who, though he disliked conferences, attended one at Genoa, making it, however, a condition that it should not derogate from the power and authority of the League. There was, in fact, little or no result from the conference.

In Italy, the seizure of power by Signor Mussolini occurred. He became Prime Minister and shortly afterwards Dictator. Earlier in the year, Cardinal Ratti became Pope Pius XI.

Meanwhile the work of the League went steadily on. In the autumn of 1921 two important questions had been dealt with. One was the Albanian question which I have already referred to. The other was the delimitation of the frontier in Upper Silesia between Poland and Germany. In both cases results were achieved which lasted until the disastrous events of 1939. The main decisions had already been given. But a good deal remained to be done in working them out and this task was substantially completed in 1922.

As far as Albania was concerned, the controversy between her and Yugoslavia was finally settled. There was more trouble over Upper Silesia. The actual demarcation of the frontier involved many practical difficulties. Commercial and social organizations were split by the proposed boundary between the two countries. Geographical features could not always be followed. A Commission had been appointed by the League to determine all such questions and after many sittings all but three had been amicably agreed. It seemed as if the Commission would have to decide these. But at the last moment, in answer to an appeal by the Swiss President of the Commission, Monsieur Calonder, the parties came to an agreement. Such, at this period, was the growing influence and authority of the League and its officers.

Another event of great importance was the Washington Conference on Disarmament. It began its Session in November 1921 and it finished in the Spring of 1922. It was very successful and arrived at conclusions on a number of points. The most important were an agreement to limit the tonnage and number of capital ships and the calibre of their guns, and another agreement to safeguard the integrity and independence of China by what was called the Nine Power Treaty. This last treaty was broken shamelessly by Japan in the Manchurian affair in 1931 and again in the present ruthless war now being waged over large areas in China. The Disarmament clauses fixed the naval ratio at 5 for the British Empire and the United States, 3 for Japan, and $1\frac{1}{2}$ for France and Italy. It was observed by all the European and American parties to it and for a time by Japan also. Later she denounced it.

The Assembly met on September 5th and with Dr. Gilbert Murray I was again Delegate for South Africa. The growing international importance of the League was shown by the number of Prime Ministers and Ministers of Foreign Affairs who attended it as delegates for their countries. Besides these, there were men of outstanding position in their countries, like Lord Balfour, Monsieur Bourgeois,

Monsieur Hanotaux, Monsieur Viviani, Signor Scialoja, Signor Imperiali and Dr. Nansen. The opening debate on the Report of the Secretary General also shewed progress. There was a tone of greater belief in the responsibilities of the League and confidence in its power to discharge them. Thus Lord Balfour declared that it was the function of the League to preserve Peace; and I urged the necessity of courage in carrying out the 'full responsibilities laid upon the League by the Covenant'.

As in the previous Assembly, a large amount of non-contentious work was done, dealing with Opium and other questions such as the White Slave Traffic, Prisoners of War, Russian Refugees — another of Dr. Nansen's activities — Near East Relief, Health, Transit, Financial and Economic questions. The first steps, too, were taken in relation to Slavery on the initiative of the late Sir Arthur Steel-Maitland, on this occasion representing New Zealand. Then there was an important Report by Dr. Murray adopted by the Assembly on the treatment of Minorities. The question was of great international importance. Millions of human beings had been transferred by the Treaties of Paris from one State to another, and in consequence very considerable racial and other minorities had been brought into existence which came within the principle of the Minorities Treaties. I have already explained what these were, and an effort was made at this Assembly to lay down for the benefit of both the Minorities and the State in which they lived the considerations which they ought to have in view in the new conditions created for them. Unhappily, the admirable terms of Dr. Murray's report fell on deaf ears. In many cases, as in Poland, the minority of Germans had belonged to a truculent ruling State before the Treaty of Versailles. Now that the position was reversed it was inevitable that bitterness should be caused even when, as in the case of Czechoslovakia, there was not any very serious ground of complaint. Sometimes, indeed, as in the case of a complaint about the educational hardship to the Hungarian minority in Rumania, a reference to the old

Hungarian laws shewed that the Rumanians had, before the Treaty, at least as great a grievance with the then Hungarian Government as the Hungarians had now. Since that time, the horrible cruelties to the Jews in Germany have enormously increased the urgency of this question.

But the two most important questions discussed at the Third Assembly were the financial assistance to be given to Austria, and Disarmament. The Austrian case was one of immense difficulty. Before the war, Vienna, a city of some 2,000,000 inhabitants, had been the chief city of a great country. By the Peace Treaties, Austria had been reduced to a little State of some five or six million inhabitants and Vienna had necessarily become far too large for it. The result was financial chaos. It had been brought before the League in 1921 and an elaborate scheme was drawn up by the Financial Committee for the assistance of Austria and the reform of her administration. Unfortunately a number of countries had claims on Austria which could not at that time be suspended, and until that was done no permanent relief by loans was financially possible. So that Austria went on gradually sinking lower and lower in the morass. Loans were granted to her by one or two countries without any system of reform to her Government, and so just relieved her for the moment and no more. At last, in August, 1922, she applied to the Supreme Council of the Allied Powers, a survival of the war. The Council was mainly occupied with German Reparations. But on the last day of its Session, August 15th, the Austrian appeal was considered. She was informed that the Allied Powers could provide no more money and that she had better see whether the League could devise some help for her. Accordingly, Mgr. Seipel, the Austrian Prime Minister, arrived at Geneva and addressed the Council of the League, explaining the desperate position in which his country was, and asking for League assistance. A remarkable scene followed. Minister after Minister of those countries which a year or two before had been Austria's enemies in the field, rose in his place and declared that help should be given to a fellow-member of the League. The matter was referred to a Special Committee. Under its guidance, the Finance and Economic Committees of the League set to work and elaborated a scheme by which, in consideration of Austria undertaking to carry out necessary reforms and to accept rigid Financial Control by a High Commissioner appointed by the League, a sum of money was provided by the banks, guaranteed by the Governments of Britain, France, Italy, Czechoslovakia — who each took 20% — and certain other Powers, which it was estimated would carry Austria through the period which must intervene before she could become self-sufficing. There were difficulties. The financial purists in England raised objections, but Lord Balfour's influence was sufficient to overrule them; Italy hung back; and so on. But the scheme went through, and well might Dr. Seipel declare: — 'Thank God we can say to-day the League has not failed us'. It is lamentable that, when political disasters came upon Austria fifteen years later, the statesmen who then controlled the League Governments showed neither the courage nor the wisdom which had distinguished the action of the League in 1922. I do not propose to trace in detail the progress of the League Scheme. It is enough to say that by the end of 1924, Austria was again paying her way and, though she had to endure, with other countries, very great financial difficulties, she never again during her existence as a State Member of the League fell into the same financial morass from which she was rescued by Lord Balfour and his associates in 1922.

This was by no means the only political question affecting members of the League which came before it. A League Commission examined various questions in Albania and made recommendations. A financial adviser to that country was appointed. Frontier questions between Hungary and Czechoslovakia, and between Hungary and Jugo-Slavia were dealt with. Other questions affecting other countries were considered; in particular, the first stages of a long and complicated controversy between Roumania and Hungary about the property of persons in territory which had been transferred from Hungary to Roumania, who had chosen to remain Hungarian citizens. In these cases, all the Council could do was to mediate and suggest settlements which were sometimes rejected, as happened in the leading case of Poland and Lithuania. Generally when matters in dispute were of secondary importance some conclusion was reached. But it often took a long time and necessitated repeated adjournments. Had the growth of the League's influence not been interrupted by the events of 1931-39, I have no doubt that controversies would have progressively become more easy to settle. In the meantime, the inevitable delay gave opportunities of triumph to these critics who seemed to take a delight in finding and exaggerating any apparent defects in the machinery of this novel and highly successful instrument of Peace.

In addition to the many non-contentious questions and the political discussions to which I have referred, the Third Assembly resumed consideration of the vital question of Reduction of Armaments. A good deal of progress had been made by the Temporary Mixed Commission in the spring and summer of 1922. The problem which had to be solved may be thus stated: —

Armaments primarily exist for defence. This was before the era of Dictatorships and every Government denied that it had any intention of attacking another State. But, none-the-less, every Government was afraid that its country might be attacked. This was particularly true of France. Within the memory of many persons still alive she had been twice invaded, and it was the prime object of every French man and woman that that experience should not be repeated. To any proposal for reduction of armaments the instinctive French reply was: — How then shall I be safe from aggression? If it was urged that all countries would be bound to disarm alike, it was still answered: — Suppose they promise to disarm and secretly remain armed? It became clear therefore that before France would agree to disarm she must receive some guarantee of safety on which she could rely. Accordingly, when the

T.M.C. met in Paris in July and August of 1922, the principle was accepted that security and disarmament must proceed *pari passu*. That is absolutely vital. Whatever conceivable doubts on this point may have existed in some minds must surely have been removed by recent events.

The Report of the T.M.C. to the Assembly insisted therefore on two main propositions. Firstly, any really effective system of disarmament must be general, at least as far as the Great Powers were concerned. Secondly, the Governments of such Powers will usually not be willing to reduce their armaments without a trustworthy guarantee of their security. There were other points in the Report such as the extension of the principles of the Washington Naval Disarmament Treaties to the States which had not been represented at the Washington Conference. There was also a recommendation that a new effort should be made to secure a satisfactory treaty regulating the traffic in arms. But the conception that security and disarmament must be linked together was the chief point which was discussed and insisted on at the Assembly.

In all the discussions I was very fortunate in having three French colleagues to collaborate with. First, there was Monsieur Viviani — a great orator. I remember him explaining to me once that he had in reality no gift for oratory and that his success in that field was entirely the result of elaborate self-training. He described to me how he had gone to the French Bar and there studied the lawsuits in progress. As soon as he got home he practised making a speech as if he had been professionally engaged in the litigation. He found that he was deficient in vigorous, epigrammatic expression, and to improve himself he took to writing poetry. He told me that he had made eight thousand verses. At the end of this exposition he sadly concluded that nothing was more fleeting than an oratorical triumph. A few lines in the newspapers that Monsieur Viviani had made a successful speech — and that was all! As a matter of fact, Viviani was quite obviously a born orator — and, it may be, nothing else.

He had a beautiful voice which he managed admirably, and he had emphatically an oratorical temperament which was apt to be unmanageable. Every now and then — perhaps, when presiding over the Disarmament Committee — he would explode rather like the Queen of Hearts in *Alice in Wonderland*. The direction of the explosion was rather incalculable, but it usually resulted in sweeping away whatever was obstructing progress.

Another colleague was Colonel Requin, since a General and member of the Supreme War Staff. He had one of those beautifully neat French minds, a little alarmed at what he considered my revolutionary tendencies, but, when he was convinced that a proposal was desirable, he could put it into the most admirable form.

My greatest ally was the late Senator Henri de Jouvenel. He was an able man and, associated with his brother Robert, a Socialist journalist of considerable brilliancy, he was regarded as a coming man in French politics. Unfortunately, his brother died and Henri, with all his brains, was not prepared to take enough trouble to achieve success. After holding one or two minor offices he also died rather unexpectedly. At this time he was at the height of his powers and took great interest in the proposal to work for disarmament coupled with security. He became one of the French Delegates and, at this Assembly and those that succeeded it, we co-operated vigorously.

In the end, the Assembly approved the plan evolved by the T.M.C. with the addition that the special obligation to give assistance against aggression should only come into force after agreement had been reached as to reduction of armaments. As I put it in my speech to the Assembly recommending this policy: —

'If you are to have a fully effective reduction of armaments it must be general. That is obvious. You cannot have a partial reduction, because it would leave the countries who reduced their forces at the mercy of those who did not reduce their forces. It must be general.

'You cannot expect many of the countries to reduce unless you give them some alternative security and it is suggested that that alternative security is to be found in what is called a Treaty of Mutual Guarantee, that is, a treaty which will give effective, real, well thought out assistance to any country that is suddenly attacked. But that guarantee if it is to be effective for disarmament must be dependent on disarmament being carried out.'

On these lines the T.M.C. was directed to prepare a Draft Treaty of Mutual Guarantee.

One other incident deserves to be recorded. I was anxious to obtain the active support of the Prime Minister, Mr. Lloyd George, and, at my request, a suggestion was sent to him that he might come out to Geneva and make an Assembly speech on behalf of Disarmament. He considered the idea and sent a secretary out to enquire into the situation. But in the end he decided not to come. I renewed my efforts later on to get Mr. Baldwin, when he was Premier, to come out, but I never succeeded. Mr. Ramsay Macdonald, when Prime Minister, came out on two occasions.

When I returned from this Assembly I found the political position much disturbed and, as I have already recounted, Mr. Lloyd George's Ministry fell, Mr. Bonar Law succeeded him, a General Election followed, and I was returned as one of the majority supporting the new Government.

During the remainder of the year, the chief questions considered at home were Ireland, which was still in confusion, Unemployment, for which no remedy was found, and the question of Reparations which, at Geneva, I had unavailingly suggested might be taken over by the League of Nations. The Government preferred to proceed with the weary round of special conferences, the formulation of new plans for payment which proved unworkable, and the continuance of useless irritation in Europe. Ultimately, as will appear, Germany settled the question by declining to pay.

The New Year, 1923, proved to be of great importance internationally. In January Mr. Bonar Law was faced with two questions of difficulty. One was our financial relations with the United States. In the course of the war the American Government, after it had become a combatant, had made considerable advances to the Allies, especially to Great Britain, to enable them to carry on the war. The money was spent on munitions manufactured in the States. During the Paris Conference not very tactful efforts had been made by France to persuade America to forego this debt. They failed and the money — a very large sum — was still owing and we were being pressed for payment. Clearly we had to pay and Mr. Baldwin, then Chancellor of the Exchequer, went to Washington to arrange terms. He brought back an American proposal which, as usually happens in such cases, seemed to the creditor generous and to the debtor grasping. Probably, granted that the advance was not to be regarded as having been expended for the joint interest of all the Allies but as an ordinary loan by one country to another, the terms were fair enough. Anyhow, the British Government agreed to them.

The other grave question was the French occupation of the Ruhr — probably one of the stupidest things that a Government has ever done. By the Treaty of Versailles a colossal indemnity was imposed on Germany and, as part of its payment, certain deliveries in kind were to be made by her. France claimed that these had not been made and that she had therefore the right under the Treaty to occupy the rich coal-producing district of the Ruhr. Very unfortunately, from the point of view of English public opinion, the occupying force consisted partly of black troops. Apart from this, Mr. Bonar Law's Government had serious doubts whether the French construction of the Treaty was correct and were quite clear that, whether strictly legitimate or not, the occupation would be futile and dangerously provocative. At a conference in Paris these views were unavailingly pressed on Monsieur Poincaré. He was one of those persons who insist on precise decisions even if they can only be reached by ignoring some of the factors in the problem. In this case the occupation cost more in money than it brought in, it seriously strained relations between France and Great Britain, it greatly increased the internal difficulties of the then German Government, and it helped to create the conditions in Germany which led to the Hitler tyranny.

I had urged at Geneva that the question of Reparations should be handed over to the League, and the Opposition pressed this view in Parliament. Probably such a solution had by then become impracticable in view of the 'pound-of-flesh' attitude of the Poincaré Government. In the result, the British Government, while openly disapproving of the French proceedings, formally adopted an attitude of benevolent neutrality, a half-measure which merely irritated the French without allaying the German indignation.

I had received many invitations to visit the United States, and as there seemed little for me to do in England at the moment, I accepted one such proposal and sailed for America on the March 21st. It was arranged that New York should be my headquarters and that I should stay there with Mr. and Mrs. Thomas R. Lamont — very charming people whose acquaintance I had made during the Paris Conference. He was at Paris during the Conference as a financial expert, being a partner in J. P. Morgan and Co. In politics he was a Republican supporter of the League of Nations, and at that time we were in full agreement in international matters. Nothing could exceed their kindness and hospitality to Philip Noel Baker, who came with me, and myself. American hospitality is in a class by itself and puts to shame all European efforts in that line. It is not enough for an American host to shower upon his guest every kind of courtesy and entertainment, but he does it in such a way as to make it appear that he is doing little or nothing.

We were in America for about five weeks, during which

time I made about fifty speeches of one kind or another, the keynote being not so much advocacy of the League of Nations as explaining what it was actually accomplishing and what we hoped it might do in the future. We travelled in a private railway car, going as far west as Des Moines, the capital of Iowa, and visiting a selection of the most important cities east of that town, from Richmond in the south to Montreal in the north. Everywhere we had large and cordial meetings about which I noted two things. One was the extreme civility of the audience, even when any of them disagreed with what I said — as must have often happened. I like questions, and answered very many. They were always courteously worded. Indeed, at Louisville, where a member of the audience asked me some perfectly fair but definitely hostile questions, my chairman was much agitated lest the questioner should be thrown out of the meeting! The other great difference from home was that I never addressed a working-class audience. I suggested that I might do so, and though the suggestion was regarded as interesting and perhaps useful, no such meeting was arranged.

I met a number of notabilities, including President Harding and Mr. William Randolph Hearst. The President asked me how I was getting on, and when I replied enthusiastically, he said that he did not doubt I should have good meetings, partly because there were many Americans who agreed with me, and partly because an Englishman could always count on a good audience in the States! It was on this occasion that I paid my visit to ex-President Wilson which I have already described. My meeting with Mr. Hearst was at a luncheon given by Sir William Wiseman — an old war-time acquaintance — to us two. Mr. Hearst was friendly enough in manner but did not conceal from me his opinion; in the first place that the League would not be accepted in the States, and secondly that I was wasting my time there and had better go home! I was also interviewed repeatedly by American journalists. By them I was treated almost always not only with the habitual American courtesy but with complete fairness. The only exception was an enthusiastic Zionist Jew who, failing to get from me any pronouncement on Zionism, patched together a number of public statements on the subject which I had made in England and represented the result as what I had said to him!

On the whole, charming as everyone was, and deeply interesting as I found the trip, I am not quite sure that Mr. Hearst's advice to me was wrong. The view of many if not most Americans is isolationist not only because that is the tradition of their country but also because they are strangely convinced that American diplomacy is no match for European craft. They love to represent themselves as a simple, generous people who are always cheated by the phenomenally skilful and unscrupulous English or Continental Macchiavelli. It follows that though they do not nowadays dislike an Englishman as such, they listen to him with suspicion, and the better the case he makes the more they distrust it. To us, with the recollection of many diplomatic defeats at American hands, the view held over there seems fantastic and we are sometimes tempted to wish that the American estimates of British diplomacy were more nearly accurate than they are. I have the highest admiration for our Foreign Service, but chiefly because they avoid what Grey used to call, with measureless scorn, 'clever diplomacy'.

I returned to England on May 5th and found a very confused situation. Mr. Bonar Law was very ill, and on May 20th he resigned, to the general regret. Mr. Stanley Baldwin succeeded him, to the great disappointment of Lord Curzon, and I joined the Government as Lord Privy Seal, on the understanding that I should deal with League of Nations questions. There was, unfortunately, a misunderstanding about this. I had hoped to be allowed a room in the Foreign Office, and thought that I had made this clear to the Prime Minister. It however did not reach Lord Curzon and when I saw him he peremptorily declined to agree to any such proposal. In vain I pointed out to him how vital it was that the League of Nations should be dealt with as part of the foreign policy of the country and that difficulties would assuredly arise unless the League Minister was working in close collaboration with the Foreign Secretary. Lord Curzon took a rigidly official view that there could not be two Cabinet Ministers in the Foreign Office, in spite of the fact that under Lords Grey and Balfour that arrangement had worked perfectly well. He was afraid of a double direction of Foreign Affairs, which his system very nearly brought about. The result was continual friction and difficulty until the first Baldwin Government came to an end. It is fair to say that for these controversies Lord Curzon was not alone to blame. But had he accepted the arrangement I asked for they would not have arisen.

I have mentioned this incident because it illustrates the official Conservative attitude to the League, both then and thereafter. It was not that my colleagues, generally speaking, were hostile to the League. The Prime Minister, Mr. Baldwin, was temperamentally in its favour. But both he and others regarded it as a kind of excrescence which must be carefully prevented from having too much influence on our foreign policy. Geneva, to them, was a strange place in which a new-fangled machine existed in order to enable foreigners to influence or even control our international action. For us to do anything to help it either with money or diplomatic action was, in their view, an effort of national altruism which could rarely be justified. It is true that those Ministers who actually visited Geneva and took part in the work of the League, like Lord Balfour, Mr. Edward Wood (now Lord Halifax) and, later Sir Austen Chamberlain, usually took a different view. But most of them never went there, and among that number were both the Prime Minister, Mr. Baldwin, and Foreign Secretary, Lord Curzon.

To me, this attitude was almost heartbreaking. As I saw the European situation, the causes which had produced the war of 1914 were bound to resume their sway. Again would grow up the fears and jealousies, the greed and ambition which had brought about that catastrophe. For the time being the recollection of the war was too vivid and the exhaustion of the nations was too great for it to be possible that a major war should break out. But we had not much time. I put it at about ten years. If, in that time, we had not built up an effective barrier against war, the deluge would be upon us. The strengthening of the League by every possible means should have been the first object of our policy. It was the only peace organization in existence. If it was not thought adequate something else should have been put in its place. No attempt to do so was made. The League was officially tolerated. It was never liked. In spite of this half-hearted support, very much of international value was accomplished at Geneva, but unfortunately not enough.

The Assembly of 1923 met in September of that year. As I have already said, I had become a Cabinet Minister at the end of May, specially charged with League affairs. Accordingly I went to Geneva at the end of August to attend the Council and to lead the British Delegation to the Assembly. Lord Balfour was not in the Government at that time, having resigned with Mr. Lloyd George in the previous autumn. So he did not go to Geneva. His absence left a great gap both in the Council and Assembly as well as in the social life of the League. His long experience and great ability gave him a unique position, and the great progress of the League during its first three years owed a great deal to him. His ascendency in our social life there was unquestioned. He enjoyed the society as much as the work. It was indeed very interesting. At the outset there were too many large and pompous dinners which were very expensive and, after the novelty of the international atmosphere had worn off, very tiresome. But the smaller gatherings were often very useful as well as very attractive. They enabled one to meet and discuss matters in a perfectly informal way and sometimes dispelled serious misunderstandings. Often they took place in hotels. But the best of them were given in private houses. Prominent among them all were the luncheons and, more rarely, the dinners given by Mrs. Barton, the widow of a British Consul, who had lived so long and so authoritatively at Geneva as to be commonly known as its queen. She was an admirable linguist and it was her delight to collect round her luncheon table fifteen or twenty of the leading personages at the League. The conversation was multi-lingual and not too serious. In such surroundings Lord Balfour was pre-eminent though others like Briand, Hanotaux, Hymans, Scialoja and Eric Drummond and his very charming wife bore their part. There were, besides, the houses of members of the Secretariat, led, naturally, by that of the Secretary General, which were valuable meeting places. Nor must the Villa Rothschild be forgotten, where the food and wine were exquisite and where the company was often interesting and sometimes exciting. Finally, my wife and I used to collect once a year at dinner at a restaurant a number chiefly of the younger members of the Assembly and of the Secretariat — to me a most attractive function.

Such was the life to which I returned at the end of August 1923. Almost immediately after I got there, Monsieur Politis, the Greek Delegate, called on me at my hotel and informed me that a serious difficulty had occurred between Greece and Italy, that Corfu had been bombarded by Italian ships and occupied by Italian troops, and that he was instructed to bring the matter before both the Council of the League and the Council of Ambassadors. The incident had arisen in this way. The Council of Ambassadors which at that time sat in Paris to deal with subsidiary questions under the Treaties of Peace was engaged in delimiting the boundary between Greece and Albania. In this connection, a commission consisting of Italian officers under General Tellini had been sent to the locality and, while driving along a road in Greek territory, on August 27th, the Italian officers had been attacked and killed. The Council of Ambassadors thereupon, on August 30th, addressed a severe remonstrance to the Greek Government. The previous day, Signor Mussolini had issued an ultimatum to Greece, on the 29th, requiring her to make apologies with various ceremonies, to find and try and execute the murderers, and to pay an indemnity of 50,000,000 lire. The Greek Government made some difficulties about some of these terms, whereupon the Italians, on August 31st, seized Corfu, killing, incidentally fifteen of some Armenian refugees who were there. Monsieur Politis informed me that he wished to raise the matter under Article 15 of the Covenant, but he did not ask for the application of sanctions under Article 16. Article 15 applies only to a dispute 'likely to lead to a rupture' and requires the Council to hold an enquiry into the dispute. It is then to endeavour to effect a settlement of the dispute. If that fails, it is to publish the facts of the dispute and its recommendations thereon. Article 16 provides for sanctions if, in breach of the Covenant, either party to a dispute resorts to war.

The position was complicated for the League by the fact that the question was already under the consideration of the Conference of Ambassadors at Paris. I therefore informed Monsieur Politis that he was entitled to bring the matter before the Council, and telegraphed home for instructions. I was, in reply, authorized to proceed to deal with the matter under the Covenant. Accordingly, when the matter came before the Council, I supported the right of the Greek Government to ask the Council to consider the question. To this the Italian delegation was vehemently opposed. There were then two distinct questions before us. One was whether the Council had the right to entertain the matter. This was the point most vigorously debated. The Italian contention seemed to be, at first, that a Great Power was not subject to the jurisdiction of the League in any matter — to quote the old phrase — of honour and vital interest. On this point the wording of the Covenant was free from doubt and when, at my request, the Secretary General read aloud the relevant passages it was clear that the Italian contention was untenable, and it was not persisted in. Another and better point was that the Council could not deal with a matter already before the Conference of Ambassadors. At first it was doubtful whether Greece consented to the reference to the

Ambassadors, and till that was cleared up the mere fact that the Ambassadors were discussing the matter did not oust the jurisdiction of the League. Another contention was that the dispute was not likely to lead to a rupture and therefore did not come within Article 15. This point was eventually, by agreement, submitted to a committee of jurists who decided that either party might declare that a dispute was likely to lead to a rupture, and that was conclusive. On the point of jurisdiction, therefore, the decision was wholly against the Italians. The other question was what reparation Greece should make. There was no doubt that a serious international offence had been committed for which the Greek Government was at least in some degree responsible. This had always been admitted and Greece had been ready to make ample apology and to try the murderers, if they could catch them, and pay some indemnity. But she was extremely anxious not to lose Corfu. In form, the Italian Government repeatedly asserted that the occupation of Corfu was temporary, for the purpose of compelling Greece to make compensation. But there were strong reasons to suppose that, in fact, the Italian Government contemplated annexation. Ultimately, the Council, at the request of both parties, referred the question of reparation back to the Council of Ambassadors, at the same time communicating to that body their suggestion of what would be a suitable settlement. The essence of the suggestion was that the Italians should forthwith leave Corfu, that Greece should make prescribed apologies, and that the amount of the indemnity to be paid should be referred to the International Court of Justice at the Hague. At first the Ambassadors accepted all our suggestions and so decided. But later they went back on their decision and our Ambassador, Lord Crewe, was instructed to agree to the Italian proposition that the whole 50,000,000 lire should be paid forthwith. Nothing was said about any Greek counterclaim for damage done at Corfu — indeed, as far as I know, no such counterclaim was put forward. There may have been adequate reasons for the British action in Paris. But I was never asked my opinion nor informed of what was done. I heard that the action of Lord Crewe was the result of direct personal instructions by Lord Curzon. In that case the incident is an excellent example of the evil of treating our League policy as something apart from the general foreign policy of the country. On the whole, however, the League succeeded in carrying out successfully its duties under the Covenant. A difficult and dangerous dispute was settled rapidly and, apart from the amount of damages, for which it was not responsible, fairly enough. Corfu was saved, and the jurisdiction of the Council was confirmed. The Greek Government expressed themselves as fully satisfied. Indeed, Monsieur Venizelos told a friend of mine that he thoroughly approved of the action of the Council.

It will be observed that all the proceedings were before the Council and not the Assembly. But the members of the Assembly, representing especially the smaller Powers, were deeply interested and, with practical unanimity, were on the side of Greece. This was a great factor in enabling the Council to maintain its action. At the end it reported to the Assembly, which approved what it had done, though there was very strong and deserved criticism of the Conference of Ambassadors.

Sanctions were not actually used, but they were known to be in reserve, and that no doubt contributed to the relative moderation of the Italian Government.

Of not less importance than the proceedings about Corfu were the further steps taken by the Assembly about Disarmament. It will be remembered that, at the end of the Assembly of 1922, the Temporary Mixed Commission had been instructed to prepare a definite scheme for the general reduction of land and air armaments. Accordingly, the Commission had held three meetings, in February, in June and in July. At first there was considerable difference of opinion, especially between the French members of the Commission and myself. But as the discussions went on the difficulties disappeared and the Commission was able to adopt in a report to the Council, who transmitted the Report to the Assembly, a draft Treaty of Mutual Assistance. It may be noted by the way that the title of the Draft is the same as that given to the recent Anglo-French-Turkish Treaty. The Draft begins by denouncing 'aggressive action as an international crime' which the parties to the Treaty undertake not to commit. It then goes on to provide that they will furnish assistance as prescribed by the Council to any one of their number who is attacked, provided it has conformed to the provisions of the Treaty with regard to Disarmament. There follow various provisions designed to make the assistance effectual and, in particular, a provision that no party to the Treaty shall be required to co-operate in military, naval or air operations except in the Continent in which its territory is situated. On the other hand, the Council is empowered to take measures to meet a menace of aggression of the same character as it could take to deal with aggression itself. Other articles save 'complementary' defensive agreements made by two or more parties for their mutual defence, and suggest the creation of demilitarized zones between Continental countries in order to prevent a sudden attack. Then come actual disarmament clauses which provide suggestions of how to set about disarmament, without going into actual detail. The scheme of the Treaty was to confine the guarantee of assistance to those who disarmed, believing that thereby sufficient inducement to disarm would be given. Certainly it was the view of the authors of the draft that, without an effective guarantee of security, there could be no hope of disarmament and that, without a reduction and limitation of armaments, a guarantee of security was impracticable. I am still of opinion that these propositions are vital to the solution of the problem of disarmament and, therefore, of peace.

The British Government were, naturally, kept informed of the progress of these negotiations though, following their usual attitude towards the League, the War Department declined to give me any technical help such as we got from the French through Colonel (now General) Requin.

The Treaty was elaborately considered in the Third Committee of the Assembly and approved by it. It was then
presented to the Assembly by the Rapporteur, Dr. Benes,
and sent on to the various Governments for their consideration. I was, unluckily, ill at the time. The Corfu question
and this Treaty had been hard work and that, combined
with other things, brought on an attack of shingles which
disabled me for some weeks. Most of the other labours of
the Assembly fell, therefore, on Sir Rennell Rodd and Mr.
Edward Wood. Some of them were of great importance.
There was the continued satisfactory progress of the Austrian
scheme; there was the beginning of a similar scheme for
Hungary; there were the first steps in the transfer of the Greek
population of Asia Minor to Greece as the result of her
disastrous war with Turkey. There were also hardy annuals
like the Saar, Danzig, Opium, White Slave Traffic, discussion
of Slavery, and all sorts of technical questions connected
with Finance, Health, Transit and other matters. There was
also the admission of two new members — Ireland, which
raised no difficulties then or afterwards, and Abyssinia. As
to the admission of Abyssinia the British Government had
considerable doubts which were voiced by Mr. Edward Wood.
In particular, there was the question of slavery in that
country, as well as the generally backward condition of her
Government. But the Abyssinian delegation cabled for and
received assurances on these points which were communicated
to the Assembly. Even so, it is doubtful whether she would
have been admitted but for the earnest support given to her
claims by Italy and, to a lesser extent, by France — who were
trade rivals for Ethiopian custom.

I returned by rail to London and arrived to find the Ruhr
question in a deadlock. The occupation by the French still
continued, without producing any adequate pecuniary result.
Efforts by Lord Curzon to come to terms with Monsieur
Poincaré had failed. I myself, when I was in Paris in July,
had seen some of the French Ministers, including the President, Monsieur Millerand, and had informally discussed the

question with them. The attitude of Monsieur Millerand seemed to me not unfavourable and I so reported to the Foreign Office. This was, no doubt, outside my functions, as the Prime Minister pointed out to me, though I cannot see that it did any harm. Certainly the continuance of the deadlock was a serious matter.

A meeting of the Imperial Conference was in progress, at which I was deputed to explain what had happened at Geneva about Corfu, and the Conference expressed satisfaction with the British action there and with the result. General Smuts made a strong speech in favour of the League. He also made a speech deploring the occupation of the Ruhr and suggesting an International Conference on the subject. Meanwhile, the American Government renewed an offer to take part in an enquiry into Germany's capacity to pay, and this was accepted by the British Government. After some negotiation, the French Government also accepted and the enquiry took place in the following year. As part of this arrangement the occupation of the Ruhr was discontinued. But unhappily, its effect on the European situation remained.

In connection with the Imperial Conference, an Economic Conference of Empire representatives was held, at which Mr. Bruce of Australia made a strong speech advocating the adoption of Protection by this country in order to make Imperial Preference effective. This speech was delivered on October 9th. On October 25th, Mr. Baldwin attended the annual meeting of the National Unionist Association and announced that, as a cure for unemployment, he was convinced that it was necessary to adopt a moderate Protectionist policy. As he had earlier given a pledge that there should be no change in the fiscal policy of the country during the lifetime of the then existing Parliament, a dissolution became necessary. Though I believe the Prime Minister had spoken of his intention to make this speech to one or more of his colleagues, the opinion of the Cabinet on the change of policy involved had never been asked. Those of us, therefore, who were more or less Free Traders were, to put it mildly, a good deal surprised, and one or two of us even contemplated resignation. However, as no definite proposal had been made we did not resign. On the other hand, I felt such difficulty in fighting a contested election under a Protectionist banner that I asked for a Peerage. In doing so, I was partly influenced by my growing conviction that my ideas of Foreign Policy, particularly as to the League, were so doubtfully shared by my colleagues that I might find co-operation with them on that subject impossible. To leave the House of Commons was a very great disappointment to me, though I had found it much less interesting since I had been a Minister. On the back bench or in opposition an M.P. can speak when he pleases, if he can catch the Speaker's eye, and say what he likes. But as a Minister — unless he is in charge of a Bill or is the Leader of the House — he can only speak as and when he is told to, and that may be on subjects which he does not like. On the other hand, the House of Commons is far more influential than the House of Lords. I remember Sir Austen Chamberlain declaring to me most vehemently that he would never take the step I had taken. Still, there is more freedom in the Upper House. Advocacy of a non-Party cause like the League of Nations may compel a man to criticize the Government of the day, even though the Party to which he belongs is indifferent or even unfriendly to that cause. And under modern conditions, criticism by a Conservative M.P. of a Conservative Government is almost certain to set the Party machine in action against him. That is an unfortunate condition of affairs and has done much to lower the reputation of the House of Commons. But it is convenient for Party Leaders and Party Whips. It involves increasing subservience of Members to those officials and adds a great burden to those who are forced by their opinions to take an independent line. It was partly, therefore, because I rightly feared that it would become difficult for me to approve Conservative policy on the League that I was driven to ask the Prime Minister to recommend me for a Peerage, which he very kindly did.

The Election took place, with the result that the Conservative Party came back as the largest Party, but in a minority if Labour — the second largest — and Liberals voted together against it. Mr. Baldwin decided to meet the House of Commons so that the Government went on unchanged until January.

I attended a Council of the League in Paris in December, where the Hungarian plan was advanced a stage. Unfortunately, this led to one of the perpetual misunderstandings with the Foreign Secretary, Lord Curzon — the details of which are not now of importance. Meanwhile there were various negotiations going on as to the next Government. Among other things it was thought possible that Labour would ask me to continue as League Minister. In fact, no such suggestion was made to me by the Labour leaders.

(E) 1924

In due course Mr. Baldwin's Government was defeated and Mr. Ramsay Macdonald became Prime Minister. He was also Foreign Minister and, though he succeeded in relieving the Anglo-French tension, it became clear as the months proceeded that the burden of the two offices was too great for any man to bear, especially if he was in the House of Commons. Meanwhile the League of Nations Union, of which I had become Joint-President with Lord Grey, hoped much from the new Government. Unhappily, Mr. Macdonald, though he supported the League of Nations in principle, never liked it. Perhaps his dislike for it was increased by a stupid personal quarrel with the League of Nations Union which led him to refuse to become an Honorary President of that body, as all others were who had occupied the post of Prime Minister.

Soon after the formation of the Government we went on a deputation to Mr. Macdonald and Lord Parmoor, who was understood to be in charge of League affairs. We were very graciously received and obtained as much as deputations usually obtain — that is, nothing. I remained a member of the Hungarian Committee of the Council and collaborated with Mr. Montagu Norman in securing for Hungary assistance of the same kind as — though by no means identical with — that given to Austria. It was equally successful. I also attended the meetings of the Temporary Mixed Commission at which we tried, with partial success, to grapple with the evils of the traffic in arms. In May I accepted an invitation to go to Holland and Scandinavia, and had a number of very successful meetings in the four countries. One of the best was at Amsterdam, where I spoke for about an hour. Half-way through there was an interval in which the audience left their seats, returning in about ten minutes, after which I resumed my speech — a curious custom, but, granted the orderliness of the Dutch, not a bad one. I spoke in English, as I did elsewhere, without an interpreter and, except at Stockholm, I seemed to be always perfectly understood. As a Dutch lady said to me in answer to a compliment on her English: 'Oh! you see we don't think we have begun to be educated unless we know the four languages, English, French, German and Dutch'. I thought, however, that some of the boys and young men looked as if they overworked. Our northern friends were charmingly hospitable, with their custom of making little speeches of welcome to their guests at dinner, to which the guest replies a little later on, and their rule by which, whenever you next meet your dinner hostess, even if it be months later, you should thank her for her hospitality. The audiences were very receptive. Indeed, a Scandinavian meeting seemed to me much more like an English or Scottish meeting than did a comparable audience in America.

While I was in Norway I met a League official who told me that the Labour Government had definitely decided to turn down the Treaty of Mutual Assistance, and this proved to be the case. There was a debate on the subject in the House of Lords in July at which Lord Parmoor announced this decision. It was based partly on the alleged reluctance of the Dominions to accept the Treaty. In fact, they would not have been much affected by it since they would not have been bound to take any action under it outside their own Continents. It was also said that it would drive the United States further from the League — a complete misunderstanding of American opinion — and that it might enable a foreign body to dictate our military strength — a fantastic perversion of the proposal. The real truth was that, at that time, Lord Parmoor thought that peace could always be preserved without the use of force — an opinion which he found unsustainable as soon as he got to the Assembly in the following September. Lord Balfour approved the Government decision mainly on the ground, so often and so fatally repeated, that we must avoid commitments — that is, definite statements beforehand of what our action would be when a crisis arose. This opinion was defended on the theory that it makes for safety. The exact opposite is the truth. We undertook in the Covenant that we would, in certain cases, join in protecting a victim State against aggression. But the undertaking was in somewhat general terms. The result has been that aggressors have 'taken a chance' that we should not fulfil our undertaking. That came off over Manchuria and, ultimately, over Abyssinia. Still more regrettably, the same thing happened over Czechoslovakia. Then came Poland and, though our position was perhaps less favourable than in any previous case except Manchuria, we felt bound to act and feverishly scratched about everywhere to get assistance from other countries which, under the Treaty of Mutual Assistance, would have been given to us as a matter of course. Had that Treaty been in operation, it is morally certain that the Italian invasion of Abyssinia and the German invasions of Czechoslovakia and Poland would never have taken place.

Lord Grey and I protested unavailingly against the Government decision which, however, was maintained and repeated at Geneva in September. Thus the French are able to claim, quite rightly, that it was the British and not they who turned down this first proposal for making effective international security and disarmament.

When the British representatives of the Labour Government reached Geneva they found it impossible to persist in a purely negative attitude and agreed to the Protocol of Geneva. I was not there and so can only give a very brief outline of what occurred.

The Protocol was based on three conceptions — Arbitration, Security, Disarmament. It proposed a complicated scheme for dealing with arbitration, which ended in compulsory arbitration in all cases. Utterances of Lord Parmoor seemed to indicate that he thought arbitration without any force to back it could solve all international disputes. But it was clear that none of the continental nations except perhaps Scandinavia would look at such a proposal. Still, general arbitration would have done one thing. It would have provided a test as to which country was the aggressor, since it might be concluded that if arbitration were rejected by one of the disputants it was that one that meant to attack. Next, the proposals as to security consisted merely in an obligation 'loyally and effectively' to carry out the provisions of the Covenant, such as Article 16. By a singularly unscrupulous proceeding on the part of the British critics of the Protocol it was described as putting the British Fleet at the disposal of the League. There was no truth in this suggestion.

The weakest part of the Protocol was the provision as to disarmament. This consisted in little more than the obligation to call a conference on the subject in the following summer. This was a vital difference from the Treaty of Mutual Assistance since that was not to be effective till disarmament was actually in the course of being carried out.

The policy of the Protocol was in my opinion a serious mistake. It was a long and complicated document carried in a great hurry and appearing to involve much larger changes than it actually did. It was seized on by the

Opposition in Great Britain as another proof of the practical incapacity of the Labour Government and, though the attack was largely unfair, yet the action of the Government in rejecting the Treaty of Mutual Assistance because it involved the use of force, and then adopting the Protocol which was equally open to that charge, was difficult to defend. Had the Government accepted the Treaty of Mutual Assistance and inserted in it simple provisions for arbitration, they would have been in a much stronger position and might well have settled the whole question. In fact, as will be seen, the British Government rejected the Protocol and once again appeared as obstructing efforts for peace to which France had agreed.

The other proceedings of the Assembly were overshadowed by the Protocol but were in themselves important. The scheme for the relief of Austria proceeded, though it experienced some difficulties. Its Hungarian counterpart was just starting and got off very well. That was, in part, due to the fact that the Commissioner in charge, the American, Mr. Jeremiah Smith, was perhaps more tactful than Monsieur Zimmermann at Vienna. Another relief scheme of a very different kind was that arising out of the wholesale emigration of Greeks from Asia Minor. As the result of the war with Turkey, Greece found herself faced with the obligation to receive upwards of a million new subjects — nearly 25% of her existing population. Greece appealed to the League for help and at the 1923 Assembly a scheme was launched whereby money was to be raised and applied for the settlement of the refugees under the control of a commission of four, of which two, including the Chairman with a casting vote, were nominated by the League. The Greek Government placed land at the disposal of the refugees and money was found — two preliminary sums of £1,000,000 each by the Bank of England. At the 1924 Assembly it was announced that the security proposed by Greece for a loan of £10,000,000 was regarded by the Bank of England as sufficient. As I shall not return to this subject again I may say briefly that the scheme proved a great success, that the population so settled in Greece is now very prosperous and has become a great asset to the country.

There was much other work done by the Assembly in connection with minorities — a great success being achieved about Polish minority questions; Mandates, Slavery, Health, Opium, Refugees, White Slave Traffic, Transit, etc. But these, being mainly technical and non-controversial, were not good 'copy' for the Press and received little publicity.

During the spring and summer of 1924, the Labour Government was going downhill. In Home affairs it was precluded by its dependence on a partly reactionary Liberal Party from doing much. In Foreign affairs it had a great opportunity and at first Mr. Macdonald's administration of the Foreign Office was much praised. But his great chance was to put himself at the head of a vigorous League policy and this, as I have explained, he failed to do. The Protocol, which might be regarded as the one constructive League effort of his Government, was not very good in itself and was put forward in such a way as to challenge opposition. Nor did he somehow produce a very good effect in Geneva when he went there. It was thought that he addressed the Assembly of the statesmen and diplomatists of Europe as if it had been an English public meeting. The truth is that he enjoyed immensely the old diplomacy, the conception that a few very eminent personages sitting in secrecy should settle the affairs of Europe. He never fully accepted the view that modern education and modern publicity makes it essential that diplomacy should carry with it the knowledge and assent of the peoples, particularly in democratic countries. For that object the Assembly is an invaluable instrument, but it requires a different technique from that which was suitable for the Congress of Vienna.

In one respect Mr. Macdonald set an admirable precedent. He was the first British Prime Minister and Foreign Secretary who went to Geneva. His doing so greatly increased the prestige of the League. Many other statesmen of eminence followed his lead. In the French Delegation, Monsieur Herriot, the Prime Minister, presided over a very distinguished body, including MM. Bourgeois, Briand, Paul-Boncour, Jouvenel, and others. I had seen Herriot in London and asked him whether he was going to make Briand his Foreign Minister. He said No! first because it would make his own position impossible, and secondly because Briand preferred to be made the French Official Delegate to the League, which he continued to be till the end of his life, whether or not he was also Foreign Minister. The incident is eloquent of the great position the League enjoyed in France at that date. The example given by Britain and France was followed by other countries, so that for the next ten years the Assembly was a collection of the leading statesmen in Europe. More distant countries were usually represented by their Ambassador or Minister in one of the European capitals. The Dominions sent either their High Commissioners in London or other statesmen, according to circumstances. Another evidence of the growing authority of the League was the spontaneous offer of the United States to attend an international convention on the traffic in arms, if one were summoned.

Still, in spite of the increase in the prestige of the League, for which the Labour Government was entitled to some credit, its popularity at home was decidedly going down. When, therefore, difficulties arose over our relations with Russia abroad and the Communists at home, the Liberals decided to join the Conservatives in turning Labour out — an incident which the Labour Party has never forgotten or forgiven. An election followed, in which a letter signed by Zinovieff, a Russian personage, urging British subjects to work for Revolution, played a great part. The letter was officially declared by the Russian Ambassador to be a 'clumsy forgery'. But I believe it was genuine, as a Committee of the incoming Conservative Cabinet, on which I served, unanimously stated. Anyhow, it gave an additional push to the swinging pendulum, with the result that the Conservatives came back

MONSIEUR ARISTIDE BRIAND

with 415 members of the House of Commons as against 153 Labour and 40 Liberals.

Mr. Baldwin formed his second Cabinet, in which Sir Austen Chamberlain became Foreign Minister, Mr. Winston Churchill Chancellor of the Exchequer, and Lord Birkenhead Secretary of State for India, thus healing the Conservative split. I accepted the Office of Chancellor of the Duchy of Lancaster, reluctantly offered to me by Mr. Baldwin, and with his consent suggested to Sir Austen that I might be his subordinate in the Foreign Office, for dealing with League affairs. But Sir Austen resolutely declared that he could not allow me any share in the direction of League policy beyond that which I should have as a member of the Cabinet, on the ground that there could not be two Cabinet Ministers in the Foreign Office. I was much disappointed but, after a good deal of hesitation, I decided to accept. The prospect was not alluring. Out of a Cabinet of twenty-one, not more than one-third could be considered as adherents of the League, and most even of these were more or less half-hearted. Sir Austen knew, at that time, very little about it and was inclined to accept the advice on the subject of the more reactionary officials in the Foreign Office. At first, indeed, he proposed to send the Under-Secretary, Mr. Ronald MacNeill, to represent the British Government on the Council which was to be held in Rome early in December. The League Secretariat vehemently protested, saying the representative must be a Cabinet Minister. As Sir Austen was quite determined not to send me, and could not find any other colleague whom he thought suitable, he decided to go himself — a most fortunate decision. It is only right to add that he very soon became one of the League's most convinced supporters and that he and I worked for the League in general agreement.

Two things happened to me this autumn. Just when the Cabinet was being formed I was elected Lord Rector of Aberdeen University, which gave me then and afterwards very great pleasure. I also received the first peace prize awarded by the Woodrow Wilson Foundation and went to

America to receive it at the end of December. It amounted to £5,000 and the travelling expenses of my wife and myself were also paid. We stopped with the kind Lamonts again, and I made two or three speeches. One of them was in answer to the presentation of the prize, which was made by Mr. Franklin D. Roosevelt. I also went to Washington, to be presented to President Coolidge, and stayed with the British Ambassador, the late Lord Howard of Penrith — a charming visit. He took me to call at the White House, and when we were received by the President the latter said: — 'Folks who come to see me have to do the talking!' However, in fact my function was that of a listener.

We left New York in a blizzard. The car could not get through the snow to the steamer, so that we had to walk the last half-mile or so. When we got there, rather breathless, we found the sailing had been put off for a couple of hours!

(F) 1925

When we got home I heard that there was an important League Committee on Opium sitting at Geneva, which had got into a tangle. My brother Salisbury had agreed to attend it for the British Government; but unfortunately was disabled by a fall from his horse. There was no one else of my colleagues who could go, and so the Foreign Office were compelled to send me. I spent an agreeable three or four weeks in January and February 1925, at Geneva, negotiating chiefly with Mr. Porter, a typical American Congressman, perpetually on his guard against the wiles of European Diplomacy. The object in view was a Convention, or, rather, two Conventions, to regulate the production and traffic in opium. There are three ways in which opium is consumed. One can eat it, and as far as I could make out it is not more harmful in that form than, say, the drinking of spirits — that is to say, it does not hurt you seriously unless you take too much of it. It used to be consumed as laudanum in this country, not only by what we should now call addicts like Coleridge and de Quincey, but very commonly as a medicine. Dr. Johnson, for instance, took it frequently to relieve his asthma and other ills. Nowadays it is not much used here. But in India it is taken in the form of pills and is alleged to be of great value against physical fatigue. I have heard distinguished Indians in the Assembly make almost lyrical speeches on its virtues!

Then, as we all know, it can be smoked. In this form it seems much more deleterious and the Chinese, who are the chief opium smokers, regard it as very pernicious. If a person becomes a constant smoker it seems to undermine his whole constitution, mental and physical. Lastly, in the forms of morphine and heroin it can be injected. This is the way it is used in many European countries, in Egypt and the Middle East, and in the Far East, and also on the American Continent. Apart from its medical value it is, in this form, unquestionably a great curse and, though it cannot be dispensed with as a painkiller, all civilized countries are agreed that its production and sale should be closely controlled. Unfortunately, the opium-poppy can be grown with great profit in many countries. It is therefore very difficult to limit its production, especially as the Indian use of it is, as I have explained, relatively harmless. However, it was no use saying that kind of thing to Mr. Porter. He and his friends were crusaders and nothing but root and branch extirpation would satisfy them. Ultimately we agreed to set up an elaborate international machinery rationing the various countries as far as we could and doing our best to bring all the manufacture of and traffic in morphine and heroin under very strict public control. Even so, a great amount of illicit dealing with these drugs goes on with the help of large and wealthy criminal organizations. The annual Egyptian Report on the subject by Russell Pasha gives a vivid picture of the devices of the traffickers and the courage and resource of the defenders of the law.

While I was at Geneva I heard that the British Cabinet

were going to consider their policy with regard to the Geneva Protocol. At my earnest request they postponed their deliberations till I could be present. Accordingly, as soon as I got back in February, there was a meeting of the Committee of Imperial Defence to consider the military aspects of the European situation. The Foreign Secretary urged on his colleagues the necessity of making an attempt to relieve the serious tension that existed between France and Germany. We were informed that there was a prospect that Herr Stresemann, then at the height of his power, might agree to a pacific policy. Recent publications have made it doubtful whether his real intention was other than to gain time until Germany recovered her strength. He never was to me an attractive personality. However, at this time his proposal was plainly acceptable. The majority of the Committee had no doubt that the Geneva Protocol ought to be rejected. During the Election many of them had denounced it with great vigour, and, for reasons which I never appreciated, it seemed to excite bitter feelings of hostility. I urged amendment rather than rejection, with no support. When, therefore, Sir Austen, seizing on the hint that had come from Stresemann, held out hopes of obtaining an agreement with France and Germany which would lessen the danger of war in that part of Europe where it seemed most menacing, I agreed to the double policy of dropping the Protocol and securing in its place what afterwards was known as the Locarno agreement. Instructions with this object were drafted, chiefly by Lord Balfour, which Sir Austen was to take with him to the next meeting of the Council. I made two efforts to modify this policy. One was to add to the specific arrangements with regard to France and Germany some kind of general clauses indicating the desirability of extending a similar policy to the rest of Europe. On this point the rest of the Committee disagreed with me. I also tried to soften parts of the instructions which seemed to imply that the coercive Articles of the Covenant could no longer be regarded as binding. As to this, Sir Austen took the same view as I did, and when the instructions came before the Cabinet they were amended accordingly.

When the instructions were read out at Geneva, Monsieur Briand did not conceal his great disappointment at the British action, a disappointment which was only in part removed by the suggestion of some special arrangement dealing with particular regions of Europe. The same thing happened later on at the Assembly, which I attended in September as second delegate with Sir Austen. Sitting by him, we listened to an eloquent speech by Monsieur Paul-Boncour in which he expressed his profound disagreement with British policy. I remember whispering to Sir Austen that the speech made me feel very mean, since I really agreed with every word of it. He made no reply. Then in the autumn Sir Austen met Monsieur Briand and Herr Stresemann at Locarno, where the agreements which bear its name were concluded. They provided in effect that Germany would make no effort to recover Alsace-Lorraine and would not resort to arms to alter her boundaries with Poland. Britain and Italy guaranteed these engagements, expressly promising to go to the assistance of France or Belgium if Germany attacked them, and conversely, of Germany if she were attacked by either or both of the other two. France and Poland also made a defensive alliance, as did France and Czechoslovakia. Germany further made arbitration treaties with France, Belgium and Poland. In all the Treaties, the position of the League was fully safeguarded. Indeed, they were not to come into force till Germany entered the League. There were also general promises to work for disarmament. Sir Austen had therefore full right to insist, as he always did, that the Treaties were intended to strengthen the League. As such they were gratefully accepted by Parliament and Sir Austen was much and rightly praised for his part in the negotiation. It was on this occasion that he received the Garter. It was one of the most shameless acts of the present German Government to repudiate the German promises then freely made, and to tear up

Treaties which owed their origin to the action of its own predecessors.

In this country I doubt if Locarno was ever popular, though at the time I thought it was. Perhaps the common people, with their remarkable political sense, recognized that a particular arrangement of this kind could not be the basis of a lasting security for peace. Certainly there is much to be said for this view. Europe is too closely bound together nowadays for it to be possible to provide effectually for the preservation of peace in one section of it alone. Europe may perhaps be separated for peace purposes from the rest of the world, though even this would not be easy. But no smaller area can be so treated. Another feature of Locarno ought to have been seen to be dangerous. It was in connection with these negotiations that the policy of no general commitments was first suggested by British Ministers as part of our international attitude. Never has any policy done more harm. Theoretically something may be said for the rejection by us of any European entanglements, though in actual fact this has always proved impracticable. But if it be granted that peace is our greatest interest and that any outbreak of war in Europe endangers the tranquillity of the whole of that Continent, then we must evidently take our share in preventing or extinguishing such an outbreak. To admit that this is both our interest and duty, and yet to refuse to tell the world and especially other peace-loving Powers beforehand what we will do when the moment comes is surely folly. I have no doubt that the Polish war was mainly brought about by this senseless system. Had we adopted in earlier years a clearer and more courageous policy, Russia would not have been estranged, the 'neutrals' would have been encouraged and it is more than doubtful whether, in that case, Hitler would have invaded Poland. The truth is that an influential section of British opinion, though it has always shewn itself ready to resist by force of arms any attack even on an outlying and unimportant part of our Empire, has never thought out the reason for doing so. The only justification is that submission may lead to more serious attacks. But if that be true, it is far more true that any unresisted armed invasion of a peaceful country is a danger nowadays to the whole international *status quo*. It is the literal truth that 'Peace is indivisible', and it was the failure fully to recognize that fact which made Locarno relatively useless. No doubt, as Sir Austen more than once said, he hoped that Locarno would be followed by other regional pacts. But he thought we had done our part and others ought to take the lead elsewhere. He seems never to have quite accepted the view that Locarno, unless in some way made part of a general peace system, was of little value. In fact, nothing was done to complete Locarno for the rest of Europe.

Two personal events happened during the early months of this year, 1925. Lord Curzon died. I had known him for very many years and though latterly we had been officially opposed to one another, there was no breach of personal relations. He was a man of many gifts, social, literary and political. He had what must be regarded as a highly successful life and had filled some of the highest offices of State. Yet he was not, I believe, a happy man. Certain peculiarities of manner and outlook, particularly a curious want of proportion, made him quarrel, sometimes bitterly, with many of his best friends. In some moods, he was, as an American acquaintance described him, 'both peevish and arrogant'. Yet he was a great figure. He had a high sense of public duty, great eloquence and almost incredible industry. He narrowly missed being Prime Minister, to his intense disappointment. It was, perhaps, this event, coupled with his continual ill-health, which made the closing years of his life miserable for himself and trying for his colleagues.

The other event was the acceptance of a peerage by Mr. Asquith. That marked the close of his political life. It is true that he attended the House of Lords and made interesting and valuable speeches. But a political leader in the Upper House can only be influential as a Party politician if he leads a numerous and effective body of supporters in the

House of Commons, and the Liberal Party in that House could not properly be so described. His work was ended, and he left behind him not only a great intellectual and parliamentary reputation but an example of devotion to his country and loyalty to his friends and colleagues which have never been surpassed.

The two great domestic political events of this year were the first beginnings of Protection and the first stages of that industrial unrest which culminated in the General Strike. There was also a very moderate increase of the Navy, not nearly sufficient unless the League had been kept in being as a serious safeguard of peace. The No Commitment policy was thought to make it less needful to have a powerful Navy. The truth was exactly the opposite. No commitments meant an anaemic League. The only alternative to a strong League was a strong Navy, and indeed strong armaments, however unsatisfactory that might be.

In this year also took place the Chinese threat to Shanghai. Since this involved danger to important commercial interests in that city, the British Government, in common with other Governments, reinforced our troops there and even examined the possibility of a general blockade of China. In fact, the Chinese commanders ultimately withdrew their troops and the incident closed.

At the Assembly that year the atmosphere was dominated by the British rejection of the Protocol and the negotiations set on foot by the Germans which resulted in the Locarno Treaties. Though there were hesitations in certain quarters about a definite endorsement of the terms of the Protocol, there was an almost universal acceptance of its principles, and a thorough-going defence of its actual terms by a considerable majority of those who spoke for it. Dr. Benes of Czechoslovakia defended it, warmly declaring that no system of regional pacts would be effective to maintain peace.

In the result, the Protocol was shelved inevitably in view of the British attitude, and the Assembly contented itself with approving the principle that aggressive war was an international crime and asking the Council to appoint a Commission to prepare for a Conference on Disarmament. It should be explained that one of the most regrettable actions of the new British Government was to bring to an end the Temporary Mixed Commission for Disarmament, by refusing to take any further part in it. I have already stated that this body had incurred the dislike of the bureaucracy since it included persons who were not regular Government representatives. They had been thought dangerously active, an impression that had perhaps been increased by the unsparing condemnation by the Commission of private manufacture of armaments. The great and not too scrupulous activity of the armament firms in defence of their pecuniary interests in the armament trade has always been an obstacle to disarmament progress. Indeed, whenever the League has shewn signs of taking effective steps in this direction, an outburst against the Geneva system was sure to take place in circles likely to be influenced by armament interests. As Monsieur Briand once said about the attacks upon his peace policy which were being made in certain well-known Paris papers — 'The pens which write these attacks are made from the same metal as the armaments of war'.

The Council duly appointed the Commission asked for by the Assembly. It was called the Preparatory Commission and I was appointed to represent the British Government. In fact, it did little, for the next four or five years. The blame for its inaction mainly rests on the French, though the British Service Departments were distinctly unhelpful. I shall have to return to its proceedings later on.

Meanwhile, the Commission appointed to supervize German Disarmament under the Versailles Treaty had reported that, with some minor exceptions, Germany had carried out her obligations in this respect. This Report was accepted by France and ourselves as showing sufficient compliance by Germany, and she became thenceforward entitled to claim that the other parties to the Treaty of 1919 should also disarm in accordance with the very definite pledge to do so contained in the letter by Clemenceau written as President of the Paris Conference on behalf of all the Entente Allies there represented.[1] It must be admitted that the Allies did little to discharge this obligation for the next seven years. The French still clung to the delusion that it was safer to keep their armaments in spite of their pledges, and the Service advisers of the British Government to some extent shared that view. On the other hand, financial considerations prevented any increased expenditure on armaments. The result was that the Germans, not inexcusably, began secretly to re-arm — a process which, under Hitler, assumed the formidable proportions which we all know. It is difficult to exaggerate the evil that resulted from this indefensible policy of France and Britain. It enabled the Germans to say that we, too, were ready not to carry out agreements made at Paris when it suited us, and that in rearming they were only imitating our action. That was not true, for we never repudiated our obligation to agree to general disarmament. Even so, our inexcusable action or inaction did strike a blow at international good faith, which ought to have been the sheet anchor of our policy. The truth is that in this as in other matters our policy was ambiguous. We ought either to have insisted that all nations should accept general disarmament based on the League and Collective Security or we should frankly have reverted to the old discredited policy of armaments and alliances. In practice we did neither.

The other activities of the Sixth Assembly were mainly of a normal character. In addition to a good deal of useful work in connection with double-taxation, tariffs, treatment of foreign nationals, the holding of an international economic conference, questions of travel and transport, opium, the protection of women and children, refugees, health, minorities, and intellectual co-operation, the great work in assisting Austria and Hungary was practically finished and that on behalf of Greece went prosperously forward.

. I was myself very largely occupied with the question of

[1] See the terms of the letter set out in Appendix at page 123.

slavery. A resolution had been passed at the suggestion of Sir Arthur Steel-Maitland representing New Zealand in the Assembly of 1922, drawing attention to the whole question of slavery. As the outcome of this resolution, a Commission had been appointed to enquire into the matter. In the summer of 1925 the Commission issued an extremely valuable report stating the extent to which slavery still prevailed and making a number of very important recommendations. At a meeting at the Foreign Office in the summer, in London, at which the business of the Assembly was being considered, I suggested that we might take up the report of the Commission and make definite proposals thereon. This was agreed to and a Convention was drafted defining slavery and the slave trade, providing for the immediate suppression of the trade, and the gradual emancipation of all slaves, and also for some restriction on forced labour. I presented this to the appropriate League Commission and it was examined article by article very much on the lines of the parliamentary consideration of a Bill in Committee. I had hoped to have got it through in time to have it ready for signature by the various Governments at the Assembly. There was, however, a great deal of discussion by those who wanted the Treaty to go further than proposed, and some resistance by those who did not want it to go so far. It is astonishing how the opinion lingers on the Continent that slaves are much better off than they would be if they were free — a wholly groundless contention — and that at any rate the rights of property must not be interfered with, in fact, precisely the contentions maintained by Boswell, about 1775, and vehemently rejected by Dr. Johnson. To finish this subject off, the Convention was again carefully considered and adopted in 1926, and was then signed by a number of Powers including the United Kingdom. Others have since joined and the question of forced labour has also been dealt with more satisfactorily than was then proposed.

I have gone thus much into this subject because the procedure adopted was both careful and effectual. True, it took two or three years. Any other form of international procedure would probably have led to no result and in any case would have taken much longer.

Two other matters of international importance came before the League this year. One was the settlement of the boundary of Mesopotamia and Turkey. By the Treaty of Lausanne this had been left to a 'friendly arrangement' between Turkey and Great Britain, failing which it was to be 'referred to the Council of the League of Nations'. It was characteristic of the casualness with which the League was treated by British statesmen that no indication was given in the Treaty of how the Council was to act. Was it to be as arbitrator, was the Council to decide by majority or by unanimity, and if the latter, was Turkey to be entitled to a vote? Accordingly, when the question was raised before the Council, Turkey raised these points and the Council decided to ask for a decision of the Hague Court upon them. That meant a postponement of action by the Council till the Court had given a decision, which reached Geneva in December. It was to the effect that the Council must act unanimously, excluding the parties to the dispute — a decision of some importance, since it proceeded on the general ground that no one can be a judge in his own cause, and would seem to apply to all quasi-judicial actions of the Council. Acting on this ruling, the Council, after considering the report of a Commission presided over by Count Teleke, decided the matter in dispute mainly in favour of the contention of Great Britain — a decision which was accepted by Turkey and in the end greatly improved the relations between the two countries.

The other matter was a serious controversy between Greece and Bulgaria. The relations between the two countries had for some time not been good, owing to controversies about national minorities in each country. On October 19th a Greek soldier who was alleged to have entered Bulgaria improperly, was shot by the Bulgarian frontier guard. Thereupon, the Greek Government, at this time under the Dictator, General Pangalos, sent, on October 21st, an ultimatum to Bulgaria demanding apologies, compensation, and punishment of the Bulgarian soldiers; and, failing to receive satisfaction, invaded Bulgaria with an Army Corps which occupied a strip of Bulgarian territory twenty miles long and five miles wide, doing much damage to life and property. Bulgaria appealed to the League on October 22nd, which took prompt and effective action. A special meeting of the Council was summoned which was held in Paris on October 26th under the Presidency of Monsieur Briand, which called on both parties to desist from hostile acts and within sixty hours to withdraw their forces from each other's territory. I believe that Sir Austen Chamberlain and Monsieur Briand were prepared to take naval action under Article 16 if the demand had not been complied with. Fortunately, it was not necessary to use force, since the parties obeyed the directions of the Council by October 29th, and the Council thereupon sent a Commission of three persons, presided over by that admirable public servant Sir Horace Rumbold, at that time our Ambassador in Madrid, to investigate and report on the whole affair. On December 3rd the Commission issued its report, acquitting Bulgaria of all blame and deciding that Greece had illegally resorted to war against her and must pay an indemnity of £45,000. The Commission also proposed certain frontier precautions to prevent any similar incidents in future. The recommendations were approved by the Council and accepted by the two countries. Thus an incident which, but for the League, must almost certainly have resulted in a Greco-Bulgarian war, was peacefully and justly terminated in some six weeks — another instance showing that where the Powers were willing to back the League with force, its machinery worked smoothly and well for peace. Doubtless if they had taken similar action when Italy invaded Abyssinia ten years later, a similar result would have followed and the subsequent aggressions by Germany would never have taken place.

It was also in this year that Sir Austen very properly took occasion to withdraw the charge made during the war that the Germans, in order to supply grease essential to them, had boiled down the bodies of those who fell in battle. I had been so far concerned in making the charge that, acting on the interpretation of a German notice, given by some of my advisers, I had authorized its appearance in a newspaper. The German Government now formally and no doubt rightly repudiated this interpretation, and Sir Austen, in withdrawing it on the authority of the British Government, naturally spoke for all his colleagues, including myself.

(G) 1926

The year 1926 began for me with a question of health. The doctors advised that it was necessary for me to have my tonsils removed. It is not a pleasant operation, and for a man of sixty-two it is more serious and disagreeable than for a child. It was the first operation I had had, and I went to a nursing home for it. My experience makes me very doubtful of the advantages of that course. If it is impossible to have an operation done at home, I incline to think it is better to go to the paying ward of a hospital. I was advised that it would take about four weeks to recover completely. In fact, it took a good deal longer, though I went back to work in about that time.

In League affairs everything was dominated in the spring and summer of 1926 by the difficulties which arose over the admission of Germany to the League. By the Locarno Treaty, German membership of the League was made a condition of the Treaty coming into force, but nothing was said as to the way in which this was to be brought about. It had, however, always been fully understood that Germany would be made a Permanent Member of the Council like the other Great Powers, and until that had been done no material change would be made in the constitution of the League. Unhappily, French opinion, which was uneasy about the German entry into the League, now suggested that Poland should at the same time be given a permanent place in the

Council, as a kind of balance to Germany. It was a most unfortunate suggestion, both because it had an air of springing on Germany a fresh condition for her membership, and because it seemed to treat Poland as her equal. It appeared that Sir Austen had given Monsieur Briand some ground for believing that Britain would support the French proposal. The Cabinet did not endorse this view, and Parliamentary opinion declared itself as decidedly hostile to it. Sir Austen temporized and, perhaps rightly, declined to pledge himself on the subject till he got to Geneva. Meanwhile, it had been arranged that a special Assembly should be called in March to admit Germany. I was rather amused to notice that the Prime Minister, in defending himself against attacks in the House of Commons, made a good deal of play with the fact that I was to accompany Sir Austen! On March 7th we reached Geneva. Here, it quickly became clear that the position was complicated. Poland's demand for a Permanent Seat induced Brazil and Spain to make similar demands on much stronger grounds. As I wrote at the time -- 'Everyone is dying in the last ditch. "No surrender" is the motto of every Delegation'. The situation was made worse by the insistence of Sir Austen and the French on discussing everything in private meetings of the Locarno Powers, with the result that all the other delegations sitting in Geneva with nothing to do, denounced everyone. In vain I urged a public discussion in the Assembly. The familiar results of 'secret' International Committees followed. In the Committee everyone was as unreasonable as they liked. There was no public opinion to restrain them. The Germans especially rejected every kind of compromise and then told their papers that all the difficulty was caused by Sweden. Secrecy in such a case merely means facility for misrepresentation. After long discussions, when all seemed settled on the terms of promising, ultimately, permanent seats to Brazil and Spain, suddenly Brazil said she that would vote against Germany's membership of the Council unless she then and there received a permanent seat also. As the Council has to be unanimous on this question, that meant the exclusion of Germany, and therefore Sir Austen, without speaking to me about it, agreed with Briand to postpone the whole discussion till September. I protested, urging once again the propriety of a full and open discussion at the Assembly, feeling fairly confident in my own mind that that was the best chance of getting a reasonable decision. It was too late. The decision had been reached and all that remained was a melancholy meeting of the Assembly at which our failure had to be announced. I felt rather bitterly on the subject. I had been brought to Geneva as a guarantee that League interests should be safeguarded. I had been very little consulted, especially at first, and the final decision had been taken over my head. It was impossible for me to do anything at Geneva without apparently attacking my own Government in an international gathering, which I was very reluctant to do. Coming on the top of other incidents, it seemed to show that I was out of sympathy with my colleagues on the broad aspect of our attitude to the League, and on my return home I tendered my resignation. When this became known to those whose opinion I greatly trusted, they unanimously urged me to withdraw it on general grounds and especially because the issue was not clear enough for it to be understood by my fellow-countrymen. Accordingly, I withdrew it. But I am not sure that I was right in doing so. I never doubted that our only hope of lasting peace was in the maintenance of a strong and efficient League of Nations, or that a clear and courageous lead by this country was essential to the achievement of that object. The kind of fumbling that went on over the admission of Germany should have shewed me that the Cabinet did not really agree with me.

In consequence of the difficulties just described, it was decided to set up a League Committee to consider the composition of the Council, and I was appointed the British representative on it. The Committee met on May 10th. There were some nineteen of us, including a charming German representative, Herr von Hoesch, then Ambassador at Paris and afterwards at London, where he died suddenly.

My instructions were to press for the appointment of Germany to a Permanent Seat on the Council, to resist the creation of any other Permanent Seats but, subject to that, to do what I could to satisfy Spain and Brazil. Quite apart from the difficulty about permanent members, something had to be done to meet the demand of the other members of the League to have a reasonable share in the work of the Council. Originally there had been four elected members. These were, in September 1922, increased to six. Even so, no plan for rotation had been agreed on, so that to a very large extent the same countries were re-elected every year. Unquestionably, this had great practical advantages. The members of the Council got to know one another, and the Council grew to be an entity with that kind of corporate opinion which the French used to call *l'esprit du Conseil* — an immensely valuable thing. It had to a minor extent its counterpart for the whole League, which was sometimes referred to as the 'atmosphere of Geneva'. A larger Council some of the members of which changed every year, made for less intimacy and solidarity of its members and consequently less vigour to resist the difficulties which began in 1931-32.

It was therefore a misfortune that we had to enlarge the membership of the Council. But it was clearly indefensible that six countries, originally chosen almost at hazard, should alone be entitled to elective seats. The plan that was ultimately agreed to was one which I put forward on the instructions of the British Cabinet. The four permanent members were increased to five, to include Germany. The six elective members became nine, who sat for three years each and could not then be re-elected without an interval, except that not more than three of the elected members could ask for the cancellation of this disability, and this could be granted by a two-thirds majority of the Assembly. These came to be called semi-permanent members. So that there were three classes of members — the Great Powers, who were permanent; other countries of importance, such as Poland and, later on, Spain, who were elective but could be indefinitely re-elected; and six other elective members who could not sit continuously for more than three years. The creation of semi-permanent members was designed to meet the views of Poland, Spain and Brazil. Poland accepted; the others did not and gave notice of their resignation from the League. Spain later withdrew her notice and remained a member, but Brazil went. She certainly had a considerable claim to be treated as a Great Power. But her claim was not so outstanding as to have made it possible to admit her alone.

Looking back, I do not see that anything better could have been done then. Once the controversy over Germany's admission had arisen, the rest of the arrangements followed inevitably. Still, it did the League an injury for which the admission of Germany did not turn out to be the ample compensation which we then all of us expected it would be.

I had been much afraid lest the postponement of the admission of Germany to September might result in her exclusion altogether. My fear was not, as it happened, justi-fied, and in September she was duly admitted after eloquent speeches by Herr Stresemann and Monsieur Briand. It is tragic to re-read those speeches now. Herr Stresemann declared that the German Government could 'well speak for the great majority of the German race when it declared that it would wholeheartedly devote itself to the duties devolving on the League of Nations'; and that 'Germany desired to co-operate on a basis of mutual confidence with all nations represented in the League or upon the Council'. Monsieur Briand, rejecting what he called the 'perilous success of prestige', looked forward to the time when there would 'arise at last a European spirit which will not be born of war and for that reason would be nobler, loftier and more worthy of admiration!' Sir Austen moved that these two speeches should be printed. But he never persuaded his Cabinet colleagues fully to act in the spirit from which they sprang.

There was nothing of striking importance in the other work done by the Assembly. As I have already said, the Conven-tion on Slavery was completed. So also was the economic rehabilitation of Austria and Hungary. The scheme for settling the million and a quarter Greek refugees from Asia Minor — amounting to some twenty-five per cent of the population of Greece — in the district of Salonica, was carried forward with a wonderful success, creditable alike to the League, to the Greek Government and to the refugees. A similar but minor scheme for Bulgaria was set on foot. The disarmament question was further debated in the Third Commission of the Assembly, and a resolution was passed urging the early summons of a General Disarmament Conference. As a step in this direction, a meeting of the Preparatory Commission was held in the last week of the Assembly, and another one which I attended in December. But the progress was slow against the military bureaucracies. Beyond this, valuable non-contentious work was done about Opium, the traffic in Women and Children, Child Welfare, Refugees, Health, Intellectual Co-operation, Economics, Finance, Transit, etc.

While the Assembly was in session an unsuccessful effort — one of several — was made to overcome American objections to participation in the World Court. It failed for reasons which were no doubt convincing to Senatorial opinion in America, but are quite incomprehensible to the average man on this side of the Atlantic. That a country traditionally in favour of arbitration as a substitute for war should refuse to give its support to by far the most effectual attempt in that direction which has ever been made, for reasons which exceeded in subtlety the lucubrations of schoolmen of the Middle Ages, only shows that there is no limit to the vagaries of human nature.

On my return to England, I found the coal controversy, which had been going on for months, just coming to an end. It had led in the summer to the General Strike — an attempt by the Trades Unions to force the Government to impose on the coal owners terms satisfactory to the miners. Though conducted without violence, it was in effect a revolutionary attempt to put organized labour above the law, which fortunately failed. It was abandoned after about ten days. There was also an Imperial Conference in progress, the most important outcome of which was a Declaration that the United Kingdom and the Dominions were 'autonomous Communities within the British Empire', completely independent of one another, 'though united by a common allegiance to the Crown' — a declaration which may have some importance as a precedent when the future of the League of Nations is discussed.

(H) 1927

In the early part of 1927 there was much discussion over the Chinese question. China had for some years been in a condition of great disorder. There was a complex system of civil war. Every province seemed to the Western observer to have its War Lord, fighting with his neighbours. In the course of these disturbances an effort was made by Marshal Chang-tso-lin from the north, to dominate the whole of China. He was met by considerable forces from the south and, in the course of the fighting, some injury was done to British subjects and their property in Nanking, and more was threatened to the large British interests in Shanghai. I have already said that British troops had been sent there to protect our property; and these were considerably reinforced in the early part of that year. Ultimately, General Chiang Kai-Shek appeared, commanding the moderate or Nationalist section of the southern armies. He put a stop to the disorders on the Yangtse, agreed in principle to compensation for damage to British interests, and summarily executed those who had been guilty of outrage. That closed the incident. A few weeks before this happened, Sir Austen decided, at my suggestion, to inform the League of what we were doing and to explain that we were not making any attack on the independence or integrity of China. At his request I drew up a despatch on these lines, which he adopted.

One other incident occurred which helped to embitter relations between us and Russia. The Russian Government had repeatedly promised not to foster revolution in this country, and on that basis had been allowed to send a very large trade delegation here, known as Arcos, to develop commercial relations between the two countries. The Home Secretary, Joynson Hicks, who belonged to the 'diehard' section of the Conservative Party, was convinced that Arcos was a centre of international sedition. He was authorized by the Cabinet to have Arcos searched and, though the results of the search were not very conclusive, the Trade Delegation was sent back to Russia. The proceeding was perfectly regular but it is doubtful whether it was wise. The theory that unscrupulous foreigners will persuade my fellow-countrymen to embark on revolution seems to me fantastic. If Arcos had any value commercially or otherwise I should not, in time of peace, have taken action against it because of any fear of its political activities.

Early in the year, a Committee had been sitting to consider what attitude we should take up about international disarmament, especially in the League Preparatory Commission. I was chairman of it and the idea was to draft a skeleton Convention setting out the general principles and machinery of disarmament, leaving the actual figures to be filled in at the Disarmament Conference. A document was drawn up which was a compromise between the views of the fighting services and those who, like myself, believed that an international agreement for the reduction and limitation of armaments was essential for the safety of European civilization and the existence of the British Empire. Even at this time, long before the rise of Hitler, it was evident that unless some international agreement was reached, Germany would re-arm, and if that happened a race in armaments would inevitably follow, with all the consequences which we have seen. The Cabinet never apparently accepted this position. They, or their friends, were fond of pooh-poohing the urgency of the problem, saying sometimes that armaments did not lead to war — which is very much like saying that alcohol does not lead to drunkenness. In one way that is true. But without alcohol there would be no drunkenness, and without armaments there would be no war. When the critics of disarmament were tired of praising the harmlessness of armaments, they would go on to say that Britain had disarmed much more than other Great Powers. Probably that was true, apart from Germany. But it was irrelevant. We are, and always have been, a peace-loving nation. For us to disarm alone will not promote peace. Indeed, unless there was to be general disarmament, we ought to have kept up our armaments fully. As has been recently shewn, a weak Britain is a temptation to an aggressive nation. No doubt the reason why we allowed our armaments to fall so low as we did was purely financial. If, by doing so, some of the Ministers thought they were contributing to the general disarmament which, by the Covenant and other international obligations, we were bound to promote, they cannot have given any serious thought to the subject.

Nevertheless, when the draft Convention, settled by my Committee, was brought to the Cabinet, its efficiency, such as it was, was further cut down. I protested, in a Minute to the Cabinet which I later used in the House of Lords. However, I proceeded to Geneva on March 21st and for some weeks battled with foreign militarists to preserve the little which their British *confreres* had allowed me. The work was disheartening and exhausting, and my wife and I tried for a little rest at Easter time by crossing the Alps to Pallanza. It was a bad plan. I was really too tired for anything except complete rest, which was not to be obtained where we went. The hotel was crowded and uncomfortable and, though the weather was bright, there was a violent and bitterly cold north wind coming straight over the snow-covered Alps. The consequence was that I had a breakdown and, when I returned to Geneva, was more or less a wreck.

When we got back to England, the doctor assured me there was nothing organically wrong but that I must for the time take things as easily as I could. For the next two months I followed this advice, though I attended meetings of the Cabinet and did other urgent work.

A few weeks later, the Prime Minister asked me whether I would accompany the First Lord of the Admiralty to Geneva, where he was going to attend a conference called at the instance of President Coolidge, to see if the principle of the Washington agreements as to battleships could be extended to cruisers and other smaller vessels.

I had nothing to do with the preparations for the Conference, which turned out to be inadequate. The French and Italians refused to attend and the negotiation was confined to America, Japan and ourselves. I gladly agreed to go, believing that it would be a fairly easy job, since I was told we were prepared to make concessions and I had always found the Americans pleasant to deal with. Going through Paris, I saw Paul-Boncour, who had been on the Preparatory Commission, and told him that I felt sure that the Naval Conference would succeed, which would help considerably the general disarmament work. When we got to Geneva, at the first plenary meeting each of the parties, without consultation between them, made proposals which were far from acceptable to the other two. That was a bad start. Next, when I urged public discussion, the Japanese said that would be hard on them as we and the Americans would be talking our own language while the Japanese would not. The appeal was impossible to resist and the whole negotiation was nominally secret except for an occasional plenary meeting. In fact, the Japanese would not have suffered, as they were ready to agree to almost any proposal which gave them about the same proportionate strength as they had been allowed at Washington, and they would easily have got that. The real controversy was between the Americans and ourselves on the cruiser question. As to other vessels, we got practically to an agreement, but on cruisers the difficulty was great. The Americans asked for equality and in principle we agreed. But we claimed that we must have a large number of cruisers, since we had large spaces to defend. We wanted, therefore, some large vessels armed with 8-inch guns, and a good many relatively small ones armed with 6-inch guns. The Americans did not want so many vessels and, in order to maintain equality, they demanded fewer small vessels and more of the larger vessels. Bridgeman and I, aided by a very able Admiral, Field, were quite agreed with one another and felt sure we could easily reach a settlement. As far as I was concerned, I wanted a limit so as to avoid any temptation to an armaments race, but it did not seem to me of any importance whether the Americans were or were not a little stronger than we were in cruisers. I had always understood that, in old days when we were counting our naval strength in comparison with that of other countries, America was never brought into the calculation since the eventuality of a war with her was so unlikely as to be negligible. Nowadays, that is more true than it has ever been. We ought to have regarded the American Navy and ours as two divisions of a great Peace Fleet, and if the Americans liked to provide the larger part of it, so much the better.

However, the Cabinet took a different view and eventually called us home to consult. They were very courteous, but it was soon quite clear that we differed in opinion. They, or some of them, were determined to maintain our Naval superiority and almost openly regretted the Washington Treaty. On those lines, no agreement at Geneva was possible and I suggested that they should send someone else out in my place to complete the negotiations. This was refused, and I then said that I was sure that the Conference would break down if we were instructed not to concede the American demand, and that, if it did, I must reserve my right to resign.

On that understanding we went back to Geneva. The Americans were quite obdurate. We did not know then that one, Shearer, had been employed by some of the armament firms in the United States to prevent an agreement if he could and that, accordingly, tendentious telegrams had been sent across the Atlantic representing the danger of concessions at Geneva. But that by itself would not have mattered. Unhappily, though, the British Cabinet were divided, their effective majority was against conceding to the United States mathematical parity, which was what the Americans had always asked for and what we had been instructed to concede at the outset of the Conference. Accordingly, that section of the Cabinet preferred a breakdown of the negotiations to a concession of parity as the Americans understood it, and they carried their way. Several compromise suggestions which we put forward were rejected and, after a few days, the negotiations finally broke down and we went home.

On my arrival in England I informed my colleagues that I must resign. The failure to reach an agreement was in itself a serious matter. In fact, it was even more serious than we knew, for up to that time Japanese policy had been essentially pacific and accommodating. A very few years later it changed its character and became unscrupulously adventurous, resulting in the Manchurian policy which began the series of international aggressions leading ultimately to the Polish war. It is at least possible that, if we had settled the cruiser question, as Japan was most anxious to do, we should have helped to strengthen the peace party in that country and the invasion of Manchuria might never have taken place. The fact that the break arose from Anglo-American differences was another serious feature, not only because any injury to our relations with the United States is to be deplored, but because such a difference is especially harmful in the Far East. It was the want of hearty co-operation between the two countries which encouraged Japan to attack Manchuria, and added greatly to the difficulty of stopping her.

But I do not pretend that I foresaw these actual consequences. I believed that without some general limitation of armaments, peace must be precarious. The Germans were insisting, as they had every right to insist, either that the other countries should carry out the promise given by Clemenceau at the Paris Conference or that they must be allowed to re-arm. It was clear to everyone that limitation of armaments would be a complicated business and if the Germans re-armed the complications might be insuperable. Unless the peace-loving Powers were prepared to make a real effort to solve the many problems involved, agreement would not be reached. And if the negotiation were to be inspired by the same spirit as that which had prevailed at the tripartite conference there would be no chance of success.

Nor was this an isolated difference between me and my colleagues. They had been opposed to the Treaty of Mutual Assistance. They had insisted on destroying the Protocol. They had abolished the most effective international committee for disarmament that has ever existed. They had dealt with the entry of Germany into the League in a most unsatisfactory manner. They allowed their technical advisers to hamper the Preparatory Commission in every way. The Prime Minister, Mr. Baldwin, and Foreign Secretary, Sir Austen Chamberlain, though they were personally friendly to me, did not conceal the fact that they had little sympathy with my conviction of the vital importance of using what I had always felt would be a short interval after 1918 in order to erect an effective barrier against war.

Fortunately for myself, I had plenty of time to think things over before my resignation was definitely announced. Mr. Baldwin was away in Canada, and it was agreed that nothing final could be done till his return, which did not take place till the end of August. During that time, I naturally thought the question over very carefully and had the great advantage of receiving verbal and written advice from my colleagues. But they insisted that there was no difference of opinion between us, whereas the opposite seemed to me quite clearly the case. Accordingly, I resigned and, receiving the usual permission from the King to make what explanations I felt to be desirable, notwithstanding the obligation of secrecy which binds all Privy Councillors, I explained first in writing, and afterwards in the House of Lords, my reasons for resigning.[1]

Resignations are harassing things. I knew that mine meant the final severance of official connection with the Conservative leaders and, ultimately, with the Conservative Party to which I was bound by very strong personal and family considerations. An incident brought this home to me very strongly. Though I had been in substantial agreement with Bridgeman all the time we were at Geneva, he strongly disapproved of my resignation and of the reasons I gave for it, and naturally said so in public speeches to which I had to make some reply. Bridgeman was a very old friend. We had been at school together and had often co-operated in political matters. He was a charming man, of considerable ability and absolutely loyal and honourable — in every respect a typical example of the best type of Englishman. As far as I was concerned, and I hope as far as he was, our difference was solely and exclusively political. But it was not without temporary bitterness, all the same.

The truth is, I was never a very good Party man. Probably but for the war of 1914, I should have gone on fairly comfortably as a Conservative official. But those four years burnt into me the insufferable conditions of international relations which made war an acknowledged method — indeed, the only fully authorized method — of settling international disputes. Thenceforward, the effort to abolish war seemed to me, and still seems to me, the only political object worth while. As time went on I became increasingly conscious that that view was not really accepted by most Conservative politicians and was, indeed, hotly and violently rejected by large numbers of the right wing of the party. Not only did they reject in their hearts the League of Nations, but they did not propose to take any step for getting rid of war. Clearly, they and I could not honestly belong to the same Party. If I had had any doubts on the point, they would

[1] My first letter of resignation, with all the reasons for it, will be found in the Appendix. To it I received no answer, but to a later letter summarizing the first I received Mr. Baldwin's letter which is also printed in the Appendix.

have been removed by what took place at the Assembly in September.

It was on September 4th that the Assembly met. Good observers remarked on the increase of the corporate feeling displayed at the meeting. The number of Foreign Ministers present was larger than ever, among them being Sir Austen Chamberlain, Monsieur Briand and Dr. Stresemann. Dominating the atmosphere of the Assembly were the questions of Disarmament, Security and Arbitration. Almost every speaker in the opening debate referred to these topics and the great majority were anxious to revive the Protocol. The one formidable opponent was the United Kingdom. Sir Austen was in his most characteristic mood. He explained the line taken by his country at Locarno. He emphasised the value for peace of the Treaties there made, and he urged that it was now for other countries to complete the work. But he added explicitly that the British Government were not prepared to extend the Locarno Treaties beyond the region to which they referred. This was coupled with eloquent eulogies on the value and importance of the League and assertions that his Government 'based its whole policy' upon it. The speech caused great disappointment. Locarno chiefly dealt with dangers of war arising between Germany, France and Belgium and, to a modified extent, threats to Poland. To the Continental statesman that was security so partial as to be almost illusory. They knew that the war of 1914, which involved most of the civilized countries of the world, began with a quarrel between Serbia and Austria over a political assassination, and they felt that something of the same kind might happen again. The outbreak of war in any part of Europe endangered the peace of the whole Continent. They were surely right, both for their countries and our own. Our greatest interest is peace and if we are to secure that, war must be prevented everywhere — at least in Europe — for once it begins no one can tell where it will stop. Sir Austen no doubt accurately laid down the policy of the Cabinet, the policy which came to be connected with the slogans — 'No commitments' and 'We have kept you out of war', which were chiefly responsible for the long series of aggressions culminating in the wars with Poland and Finland.

This, however, was not obvious in 1927. The Assembly passed a hopeful resolution urging further exertions for Disarmament, Security and Arbitration. It turned to other useful routine work of the usual description — very valuable in itself but quite inadequate as a protection against war. Much attention was given to Economics — there had been an important Economic Conference earlier in the year which had less practical success than its admirable suggestions deserved — Mandates, Slavery, Refugees, Opium, the Traffic in Women, Health, and Communications. A good observer declared that the League was 'in a distinctly stronger position than it had occupied when the Assembly met'. Nevertheless, a seed of disease had been planted in its constitution which, as the years passed, has gone near to destroy it.

In the autumn, a campaign in support of international disarmament was started by the League of Nations Union. There was a special meeting of the Council on October 21st, with delegates from all over the country. On my motion, resolutions were passed urging support for the efforts of the League Preparatory Commission, acceptance of compulsory arbitration in justiciable disputes, and organization of what is now known as Collective Security. We avoided attacks on the Government, since we were anxious, as we had always been, not to repeat the mistake made in the United States of making support of the League an issue of Party politics. Up to this date, indeed, no front-rank politician opposed the League or advocated the mutilation of its powers, and we strove our hardest to preserve that condition of affairs. For this and other stronger reasons, we always emphasised in the Council and Executive Committee of the Union, the fact that we were not in favour of disarmament by this country *alone*, but only of a general reduction and limitation of armaments by international agreement. Labour and Liberal speakers strongly supported disarmament and so, more or less, did such ministers as Sir Austen and Mr. Ronald Mac-Neill who, as Lord Cushendun, had succeeded to the position I held in the Government. But the ministerial support of Disarmament was materially weakened by refusal to accept fully collective security, for it was unquestionable that Continental nations would never agree to a reduction or even a limitation of their armaments without trustworthy assurance that they would be protected by the League members from disloyal attacks by countries who promised to disarm and then failed to do so. Limitation of armaments is essential for peace, just as arbitration must be accepted as the alternative to war, and neither limitation of armaments nor effective arbitration are practically obtainable without collective security in some form or other.

I had been urged by some of my Geneva friends to start an electoral campaign for Disarmament. That would have involved a definitely anti-Government attitude. It would not have been practical — unless I had joined the Labour Party. In England nowadays, no effective electoral movement is practicable except with the support of an organization for the purpose — that is, a Party organization. The other course was to avoid Party politics as such, and concentrate on mainly educational speeches and writings. That is what the League of Nations Union did. After the special meeting of the Council of the Union in October at which a moderate policy of international disarmament was laid down, we pressed it in a series of meetings all over the country, going on till the General Election in 1929. The difficulty of this method is that unless the Government of the day accepts the policy as advocated, criticism of their attitude becomes almost inevitable. That leads to replies from ministerial speakers which, in their turn, stir up convinced supporters of the League policy. Only constant vigilance by the officers of the League of Nations Union prevented the Union from becoming an electoral ally of the Opposition. Even so, the directors of the Conservative Central Office were highly suspicious of our proceedings. I can only say that, looking back on the course of events from 1928 onwards, I am amazed at our moderation.

A *questionnaire* had been drawn up in 1927 by a recently-formed League Security Committee at Geneva, designed to ascertain the attitude of the various Governments on arbitration and security and the relevant provisions of the Covenant. The replies were on the whole not very enlightening and the British reply was distinctly discouraging. In effect, while in principle favourable to arbitration and security, it did not recommend any step forward. As regards signature of the Optional Clause its tone was negative, and even more so in respect to general arbitration. That is to say, the British Government were opposed to general compulsory arbitration and even to compulsory arbitration of what may be called legal or justiciable controversies. On security, the plan of partial local agreements on the model of Locarno was approved, but on the terms that Britain should not take part in either making or executing them.

In the same way, their attitude to some of the most important industrial efforts at Geneva was scarcely more favourable. In particular, it became evident that they were not prepared to accept the Washington Convention for regulating hours of employment, which had been brought before the first meeting of the International Labour Office, held at Washington, by Mr. George Barnes, representing the British Government. That Government now asked for the withdrawal of the Convention and the introduction of an entirely new one.

(1) 1928

In the course of the spring of 1928 a Pact was drafted by Mr. Kellogg, then American Secretary of State, and Monsieur Briand. The purpose was to declare war to be contrary to international law, or in the American phrase, to 'outlaw war'. By the first Article, the signatories denounced war as an

N 193

instrument of national policy and, by the second, undertook never to try to settle their differences with other nations except by pacific means. No sanction was proposed for the breach of either of the declarations, and in consequence the international effect of what came to be called the Kellogg Pact has not been very great. At the same time, it may be regarded as a contribution to the building up of world opinion against war. It seemed, therefore, to me unfortunate that the British Government received this proposal in a somewhat grudging spirit. They did not reply to it for some time, and when they did it was to make comments and raise difficulties. These were in substance two. They objected that it must not apply to a war of self-defence, which it did not; and they added a rather obscurely worded objection to the effect that, in certain quarters of the globe, they must be allowed to resist any change of territorial conditions. The French also raised difficulties. However, both countries ultimately signed the Pact. This was, of course, quite outside the League, and some people objected to it on that ground — unreasonably, as I thought, since it was an American proposal. But another Agreement was, in that respect, more open to objection. Sir Austen made an agreement with the French about disarmament by which the French agreed to withdraw their objection to the method of calculating naval tonnage, which we preferred, if we would no longer oppose the French contention that trained reserves should not be regarded as part of a country's military strength. This agreement was widely disapproved, particularly by America who regarded it as an attempt by Britain and France to settle important issues in the disarmament question behind her back. It certainly was an unfortunate piece of diplomacy and, though the agreement was dropped, yet, taken with the failure of the Geneva Conference in 1927 and our reception of the Kellogg Pact, it produced for the time a certain tension in Anglo-American relations which was very undesirable. The mistake may well have been due to health reasons, for, to the regret of everyone, Sir Austen fell ill at the beginning of August, 1928, and for some four months was away from his work.

His place was temporarily taken by Lord Cushendun, who attended the Assembly, as the first British Delegate, in 1928. Meantime, I had been principally employed in making speeches in the country about the League and Disarmament. Almost always the meetings were largely attended and deeply interested in League matters. Beyond this I did not do much except to bring a Bill into the House of Lords to control the motor traffic, which was causing and has continued to cause scandalous figures of slaughter and injury to the car passengers themselves and other users of the road. Here is a case where I believe the vast mass of public opinion would welcome drastic control, but since none of the political parties will take the matter up, the motor interests, which are very wealthy and consequently very influential, have always been able to defeat any serious measure of reform. My Bill was, by these agencies, quickly snuffed out. But the problem still lacks solution.

In September my wife and I went for a pleasure cruise in the Mediterranean. We started on September 8th from Southampton and returned there just four weeks later, and enjoyed ourselves thoroughly. We had a full ship with a number of youthful fellow-passengers whose only interest in such places as Venice and Syracuse seemed to be bathing! We stopped for some hours at Gibraltar, Palma, Palermo, Cattaro, Ragusa, Spalato, Venice, Curzola, Naples, Syracuse and Algiers, and saw many beautiful and interesting things. On the whole the first prize goes to Ragusa, an unspoiled mediaeval walled town, with wonderful little streets of Venetian houses, built on a glorious coast of rocks and Mediterranean-blue sea.

Meanwhile Cushendun was leading the British Delegation at Geneva. On the whole his duties, though disagreeable, were not onerous. He had evidently been instructed to carry out the 'no commitments' policy without reserve. The keynote of the Session was the Kellogg Pact. The German

Chancellor, Müller, used it to press for international disarmament. He urged that Germany was disarmed and that all members of the League had agreed to outlaw war. Now was the time to carry out the Allied pledge to disarm themselves. Not a very easy contention to answer. Briand, who followed him, could only reply by a plea for time, based on trust in the League — the 'sole refuge of the world to shield the nations against war'. Various proposals were made to hasten Disarmament. Cushendun rejected all that were definite, and secured a pious resolution of no precise meaning. A model draft treaty for General Arbitration was agreed to but not signed, the British delegate expressing doubts of its value and preferring bilateral treaties instead. To cover the same ground as a general treaty, it was calculated that there would have to be well over a hundred bilateral treaties. There were, besides, two peace-maintaining suggestions — a German proposal enabling the international authority to require the withdrawal of troops so many miles from the frontier between two quarrelling States; and a Finnish proposal brought forward by Monsieur Holsti, who was, up to 1939, active for peace at Geneva, facilitating international loans to a State threatened with aggression. These were both a good deal considered, but neither passed. The worst thing done by the British Government was to lead an attack on the League Budget, supported by some of our Dominions. The attack was indefensible. The sum involved for the whole Empire was only some £250,000 of which about £150,000 fell on this country; the total League Budget including the I.L.O. and the Permanent Court at the Hague was just over a million and a half. The occasion for the attack was an increase of £60,000 compared with the previous year, of which £6,000 fell on Great Britain! As our national budget was then something over £800,000,000, we were squabbling over one-thirteenth of one per cent of its amount! Even if the total figure of £150,000 be taken, it was infinitesimal compared to warlike expenditure. A battleship costs not less than £7,000,000, which, if invested at 5 per cent, would provide more than twice the sum necessary to pay our contribution to the League for ever. Obviously if the League was to be regarded as of any value for peace — apart from all the very valuable non-contentious work done by it — our contribution could only be considered as almost certainly much too small. No doubt the impulse for the attack was given by the Treasury, which apparently regards itself as bound to cut down all expenditure, however remunerative. But if the Cabinet had been serious in its support of the League, it would have promptly informed the Treasury that the British Delegation would lend no support to any such attack. A half-hearted support of the League cannot be justified. Peace is the supreme interest of this country and the world. It will not come of itself without effort or expense. If the League was of no value for peace it should have been abandoned. If it was, as Monsieur Briand said, the 'sole shield to save the nations from war', no expense and scarcely any risk was too great for us to incur in its support.

For the rest, the Assembly pursued its activities in non-contentious matters, such as Mandates, Slavery, Opium, Transit, Trade and Refugees, etc. As to the protection of women, Cushendun made an exception to his usual rule and eloquently supported a forward policy. Nothing was done to put a stop to the great international scandal by which private profits were amassed from preparations for war. Even an attempt to secure great publicity about armament manufacture failed, in consequence of British opposition.

On the whole, the Session was probably the least encouraging that had taken place since the foundation of the League. It would be unfair to blame Cushendun for this. He was much liked and admired, personally. But he had to carry out his instructions, and the policy of the British Government was definitely obstructive. As Señor Madariaga said on another occasion: — 'When Great Britain stops, the League stops; when Great Britain goes forward, the League goes forward too'. Nevertheless, the general prestige of the League increased during this year. Spain withdrew her resignation and the United States, Russia and Turkey tended to collaborate more fully with the League. So did Mexico, but in other Latin American States the inclination seemed to be more towards Pan-Americanism than towards Geneva. If the League survives the present war, some co-ordination of it with the Pan-American movement should certainly be attempted.

(J) 1929

The early part of 1929 was overshadowed by an impending General Election, and in May Parliament was dissolved. All the political Parties declared, by their Leaders, that they supported the League of Nations. But the subject was much more prominently dealt with by the Labour and Liberal Parties than by the Conservatives. I wrote a public letter to the effect that the erection of trustworthy international barriers against war before it was too late transcended all ordinary political issues. A vigorous and progressive international policy was literally vital to everyone and, therefore, I advised voters, disregarding all Party ties, to vote only for candidates who could be trusted to support such a policy. Beyond this, I took no part in the election, and on May 16th I left England for Madrid, where there was a meeting of the International Federation of League of Nations Societies. It is the only time I have been in Spain, and nothing occurred there worth recording except that on Whit Sunday I saw an ecclesiastical dignitary in what looked like a State coach, escorted by soldiers, going to take part in some Church Service — quite a mediaeval touch!

From Madrid I returned to Paris, where I spoke at one or two meetings, and went thence to Frankfort, where I stayed with Mr. Merton, the eminent metal merchant. I spoke there and after the meeting Mr. Merton was good enough to take me to a shooting lodge some twenty or thirty miles off, constructed, I believe, with archaeological exactitude to represent a building in that locality of a date some centuries earlier. It was all charming and delightful, though perhaps to the English mind a trifle artificial. I met there a young professor at Frankfort University — a Czech by nationality — who gave a striking picture of the hopelessness of German Youth. Politically, they believed in nothing. All their old standards had crashed and nothing had taken their place. That was no doubt a very favourable soil for the growth of Nazism.

From Frankfort I went to Berlin, where I spoke in the Reichstag Chamber under the Chairmanship of the President of that body. It was a crowded meeting and my advocacy of the League seemed to be well received. Afterwards there was supper at an hotel and more speeches before I was allowed to return to the Embassy, where my old friend Sir Horace Rumbold was good enough to entertain me. Next day I spoke to a gathering of Zionist Jews with acceptance, and I also had the honour of meeting Dr. Einstein, who appeared to be cordially in favour of the League. The only other notability who remains in my memory was General von Seeckt, who, in talking of German rearmament, told me that he did not want a large standing army — 200,000 was, I think, the figure he mentioned — because the cost of the elaborate equipment that would be needed made it impracticable to arm more than that number properly. He, however, contemplated a large reservoir of men not militarily but athletically trained. How far all this was to be taken literally, or how it would work out, I know not. My recollection of the general atmosphere of the place then, makes present Germany almost incredible.

From Berlin I went back to England, where I found a Labour Government in office. The election had resulted in a Conservative catastrophe and Labour was the largest Party in the House of Commons, though the Liberals had enough members to turn the scale either way. Labour, therefore, had again to govern with due regard to this fact.

Some months earlier, Ramsay MacDonald had asked me

to lunch with him at the Athenaeum Club, and had then proposed that, if there was a Labour Government, I should be one of the British representatives at Geneva. I explained to him that I could not undertake to support every measure of domestic legislation which Labour might bring forward, and he immediately said there was no question of that kind. We then discussed League affairs and I found that we were substantially agreed. If anything, I was more 'advanced' than he was. I remember I expressed myself as being in favour of signing the Optional Clause even if some of the Dominions held back. The supposed reluctance of the Dominions to sign was one of the favourite arguments of the English opponents of signature. On this point MacDonald was doubtful. In the result I unequivocally accepted his offer. Accordingly, when I got back to London after the formation of his Government he sent for me and asked me if I would go to Geneva as we had agreed. I assented, only asking for a room in the Foreign Office — my experience being that unless you are part of the Foreign Office, that distinguished organization regards you as one of the 'lesser breeds without the law'. The Prime Minister said that was a matter which the Foreign Secretary must settle, and went on to expatiate on how much he enjoyed personal diplomacy. Henderson was the Foreign Minister, and with him my relations were always perfect till the Labour Government went out of office. He was the most successful Foreign Minister we have had since 1918, with no brilliant and showy qualities, but with that faculty for being right which Englishmen, like the Duke of Devonshire of my youth, possess. His political courage was great — almost the rarest and most valuable quality for a statesman. At first one was inclined to doubt whether he appreciated what was being said to him, and very often an interview ended rather inconclusively. But by the next day it was clear that the arguments had been understood and weighed, and a decision was given.

He made no difficulty about my having a room, and summarily overruled the departmental objections. His Under-

Secretary was Dr. Dalton, one of the ablest of the Labour Party, and his Parliamentary Private Secretary was my great friend Noel Baker. I will say nothing of the permanent officials of the Foreign Office and the Cabinet Offices except that they were all very competent and some of them helpful. As a team I think it may be claimed that we worked together with energy and complete mutual understanding.

The programme of the Government was cheering. International Disarmament was to be pushed forward again, and in connection with it an attempt was to be made to solve the difficulties with the United States which had brought the 1927 Conference to grief. This question the Prime Minister kept in his own hands. He saw the new American Ambassador immediately after the formation of the Government, and had conversations which were declared to be satisfactory. Later, he went to America and saw President Hoover, where they arranged to hold a Five-Power Conference in London early in January. It was also announced that a Conference with France, Germany and other interested Powers was to be held on Reparations. That duly took place at the Hague in August, attended by Snowden and Henderson, and a fresh agreement was made which was fairly favourable to the pecuniary claims of this country. It was also settled that the occupation of the Rhineland by the Allied Powers should come to an end. Though this negotiation was in a measure successful, yet owing to a certain brusqueness of Mr. Snowden, it led to some tension with France. But this did not last and by the time we met at Geneva our collaboration with her was as cordial as ever. Opportunity was taken by Henderson to improve our relations with Russia. He also attempted to reach a more satisfactory position with Egypt, and was nearly though not quite successful.

All these activities were outside the League, though consistent with its purpose. From the Hague, Henderson went to Geneva for the Assembly meeting which began in the first week in September. I travelled from London with the Prime Minister, who led the British Delegation which, besides

the Foreign Secretary, included the President of the Board
of Trade, Mr. William Graham, whose early death was a
great loss to his Party and his country; Sir Cecil Hurst, the
legal adviser to the Foreign Office; Mrs. Mary Agnes Hamil-
ton, M.P.; Mrs. Swanwick, Dr. Hugh Dalton, Mr. Noel
Baker, and myself. It was a very strong body, though the
Cabinet Ministers could only stay a few days. When they
left, I led the delegation. The weather was prodigiously hot,
and the Prime Minister, who was very much affected by the
heat and, for some reason, disliked Geneva, began the proceedings at the Assembly with only a moderately successful
speech. Its most successful passage was when he announced
that Great Britain would sign the Optional Clause. That was
known to be the policy of the Government, but it was not
quite certain whether it would be carried out then. Indeed,
only a few days before the Assembly, when certain difficulties
were made by one of the Dominions, the Prime Minister
telegraphed from Lossiemouth that we must abandon the
prospect of signature. However, under pressure from Henderson he withdrew this intimation. Beyond this question,
he spoke hopefully of the Anglo-American negotiation.
After dealing with other topics, he concluded with a warning
against delay which might cause 'nations to present not a
request but an ultimatum'. Henderson followed, urging the
overhauling of the machinery of the League Secretariat, the
general signature of the Optional Clause, the acceptance of
the treaties for financial assistance and prevention of war,
and the strengthening of the Covenant so as to make it
accord with the absolute prohibition of aggressive war involved in the Kellogg Pact. Mr. William Graham also
spoke, advocating, in a much-applauded speech full of
technical arguments and figures and delivered without a note,
the reduction of tariffs and other hindrances to international
trade. One felt, listening to these speeches which were all
warmly received, that Great Britain was giving a constructive
lead to the League suitable to her great position and authority.

There were several more interesting speeches, by Briand,

Stresemann, Hymans, Benes, Apponyi and others, which I have not space to examine. They came from men at that time wielding great authority in their respective countries and they all professed belief and trust in the system of the League. Briand made a proposal which, if it had been accepted, might have changed the history of the world, and I must say a word about that. He suggested that 'among peoples constituting geographical groups, like the peoples of Europe, there should be some kind of federal bond'. He used the word 'federal' in a very loose sense. For he went on to explain his meaning by saying: — 'It should be possible for them to get into touch at any time, to confer about their interests and to establish among themselves a bond of solidarity which will enable them to meet any grave emergency'. He left it there, saying he would return to it the following year. Several speakers commented on it, Benes saying that what was wanted was a 'new moral unit'. It may be that safety for the future must be sought along this line. Finally, Mr. Wu, the representative of China, speaking most admirably in classical English, suggested that Article 19 of the Covenant, which provides for the reconsideration of obsolete treaties, should be studied. His object was that it should be used with what was then the burning question of the so-called Unequal Treaties which gave to foreigners extra-territorial rights in China. It seemed to me an admirable suggestion; but after being examined not very cordially in one of the Assembly's committees, the Chinese Government were somehow induced to abandon it — a great pity.

Outside the plenary Assembly, the most important event was the signature of the Optional Clause first by Italy and then by the British Commonwealth, France, Greece, Czechoslovakia and others. There were certain reservations by Great Britain, not substantially diminishing the effect of the signature. Altogether some thirteen additional countries signed, making in all thirty-two, though some had not then ratified. Unhappily, in the nationalistic storm that has since burst on Europe, these signatures have been frequently ignored, shewing once again that no treaty obligation, unless it is backed by force, is sufficient to prevent war by militarist countries. Still, at the time, and as long as the peace-keeping machinery of the Covenant was kept effectively in being, it was a useful step in the great effort to substitute law for war. The Draft Treaty for giving financial assistance to a threatened victim of aggression was further considered. It was hoped to have got it signed at this Session of the Assembly. But in the end, though it was generally approved, there were so many details which raised questions that it was postponed. So also was the so-called 'Model' Treaty proposed by Germany to prevent war. As I have already said, its object was to give powers to the League to require precautions to be taken by quarrelling nations against the outbreak of hostilities. The first steps were also taken towards harmonising the Covenant and the Kellogg Pact. The latter instrument forbids the use of war as an instrument of national policy. The Covenant does not go so far. It only insists that, before war breaks out, every possible step towards pacific settlement, including the imposition of a delay for some months, shall be taken. On the other hand, the Kellogg Pact provides no penalty for its breach; whereas the Covenant requires that every political diplomatic and economic pressure shall be used against any country that, in breach of its Covenant obligations, resorts to war, and if that is not enough, the Council of the League shall advise what military action should be employed in support of the non-military sanctions. It was now proposed to require that the members of the League should in no case resort to aggressive war, so that any such resort to war except in self-defence would bring the above sanctions into operation. The technical difficulties of doing this proved unexpectedly great and here, too, a postponement became necessary. Looking back, I am not sure that the problem was approached from the right angle. In fact, though unhappily several wars have taken place in breach of the Covenant since the League came into being, I am not aware of any case where disputing nations, after carrying out all the Articles of the Covenant providing for delay and mediation, have engaged in warfare permitted by those provisions. In other words, no nation has ever crept through the celebrated 'gap' in the Covenant. Every resort to war since 1919 has been made quite clearly in defiance of the undertaking of the members of the League not to go to war in breach of the Covenant's provisions. It may be, therefore, that instead of seeking to stop the 'gap', we should have done better to clarify and make more effective the sanctions against the aggressor. Anyhow, the discussions were not finished when the Session came to an end, and I shall have to return to the subject later.

Turning to disarmament, I felt that, in anxiety to reach an agreement between France and Britain, the Preparatory Commission had gone so far that it was doubtful whether any serious Treaty of Disarmament could be made on the lines agreed upon. I therefore, with the approval of the Cabinet, proposed that the Preparatory Commission should consider how far certain principles 'have been or ought to be adopted', and I then set out the principles, some of which seemed to me to have been certainly disregarded. This was supported by Germany who, being at that time more or less disarmed herself, desired the effective disarmament of others. It was also supported by a number of the smaller Powers. But France, Italy and Japan were rather vehemently on the other side. After considerable debate, I accepted a compromise resolution drafted by the Greek, Politis, the effective part of which directed that minutes of the discussion should be sent to the Preparatory Commission for any necessary action. In accepting, I made it quite clear that this, in my view, enabled me to raise at the Preparatory Commission all the points for which I had contended!

Beyond this, work was done for making more effective the Slavery Convention, for improving the action against opium fiends, and on a number of detailed matters connected with Mandates, Minorities, Refugees, Health, the protection of Women and Children, Tariffs, the distribution of Coal, and so on.

Finally, Liberia, being aggrieved by charges against her of slavery and slave-dealing, asked for investigation by the League, which was agreed to and a Commission was sent out to examine into the question on the spot — the first step in a long attempt to assist liberty in Liberia, which proved — I will not say fruitless — but nearly so.

On the whole, then, the Assembly of 1929 showed renewed energy in the pursuit of peace. Arbitration, Disarmament and Security were all helped forward. No great political controversy was brought before it, and most of its time was spent in trying to consolidate what had been gained. The members were full of hope. The authority of the League had reached its highest point and none of us foresaw the storms and stresses which were to come upon us nor the errors with which they were to be met.

Beyond MacDonald's visit to America, and the renewal of relations with Russia, to both of which I have already referred, no important development of Foreign Affairs took place during the remaining months of 1929. But the League suffered one grievous loss in the death of Dr. Stresemann in October. Whatever may have been the ultimate motives of his support for the League, without question he gave that support, and it was very valuable. While he represented his country at Geneva, she took her full share in the efforts of the Council and Assembly to establish peace and justice throughout the world.

(κ) 1 9 3 0

During the year 1930, I was more fully employed in League matters than at any time since it came into existence. I attended the Foreign Office daily while I was in London, and took part in frequent departmental discussions about disarmament and other matters. With all my colleagues in the Foreign Office, from the Secretary of State downwards, I worked with the utmost cordiality, and I look back to my work there with the greatest pleasure. There was only one discordant note. The Prime Minister, after our first interview which I have referred to, rejected all my attempts to get in touch with him. I was anxious, particularly, to discuss disarmament, so that I might be sure that in the Preparatory Commission and elsewhere I did not misrepresent his views. I tried every device to secure an interview, and whenever we met casually he expressed a warm desire to 'have a talk' with me. Indeed, long after I had ceased active collaboration with the Government, he repeated the same phrase as we passed one another in Palace Yard. But the talk never came off. Since statements have been made as to the relations between the Foreign Secretary and the Prime Minister, I should like to say that, whatever MacDonald may have said about Henderson, Henderson, in my hearing, never spoke otherwise than with complete respect for MacDonald.

The general situation in Europe was not improving. Trade was bad almost everywhere. There had been a great speculation slump in the United States in the autumn of 1929, and that may have contributed to the general financial and economic depression in Europe and America which lasted till the end of 1931. The result of this and other things was to produce severe Parliamentary difficulties for the Labour Government. Over and over again they only saved themselves from defeat in the House of Commons by making some concession which, while it secured enough Liberal votes for a majority, greatly disgusted their supporters in the country who do not appreciate the ethics of Parliamentary bargains. It is also possible that the financial interests in the City of London were not sorry to see a Labour Government in difficulties.

In spite of these difficulties, the Government's record in Foreign Affairs was good. In the early part of the year there was a fairly successful Naval Conference in London which at least resulted in wiping out the failure of 1927 and securing an agreement on cruiser strength with America and Japan. It is true that France and Italy were unable to agree, so that the Treaty remained for several years incomplete. But the major object was secured of putting an end to the pernicious and senseless naval rivalry between Great Britain and the United States. There was also an Economic Conference at which a great and unavailing effort was made to get a Tariff Truce, that is, an agreement that existing tariffs should not be raised.

Meanwhile, I had been placed on several League Committees at Geneva, involving repeated visits there. In the early months, two of them occupied much time. One was on the re-organization of the Secretariat — a lengthy mass of detail. Besides dealing with a number of minor matters, the Committee recommended a Pensions Scheme which was adopted, and also tried to insist that members of the Secretariat should recognize and accept the position that they were the servants of an international organization and not delegates to it from the Government of the countries of which they were citizens. This created difficulties with certain States, such as Germany and Italy; with the consequence that, though pains were taken to treat the German and Italian members of the Secretariat on a complete equality with other nations, their personal influence was not great. They were not individuals working for the international objects and ideals of the League, but only the mouthpieces of their Governments. The French were not open to the same criticism nor, I think, the British either.

There was also a Committee which drew up the amendments to the Covenant needed to bring it into accord with the Kellogg Pact. It will be remembered that this had already been discussed in the Assembly of 1929, and had been referred for further consideration by this Committee. We came to a decision which, except in form, was not unanimous. When it got to the Assembly it was referred in the usual course to the regular Assembly Committee and there very considerable difficulties arose. Nominally, they were due to drafting objections. But in reality there was ground for thinking that some States were nervous lest the right of the sword should be taken completely from them. In principle they were against war and violence. But what if some State were hopelessly unreasonable ? I remember the representative of one of the Balkan States pressing this on me very earnestly. I was very far from convinced and tried unsuccessfully to persuade him that even so, the old-fashioned war would do far more harm than good. No doubt most States agreed with this view, but there was enough difficulty for the question to be adjourned till 1931, and by then the whole situation had changed.

I was also a member of the Preparatory Committee for the Disarmament Conference. But that did not sit till later in the year. Meanwhile, the Assembly itself was deeply concerned with the Briand proposal to create a European Chamber of the League. There had been a meeting on the subject of delegates of all the European States, just before the Assembly. In principle, all were favourable, but some difficulty was felt as to the connection with the League. Ultimately, on the proposal of Monsieur Motta, it was agreed that the new organization should take the form of a European Committee of the League. A resolution was accordingly passed in this sense and the new Committee was directed to draw up its own constitution, at a meeting to be held in the beginning of 1931. It is important to note that it was the smaller Powers who were most insistent that the movement should be kept within the League. Only so did they feel safe from the encroachments on their independence which they feared from any proposal originating with the Great Powers. It may be that no advance in this direction can be made unless it be started by a restricted number of States who are fully determined on their policy, and then enlarged so as to contain all who like to join on that footing.

Two other proposals were advanced a stage. The Convention providing for financial assistance to be given to a State in danger from aggression, which had been most carefully elaborated by financial experts, was again considered by the appropriate committee and unanimously agreed to. A clause

O

was added to it declaring that it was not to come into force till after a Disarmament Treaty had been accepted and, in this form, it was signed by some thirty States. It was originally a Finnish proposal, and, if it had been in force, would have been of great value in recent events.

The German proposal for separating quarrelling States by requiring them to withdraw out of reach of one another was less fortunate. The idea was accepted, but, perhaps because of its authorship, without much enthusiasm by the French Government. Anyhow, they exerted all their ingenuity to find objections, in which, I regret to say, the British naval experts gave them some assistance. The result was that the matter was again postponed.

Beyond these relatively sensational matters, a mass of very useful and less conspicuous work was done. The Judges of the Permanent Court of International Justice were elected for another nine years.[1] Arrangements were made for facilitating the giving of financial advice to States who asked for it — a power that, until the indefensible attack by Japan on China, was being of great service to the latter country. Intellectual Co-operation, Transport, Health, Refugees, Women and Children, and Prison Reform were some of the other subjects dealt with. The Minorities question also occupied a good deal of attention and, unfortunately, showed the beginning of that rise of nationalistic intolerance from the results of which we are now suffering. The discussion brought out at least two things. The first was that the existing procedure by which any minority question must be referred to a special *ad hoc* Committee of the Council was very unsatisfactory from many points of view. I am convinced that the only adequate machinery for dealing with this exceedingly thorny question must be by way of a Permanent Committee of a judicial character which, by precedents, would gradually create standards of national conduct in such matters.[2] But this will never be accepted unless the nations are prepared to apply to all Governments alike the principles of justice

[1] cf. page 121 previously.   [2] See page 120.

to minorities as laid down by the special Minorities Treaties for a few countries. The plan on these lines adopted for supervising mandates by a Permanent Commission has, on the whole, worked well even in such a highly contentious case as Palestine. A rather critical report as to the administration of that country by Great Britain as Mandatory, created some indignation at the time. But subsequent events have shewn that it was not unjustified.

Lastly, an effort was made, with only partial success, to set up a Commission to see that the Anti-Slavery treaties were being properly carried out.

At home, one of the effects of the bad times was the revival of the Fiscal question, much assisted by the Imperial Conference which met in the autumn. As to the economic case for Protection, I will only repeat[1] that I think the force of the argument on both sides has been very much exaggerated. On the Imperial side of the question, it does not seem to me that the solidarity of the Empire has been increased by Preference, and on the international side the claim of the British Empire to erect tariffs against all foreigners round the prodigious area included in it has become difficult to defend. Why, it is asked, should a country with less than fifty million inhabitants be allowed privileges of so great an extent? The urgency of the question has been increased by the grave mistake made at Versailles in depriving Germany of all her colonial possessions — a mistake now very difficult to remedy. It is a thousand pities that we should have, as it were, underlined the inequality of the position by insisting on securing for ourselves special commercial advantages in large parts of the Empire which we had previously shared with others. That policy, which received a great impulse that autumn, helped forward the great current of Economic Nationalism which, in its turn, fostered the similar political movement which we know as Totalitarianism.

While I was in England after the Assembly, I was very

[1] See page 32.

much surprised and exceedingly gratified to read in the *Times* of October 25th the following letter: —

'*To the Editor of "The Times"*.

Sir,

We desire to give hearty commendation to a project which has just been initiated to pay a tribute to Viscount Cecil of Chelwood for his unique services to the cause of international co-operation and goodwill. The formation and maintenance of the League of Nations are due to the labours of many distinguished men of many nationalities, but it has fallen to Lord Cecil to devote himself single-mindedly to strengthening the League and promoting an intelligent understanding of its work among all classes of his fellow-citizens.

A Committee has been formed for the purpose of presenting Lord Cecil with his portrait, in the hope that it will eventually become a public possession in the National Portrait Gallery.

Yours, etc.,

J. Ramsay MacDonald,
Stanley Baldwin,
D. Lloyd George.'

I was aware that some of my friends had kindly proposed to make a presentation to me, but I had no idea the plan was to receive such an imposing and flattering endorsement.

At the beginning of November, I returned to Geneva to take part in the Preparatory Commission for Disarmament. Up to that time, one of the chief difficulties was to induce the French Government to realize and act upon the proposition that there must either be a general international disarmament as promised at the Paris Conference, or the Germans would certainly re-arm. French Ministers were much too intelligent not to admit the force of that contention, but when it came to the point of taking a definite step towards a Disarmament Treaty, they shrank from positive action. Doubtless the governing motive was distrust of Germany. They believed — rightly, as we now know — that the Germans had already made some preparations for secret re-armament and they feared that, whatever the Treaty said, they would continue that action; whereas the French and British would honourably fulfil their obligations to limit or reduce their arms. If we had been prepared to say emphatically that we would agree to adequate provisions of international control, and real collective security, to protect them from such an eventuality, the situation would have been simpler. But that was just what British statesmen were reluctant to do. There were other difficulties. Each country had its own public opinion to consider. The Americans were very sensitive about any inspection of their armaments by foreigners. Yet without some form of supervision there was no guarantee against disloyal action. The Russians were much more concerned with representing themselves as the only really pacific Power than in collaboration to reach some practical if moderate step forward. The British Admiralty was indifferent as to military disarmament but looked with great suspicion upon any attempt to apply the same principles to the British Navy, and the British Air Force, for reasons which I never understood, thought that any attempt to define an air unit was exceedingly dangerous. It was therefore clear that in carrying out the instructions of the Assembly, which were to prepare a draft Treaty for the consideration of the Disarmament Conference, we should have to content ourselves with establishing the principles and machinery of disarmament. The numbers of personnel, the size and strength of the arms, all, in fact, which would make the Treaty a practical limitation, would have to be left to the Conference itself. Even so, it took some five weeks of discussion and drafting before the skeleton document I have described was agreed to — subject to *caveats* by several Governments announcing that, at the Conference, they would press for this or that amendment.

It is not worth while to consider further this outcome of years of hard work and discussion; because before the Disarmament Conference met there was a new British Government, storms were brewing in Germany, and the French had moved to the Right. The result was that the proposals of the Preparatory Commission were scrapped and unfortunately no serious or successful attempt was made to put anything in their place.

That stage was not reached till the spring of 1932. In the meantime, the Council decided that the Conference should meet on February 2nd, 1932, and that Henderson should be its Chairman. I was not very happy at the choice. I doubted whether a Foreign Minister, as he then was, of a Great Power was quite the right man for the job, and should have preferred Dr. Benes. However, the Germans would not have him, and Henderson was appointed. As will appear, the situation before the Conference met had become such as to make his position almost impossible.

I returned to London and found considerable doubts among my friends as to whether, at Geneva, the French contention about disarmament had not been unduly favoured. There may have been some force in this, but the French were at that time unquestionably the most powerful military Power in Europe and without their assent no draft Convention could have been obtained and consequently no meeting of the Disarmament Conference would have taken place. Further, it was not sufficiently realized that within the framework of the Convention any degree of disarmament agreed to by the High Contracting Powers could be established. The urgent problem to tackle was what should be the nature and extent of the actual limitation of armaments at which we should aim. On that point various discussions took place and considerable progress was made. It was, for instance, shewn by an expert committee at Geneva that it was technically quite possible to provide a limitation on armament expenditure for each country, not with a view to contrasting the amount spent in one country with that spent in another, but in order to make clear as to each country that the amount of its armament expenditure in any given period did not exceed the limit agreed on for that country. Probably the most important practical proposal proceeded on different lines. The object of all disarmament is to diminish the power of attack. Security means that those who enjoy it are confident that they can defend themselves against all comers. The course of invention had tended to increase the defensive powers of modern armaments. Experts say that an attacking force must be at least three times as strong as the defenders if it is to succeed. If, by a Disarmament Treaty, the advantage of defence could be still further increased, a great step would be accomplished. Against modern fortifications on land, rifle fire or machine guns or field artillery are relatively ineffective. In order to conquer a force adequately entrenched and armed with the weapons just mentioned; heavy artillery and aircraft, and tanks are essential. The proposal was therefore made to abolish large guns, aircraft and tanks. On the sea the problem was a little different. Obviously warships themselves are useless for invasion. The effective offensive operation by sea is or may be blockade — that is, the destruction of sea-going commerce. There is no class of warship which is in this sense essentially defensive, but the abolition of the submarine and of the larger battleships would be a step in the right direction. The whole suggestion, therefore, was to prohibit altogether as weapons of war aircraft, tanks, large guns, submarines and large battleships. There was a precedent for this, since the Treaty of Versailles had forbidden these weapons to the Germans, who had not at this time re-armed, so that to extend the prohibition in question to all countries would make at once for disarmament and equality. Moreover, total abolition of certain classes of armaments is a simpler proposition than to arrange a ratio in armaments between the various nations, and it is easier to enforce once agreed on. It was reasoning of this kind which induced a committee of the International Federation of League of Nations Societies to agree to urge this policy on the Disarmament Conference when it met, and the proposal was confirmed by the annual meeting of the Federation which took place at Budapest in the summer of 1931.

I spent a great part of my time abroad during 1931. Apart from visits to Geneva, in the summer I went to Vienna to attend an International Rotary meeting. The meeting was, from a Rotary point of view, very successful. But the weather was very hot and the audience was far more interested in its own rather Babbitian ceremonies than in anything I had to say to them. All the same, I had a delightful visit to the British Legation, where I was entertained with all their wonted charm by Sir Eric and Lady Phipps.

From Vienna I went on to Prague, where I had the great pleasure of meeting again Dr. Masaryk and Dr. Benes. Their personalities are too well known to need any description by me. It is enough to say that the whole atmosphere was one of high-minded patriotism and devotion to peace. I was taken to see a castle where the Archduke Franz Ferdinand had lived, which had been left untouched as it was in his time. It was a modern villa, filled with trophies of the chase, a collection of arms and a great number of rather crude religious statuettes. The contrast with the Government atmosphere at Prague was striking!

From Prague I went to Heidelberg, where I had been invited to address the University. The general political opinion was what we should call Liberal and I was assured that the Nazi movement was declining! The professors were attractive people but it was noticeable even with them how difficult an understanding with Germany was. Whenever, in the course of discussion, I made a concession, I was immediately told that the subject of it was of little importance, though until that moment it had been most strenuously urged.

On the whole, nothing that I saw or heard at Vienna, Prague or Heidelberg indicated great international changes or the downfall of the League.

From Heidelberg I returned to London to find a very

unquiet situation. The central international fact was the deep and widespread economic and financial depression. Every European country suffered. The position in Germany was particularly bad. Her Prime Minister, Dr. Brüning, and her Foreign Minister, Herr Curtius, visited London in order to obtain assistance and also to represent that unless some international consideration was shown to her, the extremist parties — National Socialists and Communists — would inevitably gain strength. The German Ministers, and especially Dr. Brüning, a religious Roman Catholic, impressed all who met them.

In America the situation was also bad, though not yet in anything like the same degree, and in England it grew steadily worse through the spring and summer.

In these circumstances, it is not surprising that what used to be called the propertied classes became very anxious and their anxiety was reflected in the House of Commons. It was obvious from the debates and divisions that the Government was losing ground, and three of the Ministers resigned office for various reasons. To pacify public opinion, in March an Economy Committee, presided over by Sir George May, was appointed; but none the less anxiety still continued and Snowden, the Chancellor of the Exchequer, who had earlier in the year been disposed to minimise the seriousness of the position, in a speech on July 29th took a very pessimistic attitude. Rumours had become prevalent of a ministerial crisis to end in some kind of National or Coalition Administration, which grew in intensity when the Report of the May Committee was published on July 30th. The Report spoke of a probable deficit in the Budget of some £120,000,000 and urged economies including a diminution of the amount paid for unemployment benefit. It was this recommendation that split the Labour Government. MacDonald, Snowden and Thomas accepted it, but the majority of their colleagues, led by Henderson, felt that it was quite impossible for Labour ministers who had always taken the line that the so-called 'dole' was really too little, to propose its reduction. Thereupon

MacDonald with all his colleagues resigned, and he accepted the mission to form a new Government in which Conservatives as well as sections of opinion avowedly more to the Left were represented. It was a momentous decision. It smashed the Labour Party and handed over the Government of the country to groups which, as the months went on, became more and more Conservative in their political complexion. No doubt the national position was difficult and probably appeared to MacDonald more difficult than it actually was. Even so, it is doubtful whether a minister who has been placed in power by a political party to carry out their policy is justified in remaining in office against the will of those who placed him there, to carry out a policy of which they disapprove. It would have been better if he had advised the King to send for the Conservative Leader, offering to support him as a private member in all measures that might be needed to meet the emergency. The result of what happened has, in fact, been in several ways unfortunate and, in foreign affairs, disastrous.

CHAPTER IV

DOWNHILL

(I) MANCHURIA

THE resignation of the Labour Government took place on August 24th and the Assembly was to meet on September 7th. Evidently outgoing ministers could not take part in the British Delegation and the new Government were too much harassed to do so either. Accordingly, I was asked to go to Geneva, my own political attitude being one of reluctant support of the new Government. I agreed, provided I was given adequate assistance, and Lords Lytton and Astor, with Mrs. Alfred Lyttelton and Sir Arthur Salter, were appointed as members of the Delegation.

Meanwhile, two events of international importance had occurred. The German and Austrian Governments proposed to make a Customs Agreement which it was thought would ease the financial position of both countries. The French vehemently objected on the ground that such an agreement was inconsistent with the independence of Austria which had been guaranteed by Treaty. At the suggestion of Henderson, the question of whether this contention was well founded was referred to the International Court of Justice at the Hague, who, by a majority of eight judges to seven upheld the French contention, the Italian judge being one of the majority and the British judge being on the other side. The decision has been very much attacked as 'political'. It may have been affected by national feeling, for judges do not leave all their prejudices behind them when they take their seats on the judicial bench. I can only say for myself that the question seems a difficult one of interpretation on which perfectly honest and impartial men might take different views. In fact, the Germans withdrew the proposal before the decision was actually given.

The other international event was an announcement by President Hoover that the American Government would not demand payment of any Governmental debts due to her for twelve months if other Governments would do the same. After a rather unfortunate hesitation of France, all the interested Governments assented to this proposal.

The Assembly met under the shadow of the financial depression. As this proved to be the turning point in the fortunes of the League, it is well to remind ourselves that it had been in existence for more than ten years, and during that time had grown to a position of unprecedented international authority. Not only had the League itself, with its sister organization, the International Labour Office, carried through a series of social and humanitarian reforms of great value, but it had succeeded in a dozen or more cases in settling international disputes which, but for its intervention, might easily have led to war. It is true that in one or two instances it had not been completely successful — notably in the dispute between Poland and Lithuania. But except in that case, its recommendations had always been complied with, even when something in the nature of hostilities had actually begun. Further, it had set up the Permanent Court of International Justice, which had given some twenty or thirty decisions and opinions which had in every instance been accepted by the Powers affected. Latterly, the members of the League had been engaged in extending the jurisdiction of the Court and in making efforts to buttress the maintenance of peace — first, by the Locarno agreements, and later by more general measures for lessening the probability of war. Finally, a real effort towards the reduction and limitation of armaments was being made and the date of a World Conference on the question, larger than any that has ever taken place, had been actually fixed. Russia and America, though still outside the League, were taking part in the Conference, and in other ways were shewing that the dislike of the League they had originally displayed was considerably modified. The other Great Powers were all members of the League, nor

had any of them — and, still less, any of the smaller Powers —
expressed any doubt of the wisdom and practicability of the
Covenant. In a word, during the first decade of the League's
existence it had achieved almost unbroken success. Perhaps
this very fact concealed from the statesmen who now had
the responsibility of leading and directing this great experiment that it was in truth of a revolutionary character and
would require the exercise of much courage and foresight
if it was ultimately to achieve the objects for which it was
brought into existence.

The chief part of the speeches in the Assembly of 1931
were naturally directed towards the economic question. In
the Assembly itself the general burden of the oratory was that
want of confidence was the chief cause of the depression, and
that disarmament was its best cure. The French, however,
insisted on security as a pre-condition, while the Italians and
Germans thought further security unnecessary. Events have,
I think, shewn that the French were right. In committee,
Sir Arthur Salter made an excellent technical disquisition.
He was answered by Monsieur Flandin in a purely negative
speech suggesting that nothing could be done. Just at that
moment, the British Government decided to abandon the
gold standard, and Monsieur Flandin, meeting me at a
luncheon party, explained that England must now consent
to be a second-class economic Power! It sounded as if he
thought that France, freed from the economic rivalry of
England and the military rivalry of Germany, would now
dominate the world. It was before Sir Arthur Salter had
spoken; but Monsieur Flandin had got to know what he was
going to say, and wanted me, as head of the Delegation, to
forbid it. I naturally did nothing of the kind.

Beyond this, there was some talk of an armaments truce
till after the Disarmament Conference had met. This was a
proposal of Signor Grandi, the Italian delegate, who had
made a considerable position for himself at Geneva. But the
practical difficulties of the proposal proved too great.

A good deal of useful non-contentious work was done,

particularly about slavery and about opium, on which a further Special Conference had taken place. But this was all thrown into the shade by events in the Far East.

On September 21st, Mr. Sze, the Chinese delegate, informed the Council that three days earlier Japanese troops had occupied Mukden, the capital of the Chinese Province of Manchuria; and requested the Council to take action under Article 11 of the Covenant, 'to safeguard the peace of nations'. The Council was unfortunately constituted to deal with so grave an event. No French or British Minister was present. Herr Curtius left almost immediately after the question was raised. The Polish and Yugoslavian Ministers had also departed. The President was the Spanish Delegate, Senor Lerroux, who, I believe, had a considerable position in his own country but had no experience of Geneva. I was particularly awkwardly placed, without instructions and not even in close political alliance with the actual British Government. Japan was represented by M. Yoshizawa, who laboured under the disadvantage of being unable to express himself fluently in either French or English. Usually he remained almost silent while the Chinese delegate made admirable speeches in faultless English, suggesting various steps that might be taken. At the end of any such utterance, M. Yoshizawa was accustomed to say very slowly in rather uncouth French: 'Malheureusement, je ne suis pas de cet avis!' Occasionally, however, he read from documents sent to him by his Government, and in this way the Council gathered that in the Japanese view the incident was not serious, that Chinese troops had blown up the Southern Manchurian Railway — a charge that turned out to be untrue — which by Treaty belonged to Japan as the successor in those parts of Russia, that this was only one of many similarly hostile acts by the Chinese, including the murder by bandits of a Captain Nakimura, and that the Japanese military authorities had taken steps to re-establish order. He assured the Council that Japan had no territorial ambitions in China and intended to withdraw its troops as soon as the safety of Japanese life and property was assured. The Chinese, indeed, took a very different view of the case, alleging considerable material destruction by the Japanese troops, with serious casualties including women and children. In the end, the Council passed what might be called the usual resolution, taking note of the Japanese assurance that they had no intention to annex any part of China, and urging the parties to abstain from further violence and to withdraw their forces from one another's territory. The Japanese accepted the resolution, but urged that the difficulties between them and the Chinese in Manchuria, which were said to be of long standing, should now be settled by negotiation between them. The Chinese were unwilling to accept this as long as the Japanese were in occupation of their territory. But they professed themselves as quite ready to agree to any recommendation made by the Council, whereas even at this stage the Japanese rejected any interference by the League. I pointed out that the duty of the Council was confined to preventing hostilities and it had no jurisdiction to compel any general settlement of the dispute, which was the business of the parties.

At the beginning of the controversy, I had suggested that the United States should be kept fully informed of the proceedings, and we received through Mr. Hugh Wilson, the American Minister at Berne, a very cordial message of sympathy with our resolution and a promise of diplomatic support.

That was as far as we could go at that time, and we therefore adjourned for a fortnight, receiving positive assurances from M. Yoshizawa that the Japanese forces were being withdrawn to the zone on each side of the railway which they were, by Treaty, entitled to occupy. It seemed to be a minor incident which would be settled by the time we met again. We did not then know that so far from being of slight importance it was a carefully prepared first step in a large policy of aggression favoured by the Japanese army, which has not yet come to an end. At that time there was going on a struggle between the civil and military parties at Tokio,

An ordinary political Cabinet was in power, who adhered to the old foreign policy of Japan, the keynotes of which were friendship with Britain and support of the League of Nations. Step by step, the soldiers imposed their views of policy, not hesitating to contrive the assassination of some civilian ministers who opposed them. But they moved cautiously — at first professing their anxious desire to avoid any acts hostile to China, at the same time trying one aggressive step after another to see whether the League Powers and America would take any effectual measures to stop them. When they found that they were met with nothing but remonstrance they became bolder, and occupied four Northern Chinese Provinces, including a territory as large as nearly half Europe.

However, we did not know then what was going to happen. We left Geneva, and I spent the fortnight's interval in paying a visit to Rome, where I had been invited by an Italian friend, with the full approval of his Government, to make a speech on the League of Nations. The visit was delightful, the weather was perfect and the friendliness and hospitality of Signor Grandi[1] were wonderful. I made my speech at a luncheon of notabilities, and I had a brief interview with Signor Mussolini at which nothing of importance passed. To speak frankly, his demeanour and the setting of the interview were too theatrical to be very impressive. I also had the honour of being received by the Pope[2]. It was a great experience. Nothing could exceed the kindness and courtesy of His Holiness. We spoke about a number of things, including disarmament, and his chief anxiety was lest the Bolsheviks should overrun a disarmed Europe. At that moment there did not seem, as I ventured to say, much chance of that happening. He told me that he had inserted into a recent pronouncement some words favouring disarmament, but he evidently feared that it would not succeed. However, he more than once used the French word 'Espérons' — (the conversation was in French) and expressed his warm approval of the action that I had taken and was trying to take. I was

---

[1] Then, Foreign Minister   [2] Pius XI

there for about three-quarters of an hour, and as I left he expressed the hope that if I were again in Rome I would come to see him. I do not think that I have ever met anyone from whom there radiated such an atmosphere of saintliness.

I returned to Geneva, where the Council reassembled on October 13th. Lord Reading this time attended, as did Signor Grandi, while Monsieur Briand by arrangement took the place of Senor Lerroux. The Council also, in spite of the protests of Japan, welcomed the presence as an observer of Mr. Prentiss Gilbert, the American Consul General at Geneva. Unluckily, the members of the Council were induced to give a tactlessly warm welcome to Mr. Gilbert, with the result that the Isolationists in America secured a discontinuance of the experiment!

It immediately became clear that so far from withdrawing her troops, Japan had greatly extended their occupation and had even gone so far as to bomb from the air a Manchurian town. That was before the public conscience had become hardened to such proceedings, and the Council passed a vote of regret at the incident — which did no good. It now began to look as if the original account by the Japanese of their action and objects was not to be relied on. I therefore obtained the leave of Lord Reading to get together a small unofficial Committee to consider what could be done if Japan was obdurate. There were four of us, all with considerable experience of the League. We drew up a short report, pointing out that up till then the proceedings had been under Article 11 which is the preventive Article. But in view of the present attitude of Japan, Articles 15 and 16 might have to be invoked. These are the Articles which provide for sanctions, diplomatic and economic in the first instance. Our report said that no such sanctions could be effective unless the United States would join in them, and that therefore the first step should be to ascertain what attitude she was prepared to adopt. If it was favourable, we made suggestions as to what might be done. The truth is that Japan is very vulnerable to economic sanctions. She has comparatively few internal resources for the manufacture of armaments and can only import the materials needed if she can maintain her exports. Since the United States and the British Empire take a very large proportion of those exports, action by America and the League Powers in refusing to accept them must have been very effective. When Lord Reading understood what we suggested he was much disturbed and begged me to take no further action of that kind and naturally I obeyed. His anxiety was caused by the financial position, which was very precarious. To him and to his colleagues it seemed a matter of relatively small moment what happened in Manchuria, where Britain had no territorial interests and very little trade. The infinitely larger British interest in maintaining the law of peace was never appreciated by the 'National' Government till recent events forced ministers to reconsider their point of view.

In the result, the Council passed a Resolution calling upon Japan to withdraw her troops by November 16th. As soon as withdrawal was complete, direct negotiations between the parties were to begin. I was not consulted about this resolution, which was settled by Lord Reading in concert with members of the Secretariat. M. Yoshizawa rejected it, so that it only ranked as an expression of opinion by the other members of the Council. Obviously, unless it was intended to enforce the time limit, it was a mistake to insert one.

Meanwhile, on October 6th, Parliament had been dissolved. The General Election resulted in the virtual destruction of the Opposition, which only secured 56 seats as against 558 for the Ministerialists. No doubt this was chiefly due to the attitude of the three Labour Leaders, headed by Mr. Mac-Donald. But attacks made by Labour speakers on the Bank of England and other great financial interests did not assist their cause.

Mr. MacDonald thereupon reconstituted and enlarged his Government — the most important change from the League point of view being the substitution of Sir John Simon as

Foreign Secretary instead of Lord Reading. However, we did not then know its importance.

The Council met again at Paris on November 14th. I represented the United Kingdom, though Sir John Simon paid one or two visits to Paris during its session. It quickly became clear that he was not prepared to take any step to compel Japan to leave China — not even to urge that a diplomatic protest should be made by withdrawing the envoys of the League Powers from Tokyo. When I pointed out that, if we were to do nothing to make the time limit, which expired on November 16th, a reality, it would have been better not to have committed ourselves to it, he agreed but adhered to his attitude. It was clear that in these circumstances Japan would not comply with League admonitions. Since we left Geneva she had considerably extended her occupation and she continued to do so for many months to come. Nevertheless, we spent several weeks in Paris trying to hammer out some kind of agreed Resolution which would mitigate the great wrong done to China. Accordingly, after lengthy discussions, we did arrive, on December 10th, at a resolution which was accepted by the Japanese and would have saved something from the wreck if they had carried it out in good faith. It reaffirmed the resolution of September 30th, and pledged the two parties to refrain from any initiative which might lead to further fighting. But the Japanese reserved the right to take action against 'bandits'. It was further agreed that a Commission consisting of representatives of Britain, France, Germany, Italy and the United States should examine *sur place* the situation and report to the Council the facts, with recommendations for a solution. Unhappily, the military party in Tokyo had now become supreme. They had got rid of the previously existing Government, and during the next few months they proceeded with their conquest of North China without paying the slightest attention to the League remonstrances. However, we could do no more, unless the League Powers and America were prepared for sanctions.

A few days before I left Paris, I attended a large meeting

at the Trocadero in support of the League generally, presided over by Herriot, with Henry de Jouvenel as one of the chief speakers. It was designed for all sections of opinion and for all nations. Unfortunately, the anti-League pro-armament people determined to break it up, with the connivance of Laval's Government. All the speakers except the Italian and myself were howled down, and there was a good deal of fighting in the body of the hall, with that kind of light-hearted ferocity which a French crowd seems to enjoy. It attracted quite a lot of attention in French political circles, and I think helped the Parties of the Left.

When I got home, we had an Albert Hall meeting, with Lord Grey in the chair, at which we took what turned out to be a much too favourable view of the Manchurian question — believing that our Paris resolution would in fact be carried out. I notice that in the letters I wrote at the time I was not, privately, very sanguine because I thought the Japanese had adopted not only the technical skill of their German military instructors but also their principles of international policy. Holding this view, I tried to persuade the Foreign Office that we ought to take a stronger line in support of the League. I was told that nothing could be done without American assistance which would not be forthcoming. When I asked if enquiries had been made at Washington my informant — not the Secretary of State — told me that in conversation with the American representative he had thrown a fly over him but he did not rise — a characteristically inadequate attitude towards League affairs! However, one excellent thing was done. Sir John Simon persuaded Lord Lytton to go as our representative on the Manchurian Commission. No better choice could have been made — as the event proved.

Before I go back to other League matters, I will finish the story of Manchuria. On January 7th, 1932, Mr. Stimson, the American Secretary of State, sent a dispatch to the Governments of China and Japan asserting American rights to secure the integrity of China and the maintenance of unimpeded commerce there, called the Open Door, and warning them that the United States would not recognize any situation brought about by violence. This note was communicated to the interested powers, including Britain, asking for their support. In our reply, we ignored altogether the mention of the integrity of China, and merely said that as Japan had announced her intention of respecting the principle of the Open Door, we did not propose to send any Note, but would invite Japan to confirm her previous assurances.

In the face of this reply, which must have been read in Japan as a clear intimation that we should not do anything to secure the integrity of China, it is difficult to believe that we had been anxious to prevent Japanese aggression and were only prevented from taking action in that sense because we felt sure that America would not help us! The truth is that the British Government recognized no duty to take action beyond remonstrance for the maintenance of peace under the Covenant of the League, nor did they believe that our Treaty obligations to China required us to take any active steps to preserve her integrity. No doubt the position was difficult. Of the three Western Powers chiefly interested in the Far East, two — the United States and Russia — were not members of the League and therefore not bound by the Covenant; and the third — the British Empire — had possessions in the Far East such as Hong Kong, which we could not unaided defend against Japanese reprisals. It might certainly be argued that without the assistance of the American fleet, coercive action against Japan was impracticable or at best hazardous. But, particularly in view of the American Note, it was of the first importance that our position should have been clarified. We could have said that we accepted the Japanese point of view and did not propose to take any coercive action to stop her invasion of China. That would have been difficult to defend in view of the constantly reiterated statements of British Governments that they supported the League. But it would have been clear and straightforward. Or we could have said that we were anxious to do all we could to prevent the continuance of Japanese aggression, that we would therefore join in the proposed *démarche* at Tokyo, but that we doubted whether it would be effectual and should therefore like to know what attitude the American Government would adopt if that should turn out to be the case. It may be said that we could not do anything till the Lytton Commission had reported. Certainly we could not, till then, propose any detailed settlement of the Manchurian question. But it was already abundantly plain that the Japanese militarists were breaking and would continue to break their obligations under the Covenant and until that attitude was abandoned there was no hope of any peaceful settlement in the Far East except, indeed, by the complete submission of China. Unhappily, we took neither of these courses. Instead, we continued to call upon Japan to comply with the provisions of the Covenant and the Resolutions of the Council of the League — in most of which Japan had concurred — and when she ignored these appeals we did nothing. If the object had been to bring the League into contempt and encourage other aggressive Governments to attack their neighbours, we could not have done anything more effective.

The result of our action was quickly seen. As the only method of protecting herself against Japanese attacks, the people of China had organized a boycott of Japanese trade by which that trade was reduced by more than one half, Beyond that, no violence to Japanese residents had taken place. On January 18th, however, a Chinese mob in Shanghai maltreated five Japanese monks, one of whom was killed. An ultimatum from a Japanese admiral followed, demanding punishment of the assailants, compensation, and dissolution of anti-Japanese organizations. After a little haggling over the last of these demands, the Chinese Mayor of Shanghai, five hours before the expiry of the ultimatum, agreed to all its terms. But the Japanese Navy had had no share in the slaughter and destruction in Manchuria and were not to be baulked of their opportunity to show themselves as ruthless as the army. Accordingly, a Chinese suburb of Shanghai called Chapei, crowded like all such Chinese cities, was bombarded, and Japanese marines forced their way into it. There was some resistance, which was easily overcome and gave an excuse for fresh slaughter. This went on intermittently for some weeks. Japanese forces were increased and the Chinese sent some of their regular Army to make heroic but unavailing efforts to resist, with very inferior equipment. But Japan had overlooked the fact that in one respect the situation at Shanghai was very different from what it had been in Manchuria. There, the only issue raised was that the Chinese had been fighting to repel a lawless invasion of their Northern Provinces and had expressly relied on the support of the League in doing so. Whatever fine-drawn distinctions might be drawn between one form of fighting and another, no honest man could doubt that Japan had 'resorted to war' in breach of her undertakings under the Covenant, or that the other members of the League were bound to take action under Article 16 to assist China. But nothing had been done beyond sending the Lytton Commission to enquire.

At Shanghai, Japanese action not only brought fire and sword to the destruction of Chapei and its inhabitants, but in doing so threatened the safety of Western interests. We and others had invested very large sums in the Foreign Settlements of Shanghai. The maintenance of the law of peace under the Covenant might be belittled as 'idealism'. But the protection of British property was a British interest. Accordingly, warships were sent there, such reinforcements as were readily available were also despatched, meetings of foreign representatives in Shanghai were called. All talk of the possibility of Japanese reprisals on Hong Kong was forgotten. And what happened? A British admiral presided over a Conference, a British ambassador devised formulas, and in a little while Tokyo became convinced that the Western Powers were in earnest and the Japanese naval and military reinforcements were withdrawn without having secured any stoppage of the Chinese boycott. The Japanese invasion of Shanghai came to an end, but at the cost of destruction of property estimated by the Chinese at £95,000,000 and the loss of not less than 10,000 Chinese lives, including very many women and children. The Japanese also lost 634 killed.

Meanwhile, on February 16th the Council of the League passed a strongly worded remonstrance which was accepted by China, and refused by Japan on the ground that it was 'neutral' intervention. At this Council Britain was represented by Mr. Thomas in the absence through illness of Sir John Simon. I was in Geneva on other League business, and Mr. Thomas consulted me. I found him much more sympathetic than Sir John. The only result of the remonstrance was to show that the other members of the League — the much-despised smaller Powers — were then, as up to that date they always had been, anxious that the Covenant should be supported.

A few days later, on February 19th, China asked for a special Assembly to be called, which was done, for March 3rd, in spite of Japanese protests. Meanwhile, on February 24th the American Secretary of State sent a letter to the Senate which concluded by a statement that America would not recognize a situation created by a disregard of the Nine Power Treaty and the Kellogg Pact and that if other countries took the same view it would result in the final restoration to China of the rights of which she had been deprived. The letter no doubt assisted the conclusion of the terms under which the Japanese withdrew from Shanghai.

The Assembly met on March 3rd, and on March 11th passed resolutions unanimously, except for the disputants whose votes under the provisions of Article 15 are not counted, re-affirming the autumn resolutions of the Council, supporting the line taken by Mr. Stimson, asserting that the Manchurian question, equally with the Shanghai aggression, was within its competence, and appointing a Committee to follow events and report to the Assembly, which adjourned but did not close its session.

So far it had been established that the Japanese had occupied Manchuria in pursuance of a considered plan of aggression, and had done so in defiance of their Treaty obligations in the Covenant and other documents. Indeed, as time went on Japan ceased to dispute this, but argued that China had no organized Government — though Japan had, just before, voted for China to be a member of the Council — and that the Covenant must be treated as 'flexible'. It had, further, been ascertained that no mere remonstrance, however unanimous, even if supported by America from outside the League, made any difference to Japanese policy. If, however, there was evidence that, on any point, the Peace Powers were prepared to take serious action, as at Shanghai, Japan would comply with their demands. Nothing that occurred later modified these conclusions. The Lytton Commission reached the Far East in March. It held a number of meetings and examined many witnesses. It heard the arguments both of Japan and China, and it arrived at a unanimous report. It was certainly a great achievement to get five impartial persons, drawn from Britain, the United States, France, Germany and Italy, all to agree on a document which clearly established the responsibilities of the parties, showed that the action of Japan was not approved by the population, destroyed the original pretext of Japan that Chinese soldiers had blown up the South Manchuria Railway, and then proceeded to set forth a settlement which, in the view of the Commission, would safeguard the integrity of China while securing the treaty rights of Japan. The Report was completed on August 24th, 1932, and presented a few days later.

Meanwhile, confused fighting had been going on not only in Manchuria but in other provinces of North China. In every case the Chinese were inevitably defeated by aircraft and other products of modern civilization to which they had no adequate means of reply. Numbers of them were killed and wounded for venturing to defend their own country, large tracts of which were militarily occupied by Japan. On August 8th, Mr. Stimson made another speech, which was interpreted in some quarters as meaning that America was prepared to support League action. The reply of Japan was to 'recognize' Manchukuo as an independent State under a puppet Chinese ruler, the armies and government machine of that region remaining under the control of Tokyo.

At the regular Assembly of 1932, the Far Eastern question was only referred to in detail by the Chinese delegate who thanked the League for what it had tried to do to stop the invasion of China, and also for the assistance it was giving through its officials to her social and financial reconstruction. Other speakers said little about it. I, attending for the last time, as British delegate, and speaking on behalf of the British Government, was forced to confine myself to platitudes.

The Lytton Report was not published till October 1st and the Japanese, after six weeks, issued a criticism of it. The Council met in November and, after hearing speeches from the Chinese and Japanese representatives, were informed by Lord Lytton, who was present, that his Commission did not want to alter or add to the Report. The Council thereupon transmitted it to the Assembly which met specially to consider it on December 6th. The Chinese broadly accepted the Report. Japan rejected it, brazenly asserting that she had not broken the Covenant, which must be 'flexibly' treated, and that in any case, Manchuria was essential to Japanese interests. Monsieur Paul-Boncour, for France, followed by the great majority of the delegations, condemned Japan, stood by the Covenant, and accepted the Lytton Report. The British delegate, Sir John Simon, supported more or less by Canada, Australia and Germany, made a forensic defence of Japan, and, according to the account of some of those present, was formally thanked by M. Matsuoka, the Japanese delegate. Whether that was so or not, it was that speech which made it finally impossible to take any effective action on behalf of the central doctrine of the Covenant, as it must be of any system of international peace, that aggression is an international crime which must be prevented or arrested as soon as possible.

The League still continued its efforts to induce Japan to

accept the Lytton solution, and at a further meeting on February 24th, 1933, the Assembly unanimously accepted a resolution which, in substance, endorsed the Lytton Report and declared that though before September 18th, 1931 (when the Japanese aggression on China began) both countries were responsible for the tension that existed between them, after that date Japan was alone responsible for what had happened. The Assembly urged conciliation, to which Japan replied by giving notice of resignation from the League and continuing her previous policy. The United States endorsed the League action, so that with the exception of Russia, which certainly did not differ, Japan was condemned after full and elaborate enquiry by the whole civilized world. The British Government was a party to this condemnation. Nevertheless, four days later she laid an embargo on the export from Britain of munitions of war to both China and Japan. In form, this was to declare that both countries were equally guilty, which was in contradiction to the resolution of the Assembly for which Britain had voted. In substance, it was even worse, since it was an advantage to Japan. She was fully armed. China was not, nor had she the means in her own country for remedying that inequality, and the British embargo increased her difficulty in doing so by imports from outside. This was so indefensible that in a week or two the embargo was withdrawn.

The virtual surrender by the League to Japan had the most serious consequences. Locally, so far from 'appeasing' Japan, it encouraged her to further aggression. She invaded the Province of Chihli in which the old capital of China, Pekin, was situated, and though she did not actually occupy that city then, she dominated it by the near presence of her armies. She further resented and protested against the assistance given by League experts to what may be called Nanking China.

But this was only a small part of the harm done by the Manchurian fiasco. Its repercussions all over the world were felt. It contributed to the failure of the Disarmament Conference. It hampered the League's efforts to restore peace in the Chaco war. Above all, it encouraged aggressive Powers in Europe — first Italy and then Germany — to set at naught the barrier so laboriously erected at Geneva against aggression, and brought us step by step to the present intensely grave position. Well might Dr. Wellington Koo say to the Assembly of 1933: — 'The absence of any effective action by the League had encouraged those who all along had been proclaiming the belief that might is right'. The next chapter in the Far Eastern tragedy, the invasion of central China by Japan did not begin till 1937, and must be dealt with later.

(II) THE DISARMAMENT CONFERENCE

Though I was not a member of the National Government, I was still one of its Independent Conservative supporters in the House of Lords, and acted as a British delegate on certain League Committees at Geneva and even represented them at the Assembly of 1932. It was in this capacity that I continued to preside over the Liberia Committee which strove to reform the Liberian Government, to enable it to suppress slavery, and to assist it to get funds for that purpose. Ultimately, Liberia preferred to repudiate her debts and reject the League proposal for reform.

I was also elected President of the Federation of League of Nations Societies for 1932-33.

In the autumn of 1931 I was asked whether I wished to be one of the British Delegates to the Disarmament Conference which was to meet in February 1932. I replied in a letter that it must depend on the policy of the Government, which, in my view, should aim at reduction of armaments and not merely limitation, and should provide for the equality of all nations, including Germany. I suggested that this might be done by forbidding to all nations those armaments which, by the Treaty of Versailles, had been forbidden to Germany — that is to say, military aircraft, submarines, warships over 10,000 tons, large land cannon and tanks. But I agreed that there might be other ways of carrying out the principles of reduction and equality. I do not know whether that letter was conveyed to the Government. In any case, I received no reply. But when I reached London, the Foreign Secretary, Sir John Simon, was good enough to discuss the position with me, at three interviews. I pressed very strongly to know what was the disarmament policy of the Government. I had found the position at Paris during the Manchurian discussion very galling, when I had to carry out a policy which seemed to me mistaken, and I did not wish for a repetition of that experience over disarmament. Ultimately, I gathered that the view of the Government was that Britain had done enough in arranging with the United States and Japan for naval limitation and were not inclined to take any initiative about land or air armaments. They would, however, be prepared to support any reasonable scheme presented by others. Such an attitude seemed to me insufficient. The reduction and, still more, the limitation of armaments I thought vital for peace. It is no doubt easy to argue that war may break out whether the nations are well or badly armed. But even if that be so, unless some way can be found for the international limitation of armaments, an arms race is bound to take place. Each nation on the Continent watches anxiously the extent of the armaments of its neighbours. It knows from bitter experience that as soon as there is a definite armament superiority, the temptation to an ambitious Government to bully its neighbours becomes irresistible. Accordingly, each country is tempted to increase its armaments, with or without alliances, to try to ward off the danger. That leads to increases by its rivals, with all the accompanying growth in the burden of taxation for both countries, and so it goes on. A state of international unrest is created, greatly added to by the necessity for each country to defend its growing expenditure by pointing out the threatening policy of others and by dwelling on the deplorable international characteristics which make them dangerous. Very soon, an atmosphere is produced in which everyone talks of war and when that happens war almost always follows.

This is no fancy picture. People of my age have seen the process going on more than once — a kind of automatic drive towards war, which, when it breaks out, is justified to the peaceful majority in each country as a war of self-defence, as indeed on one side or the other it usually is.

The only remedy is an international limitation of armaments; but though such a limitation is obviously in the interest of every peace-loving State, it is exceedingly difficult to reach an agreement for that purpose, particularly on land and in the air. I felt certain that unless the British Government was ready to use the whole of its influence and even to accept serious responsibilities, it was improbable that any such agreement would be reached. It was evident from what was said to me that some of the Government had little or no belief in international disarmament. They even thought it a rash proceeding to attempt it and held that we should do better to follow our own course free from entanglement with the perfidious foreigner. In these circumstances I could only stand aside with a hope that events might convert the Government to a more positive policy in which case, if wanted, I should be at their service.

The Conference met on February 2nd. There were a number of movements to demonstrate support of definite action for the limitation of armaments, including a monster petition organized by the Women's Societies with, I think, eight million signatures. The Federation of League of Nations Societies claiming to represent some 1,500,000 members also desired to put forward their proposals. It was accordingly arranged that the Conference should hold a preliminary sitting at which these various bodies should be heard. Among them, I, as President of the Federation, was allowed twenty minutes in which to explain its views. Accordingly, I developed, as far as I could, in that time, the proposal to extend to the world the prohibition of aggressive weapons then imposed on Germany. There were other subsidiary proposals which need not now be discussed. The plan was very warmly received by those present including the French delegation which, led by Monsieur Tardieu, markedly applauded. Several of the delegates afterwards expressed to me their agreement on these general lines, including to some extent Sir John Simon. In the opening debates of the Conference itself, some variant of the idea of prohibiting certain aggressive weapons received wide support from many if not all of the delegates. But as the discussion proceeded it was plain that there were serious differences of opinion underlying this apparent agreement. There were a few countries, of which Japan was the most important, that had no desire for disarmament by land or air. She had joined in the Washington Naval Treaties because on the sea she was vulnerable. But in other respects she was not, and a limitation of her army or air force would only mean that she might be hampered in carrying out such aggressive warfare as that in which she was engaged in China, at the very moment that the Conference began its sessions.

Apart from Japan, the Governments and still more the peoples of almost all countries were anxious for limitation in some form, but not always on the same grounds. Dr. Brüning, then Chancellor of Germany, claimed it in the name of equality. By the Treaty of Versailles, German armaments had been cut down drastically and she had been promised, as I have already pointed out, by the Treaty itself and even more specifically by a letter written to the German representatives by Monsieur Clemenceau on behalf of the victorious Powers, that when Germany was disarmed they too would disarm in the same way. Indeed, one of the chief reasons for the meeting of the Conference was to enable that pledge to be carried out. Germany therefore was on very strong ground. She was not asking to be freed from any of her Treaty obligations, as she was in many of her complaints. She was for once insisting on her Treaty rights. It had been stated by the International Commission appointed to supervise her disarmament that it had been substantially performed.

Ample time had been given for the Allies to do their part and for one reason or another they had evaded their obligation. Now it was to be carried out and, if not, the Germans demanded the right to re-arm. To try to keep her in a permanent condition of inferiority would be a breach of faith and manifestly injurious.

No one seriously disputed this contention. It was true that at one time Sir John Simon argued that even a failure of the other countries to disarm did not free Germany from her promise to remain disarmed. But everyone knew that such an argument was, in practice, unsustainable. Nor did the French rely on any ground of that kind. They fully admitted that a general reduction and limitation of armaments was right and proper; and though they did not formally concede that if no such disarmament took place Germany would have a legal right to re-arm, in private conversations they always agreed that such a right did morally exist. Their contention was different. They said that twice in the previous forty years France had been invaded by Germany and that she was entitled to protection against a repetition of that horrible experience. As long as her armaments were greatly superior to those of her Eastern neighbour she was in no danger. Even if she could rely on a real equality she might be fairly safe. But once she disarmed, what guarantee had she that Germany would not secretly re-arm? Her advisers rightly believed that some degree of German re-armament was already in progress. In any case, the population and resources of Germany — what was called her potentiality of war — were greater than those of France. To ask France to disarm without some effectual security against invasion was to ask an impossibility. If it were answered that France had the security of the Covenant of the League of Nations and its sanctions against aggression, there was the tragedy of Manchuria and Shanghai being enacted before their eyes to warn everyone what might happen to a perfectly innocent member of the League who relied on its protection. It was here that the British attitude became so fatal. Britain was the most powerful member of the League. She was regarded by all nations as its principal mainstay. To her they all looked for a definite pronouncement on this subject — and they looked in vain.

Germany and France had each got a strong case and unless both could be satisfied, no agreement on disarmanent was possible. There was no lack of suggestions. It is unnecessary to go into them in detail for they all broke down on the same point. The Germans would not agree without equality; the French insisted on security; and the British, followed by some others, refused to extend their obligations in that respect. Various formulas were suggested. The favourite one was to have, by way of security, a solemn declaration that none of the parties would attack any of the others — which the French regarded as quite inadequate. Recent events have fully justified their scepticism. Another plan was, in deference to the French, to limit armaments generally while keeping the Germans, for a period, in a position of inferiority and allowing them to re-arm a little in order to soothe their *amour propre*! Naturally the Germans would not accept this.

Meanwhile, events in Germany were moving disastrously. In the summer of 1932, Brüning, unable to show his fellow-countrymen any evidence of success in foreign affairs, resigned. He was replaced by von Papen, who, after a few months, gave way to the intrigues of his colleague General Schleicher. To avenge himself, Papen made terms with the Nazis and, after a few fatuous manœuvres, found that he had installed Hitler as Chancellor. That was in the early part of 1933, and thenceforward disarmament was doomed, though the end of the Conference did not come till the autumn of that year, and indeed formally not even then.

It may be said, no doubt, that in view of the strong nationalist current that overwhelmed Germany later on, the Conference was bound to break down. But it must be remembered that in the summer of 1932 the international position seemed very favourable. The Nazis were still in a considerable minority in their own country. Brüning was

Chancellor of Germany, Grandi was Foreign Minister of Italy, the French were having one of their periodical swings to the Left, and President Hoover had made proposals which certainly seemed very encouraging. If at that time the British Government, supported as it was by an overwhelming majority in Parliament, had courageously declared that in return for a genuine scheme of disarmament, based on equality, it was prepared to join in guaranteeing disarmed Powers against disloyal attacks by any Power which, after accepting the Treaty, had secretly re-armed, an agreement would, I believe, have been reached.

I had not been much at Geneva during that summer. I had been at Paris for the Annual Meeting of the Federation of League of Nations Societies, and also to attend the funeral of Briand. His illness and death were a great misfortune for the cause of peace for which he consistently worked with all his very remarkable political skill and eloquence. He was a man of great charm with one of the most beautiful speaking voices I have ever heard. At the end of his life he was bitterly attacked by the newspapers belonging to the Comité des Forges. I remember his saying in a speech[1]: 'The pens that wrote those attacks were made of the same metal as was used for weapons of war'. It was in reference to the same kind of attack that, meeting me accidentally at the Nord station, he said with his delightful smile: — 'Et quelle mauvaise tour allons nous faire maintenant!' In spite of all criticisms he was, even in his last illness, so powerful with the French people that I was assured that no Ministry could remain in office if he disapproved of it.

(III) 1932

I have already mentioned that I was one of the British delegates to the Assembly of 1932. It was rather a depressing occasion — a great contrast to 1930 or even 1931. The two

[1] See page 171.

great international questions of the day — the Sino-Japanese war and the Disarmament Conference — were being dealt with outside the normal working of the League. A German delegation was present but took little or no part. The two first delegates of Britain, the Foreign Minister and a Cabinet colleague, Sir E. Hilton Young, left me to make the chief speech for the delegation, which was a pity. The Ottawa Conference had just arrived at decisions which indicated little regard to international feeling, and this slighting of the League Assembly confirmed the impression of British aloofness. Monsieur Herriot, the French Prime Minister, made an eloquent pro-League speech. But in spite of that the general atmosphere showed, as I said at the time, 'a slackening in the enthusiasm for peace' which could, perhaps, only be renewed by 'an agreement for a substantial reduction of armaments'.

The actual work done by the Assembly was not very important. There was an optimistic reference to the war between Bolivia and Paraguay, known as the Chaco War — a tragically futile expenditure of blood and treasure in a locality which was almost impossible for peace efforts from Geneva to reach unless directed with much greater energy than was in fact shown. There were discussions, useful but unexciting, about health, communications, minorities, etc. Perhaps the most valuable actions taken were an agreement to appoint an Advisory Commission of experts to supervize the execution of the Slavery Convention; and the admission of Iraq as a member of the League and the consequent end of the British Mandate over that country.

Another League event of great importance was the resignation of the Secretary General, Sir Eric Drummond. His services to the League had been very great. The termination of his connection with it coincided with the end of its period of growth and prosperity. His successor, Monsieur Avenol, has had the melancholy experience of guiding an organization which year by year — through no fault of his — declined in authority.

The closing weeks of 1932 had been occupied at Geneva in devising a formula giving Germany a sufficient promise of equality in armaments to enable her to resume her place in the Conference which she had left in the previous summer.

(IV) 1933

In the New Year, at the end of January, 1933, I went to Geneva to preside over the League Committee on Liberia which was still in being, and to sit as a member of another Committee on the Composition of the Council. While I was there I saw a number of people, including Mr. Eden, who was attending the Disarmament Conference. It was clear that in spite of the return to it of the German representatives, the Conference was in a very bad way. The only chance to save it seemed to be the presentation of a definite scheme for disarmament, and this point of view was conveyed by Mr. Eden to the Cabinet. The result was the visit, in March, of Mr. MacDonald and Sir John Simon to Geneva, with such a scheme. The Prime Minister presented it to the Conference in what I was told was a not very successful speech. But the fate of what came to be known as the MacDonald Scheme did not depend on its presentation. It failed because, though it did provide for German equality, it did not provide for French security. In consequence, though it was received by the delegates with international courtesy, and was even given a first reading, it never really came alive.

Having presented this scheme, the two British Ministers went on to Rome to discuss with Signor Mussolini the Four Power Pact. The story of that attempt is instructive. It was originally put forward as a proposal for the revision of treaties and the reorganization of Europe, though the language used to describe its purpose was always vague. Protests were immediately raised by the other Powers including Russia, who had not been consulted. Thereupon a process of dilution ensued. Assurances were given that no country's interest was to be affected without her consent and least of all was the new Pact to interfere with the jurisdiction of the League. Indeed, it soon came to be represented as little more than an aspiration by the four Powers that everyone would behave in an exemplary fashion. Had the eminent statesmen concerned been content to utilize the League machinery, their objects, which were in themselves admirable, could have been attained without the heartburning which in the end destroyed them. But at this period one of the chief objects of the British Government seemed to be to lessen the prestige and authority of the League. Important international matters were therefore increasingly removed from its cognisance.

Another instance of this tendency occurred in connection with the World Economic Conference. There had been a good deal of talk for some time past of the necessity for making another effort to re-establish economically the world in general and Europe in particular. Accordingly, at the instance of the British Government a conference to discuss this question was summoned to meet, not at Geneva under the auspices of the League, but in London, under the chairmanship of the Prime Minister. It was early decided that the problems of inter-governmental debts and reparations were not to be considered. But it was hoped that tariffs and other similar obstacles to international trade might be mitigated and something might be done to stabilize currency. In fact, neither object was attained and the conference separated at the end of the summer leaving the economic position where it was.

One subsidiary purpose was however achieved, though it had nothing to do with the Conference as such. Earlier in the year some British engineers working in Russia had been arrested by the Soviet Government and charged with sabotage and anti-revolutionary action. British opinion was deeply moved. Not only did the accusation seem in itself incredible, but there was a profound distrust in our country of the methods and impartiality of Russian justice. Accordingly, diplomatic protests were made and when, after a trial which did nothing to remove British anxiety, the prisoners were convicted and some of them were sentenced to considerable terms of imprisonment, lenient though they were according to Russian standards, the Government with the full assent of our public opinion obtained statutory powers to impose an embargo on Russian trade — a power which was immediately exercised. It is interesting to note the difference in the attitude taken up towards this invasion of British interests and that adopted towards the far more serious international injury inflicted on us by the Japanese occupation of Northern China. That British subjects should be unjustly imprisoned is no doubt an important matter and I have no criticism to make of the action of our Government about it. But an unjustifiable aggression on a people whom we had promised to defend, in defiance of a system of international justice which the aggressor had promised to observe, was an infinitely graver attack on British interests. It is true that no British subjects were directly assaulted by the Japanese militarists, nor was any British property immediately occupied, but the ultimate consequences to the lives and possessions of British subjects and to the prosperity and well-being of the world were disastrous. No impartial person can doubt that the failure to stop the Japanese Manchurian adventure was an essential cause of most of the international evils that have since happened, culminating in the Polish war. In point of fact, the Russian embargo, so far from substantially embittering our relations with the Soviet, or creating any danger of war, led to the release of the imprisoned men. It was during the Economic Conference that this result was reached, in a conversation between Monsieur Litvinoff and our Foreign Minister. I have no doubt that international action of similar vigour against Japan in 1931-32 would have had an equally satisfactory result.

In May I returned to Geneva for the two League Committees on which I represented the British Government. While there, I saw a number of people and occasionally attended the Disarmament Conference. One conversation which I had with Dr. Benes is worth mentioning. He told

DR. EDUARD BENES, PRESIDENT OF THE CZECHOSLOVAK REPUBLIC

me that Hitler's foreign policy was to absorb Austria and Czechoslovakia, to create an independent Ukraine as a counterpoise to Russia and Poland, to suppress the Danzig Corridor and reduce Poland to subservience. This was on May 17th, 1933, so that our Government must have had plenty of warning from one of the shrewdest brains on the Continent what they might expect in Central Europe. It makes our action in 1938 and 1939 still more incomprehensible.

While I was in Geneva, President Roosevelt made an offer through his 'ambassador at large', Norman Davis. As I read it, it seemed to me that the President promised that in the case of any action by the League, America would be ready to consult with the League Powers, that she would not interfere with a League blockade against an aggressor, and that she would regard invasion as the test of aggression. This appeared to remove one of the chief objections, which at that time was urged, against our pledging ourselves to support League action against an aggressor, that it might bring us into collision with America. I hoped therefore that we should immediately have greeted Norman Davis's statement with enthusiasm. Even if it had turned out that my reading of the American declaration was too favourable, we should have shown that we were ready to accept the collaboration of America as far as she would go. I gathered, however, that the British delegation belittled the American move — perhaps because it added to their difficulty in rejecting the French demand for security as a condition of disarmament.

It was about this time that I wrote a letter to a distinguished correspondent in England in which I said: — 'The failure to preserve the peace in the Far East must have and has had very serious repercussions in Europe'. I then went on to quote French statesmen who had said: 'the proved ineffectiveness of the League in the Far East makes it impossible for the French to rely on the Covenant in Europe, and therefore they must maintain their armaments'. I ended by saying: — 'The whole question is whether the peace-making and peace-preserving machinery will, or will not, work. I am confident it will work if it is properly used, but I am also confident that if the foreign policy of this country continues to be directed in the same spirit in the future as in the past few months, the League and all the machinery for which it stands will either perish altogether or become so anaemic as to be useless.'

From Geneva I went to Montreux to preside over the annual meeting of the Federation of League of Nations Societies. We stopped in a charming hotel where I had a delicious room looking out over the lake. The proceedings were not very exciting, the most interesting incident being a controversy between the Palestinians and the German delegation as to exactly what we should say about the persecution of the Jews which was then beginning in Germany. In the end the Germans assented to a resolution of reasonable strength, though the younger members of their delegation were much dissatisfied. Hitler's Government had not then taken up a definitely anti-League attitude, though he doubtless meant to do so — Dictators who worship force must evidently hate any organization that opposes it. But so far, they were not sure that they were strong enough to fight the peace Powers of the world.

When I returned to London, I received an invitation from the Foreign Secretary to join the British delegation to the Assembly in the autumn. I had not expected such an invitation, and had agreed to take part in an Empire Conference in Canada which was being organized by the Royal Institute of International Affairs. The plan was to get delegates from the self-governing Dominions and India to meet a delegation from the United Kingdom at Toronto in September, and to discuss Imperial relations, particularly with reference to Empire Foreign Policy. After consideration, it seemed to me that the opportunity for attending the Geneva Assembly was not a sufficient reason for throwing over this agreement to go to Canada. Neither disarmament nor the Far Eastern question were to be discussed at the Assembly, and most of the other business was not of first rate importance. There was, indeed, one other League matter in which I was much interested, but that had been already disposed of by the Council. I refer to the Anglo-Persian difficulty, which arose from an arbitrary decision of the Persian Government to put an end to the concession of the Anglo-Persian Oil Company. The incident forms a good example of the smooth working of the League machinery under favourable circumstances. The question was brought before the Council and was referred to a Committee of which Dr. Benes was the *rapporteur*. After a few weeks' discussion, a new agreement between Persia and the United Kingdom was drawn up which was accepted by both parties. A reactionary friend of mine expressed regret that the existence of the League had prevented a settlement of the old type, dictated by British naval pressure! But the event has shown that the settlement by League mediation was quite satisfactory and has since endured without any fresh difficulty. It constituted a step towards organized peace — the conception which is repugnant to those trained in the old school of international anarchy.

Accordingly, on September 1st I sailed from Liverpool. My visit to Canada was a very pleasant experience. All my British colleagues were charming, and we spent three or four weeks in discussing how best Imperial Foreign Policy could be carried on, by arrangements which would provide as far as possible for joint action by the component parts of the British Commonwealth without compromising their full independence.

One complication was the fact that, from the point of view of international law, foreign countries were entitled to treat the whole Empire as one entity, involving the responsibility of each part of it for international action taken by any other part. This was no new difficulty. It had been discussed for years by those who advocated Imperial Federation, and all sorts of Federal Constitutions had been drawn up by which the Federal Government representing the Mother Country and all the self-governing Dominions should be constituted to direct the Foreign Affairs of the Empire. Lord Milner and the group known as the Round Table had given a great deal of thought to the subject and I remember I at one time attended several of their discussions about it. In the United Kingdom the proposals had a respectful and not unfavourable reception. But it was found that the Dominions had an unalterable objection to any system by which they should be compelled to accept decisions arrived at by an organization which, for technical reasons, would have had to have its head-quarters in London. At Toronto we found this feeling quite unabated — the strong Canadian delegation which included all parties in the Dominion being unanimous against giving to Canadian representatives in London any power to bind the Canadian Government. And almost, if not quite, all the other Dominion delegates took the same view. On the other hand, the great majority were favourable to Dominion participation in the League of Nations. They accepted a national responsibility for maintaining world peace and were quite ready freely to co-operate with the United Kingdom for that purpose, provided that the Dominion Governments should remain free to decide in what manner they would participate in the necessary action. I myself felt hopeful that a system of Empire consultation in London might be worked out, preferably under the aegis of the Foreign Office, similar to that which had very successfully grown up at the Geneva Assemblies for the international action of the British Empire Delegation.

We passed no resolutions, but a report was drawn up in which these matters were fully discussed. I do not know that it led to any specific Imperial reorganization. It is at least a practical warning of the difficulties which beset the path of an International Federal reformer.

Certain personal memories of my stay in Canada remain. One was of the exceeding kindness and hospitality which were shown to every one of us. Another was of a visit to Niagara, which convinced me that even the greatest of waterfalls has little honour in its own country. A third was of a perfect afternoon which I spent by the side of Lake Ontario at the country cottage of Dr. Glazebrook. And I will add as my last recollection my appreciation of the delicious melons — in a different class to any I have eaten elsewhere.

Before I left Canada, I received an urgent telegram from the Foreign Office to go to Geneva as soon as I could to wind up the Liberia affair, which I accordingly did as soon as I got back to England.

The Assembly was over. On the personal side, it had been remarkable for the attendance of Dr. Goebbels, who came there protected by a 'body-guard of large, powerful men'. Dr. Dollfuss, soon afterwards to be assassinated by the Nazis, was also there and received a warm welcome. Dr. Goebbels did not address the Assembly, but he made a speech to the press in which he justified racial discrimination and glorified war. Naturally, men who held these views, as did all the Nazi leaders from Hitler downwards, hated the League and worked with German persistence for its destruction. Much was said in the Assembly about the diminution of the authority of the League, attributed, by many speakers, to its failure to protect China, or rather to the want of support given by its most important members to the League system, of which that failure was a cogent example.

Beyond that, there was a reference to disarmament, but no positive action, since the question was in the hands of the Disarmament Conference. There were also appeals to the Great Powers to give a lead, notably by the South African delegate, Mr. te Water, who had been elected President of the Assembly in recognition of his vigorous support of League policy on all occasions. Unhappily, these appeals met with no response. On the contrary, the British Government thought it right again to make a vigorous attack on League expenditure, which resulted in a saving of some £6,000 of which the British share was £600! As has often been pointed out, the total British annual expenditure on the League was very small — something like 0.14 per cent of our annual income. No foreigner could believe that we were really anxious about such a sum and they naturally put down the Government's action to a desire to show how little it cared about the League.

Yet even in this year of depression, good work was done by the League whenever it was given the chance. I have already referred to the Anglo-Persian controversy. Besides that, it began the settlement of a very threatening dispute between Peru and Colombia over a place called Letitia, and it tried to bring to an end the tragic Chaco war. In the Letitia case, the favourable result was directly due to a threat of sanctions. In the Chaco, the long continuance of the fighting resulted from inability or unwillingness of League members to use the same means of persuasion.

Of the other work, I will only mention the creation of a body to deal with Jewish refugees from Germany, which consisted of a High Commissioner (the American, Mr. James Macdonald) and a Governing Body representing fifteen Governments. Why it was called a Governing Body I never made out. It had no powers. With great reluctance I accepted the chairmanship of it and we met first at Lausanne and afterwards in London. In order to conciliate Germany — that Sisyphean task — it was separated from the League, in spite of the fact that different aspects of the refugee problem were already being dealt with by League machinery, including the Nansen Office, and that there was at Geneva a great fund of experience in dealing with refugee questions. Nevertheless, we did our best. Mr. Macdonald, the High Commissioner, began by vainly trying to induce the Hitler Government to take some share of the burden imposed on other countries by its policy of ruining and maltreating the Jews and so driving them, penniless or nearly so, out of Germany. The chief sufferer was France, who allowed these miserable people to come freely over her frontier and spent large sums of money, some of which came from English and American sources, in keeping them from starvation. But other countries suffered also. Unhappily, the mere feeding and lodging of the destitute was no remedy. It kept them alive, but that was all. Our task was to try to find some permanent relief either by absorption in the countries to which they had been driven, which was almost impossible, especially in bad times, or by settling them in some part of the world less overcrowded than Europe. To aid in this work the Germans absolutely refused. They saw no reason why German Jews should be saved from starvation; indeed, they were inclined to claim credit for not having massacred them straight off. Seldom has a greater national crime been committed. No kind of charge was proved or even seriously attempted to be proved against the men, women and children who were so oppressed. Many of them had done notable service to Germany in science, in law, in literature. Some had served with distinction in the German army and, though a pretence was made of recognizing military service as a mitigation of the crime of being a Jew, it meant little more than a postponement of ruin. When his failure in Berlin became manifest, the High Commissioner turned to South America. But he was not able to do much there. Still, here and there something was achieved. In particular, considerable numbers were received in Palestine. But on the whole we failed. Indeed, the Governing Body was quite powerless. We consisted of representatives of Governments, generally not personally very influential, and though we laboured to draw up schemes for dealing with this tremendous evil, whenever any real, constructive suggestion was made, the members of the Governing Body could do nothing except refer it each to his Government — that is, to some clerk who earned his salary by making objections. Had we consisted of persons whose action did not involve directly the responsibility of Governments but had been chosen for their knowledge of or interest in the subject, we could at least have drawn up a complete scheme which could then have been referred to the Council of the League and publicly discussed there, so that all might know which were the Governments which were obstructing progress. That has been the way in which considerable results have been obtained in such matters as the control of narcotic drugs and the extirpation of the white-slave traffic. As I have already mentioned, in the earlier stages of the disarmament controversy excellent work was done by a similar committee. But the bureaucracies regard such machinery with considerable suspicion and normally resist its employment. They greatly prefer dealing with international questions through what a distinguished member of the Foreign Office used to call 'the usual channels'. That at any rate prevents unduly rapid action. Hence, in the recent effort begun at the Evian Conference in July, 1938, the same old plan of action by a body representative of Governments was again tried with the same lamentable failure.

Our Governing Body lasted till December, 1935, when in concert with Mr. James Macdonald, I urged its abolition.

(v) 1934 AND THE PEACE BALLOT

The year 1934 was better for the League than the years 1932 and 1933 — that is to say, the rate of descent was less rapid. Its political machinery was on more than one occasion used with success, while its non-contentious work went on smoothly and well. On the two big questions of the Sino-Japanese controversy and Disarmament, nothing encouraging occurred. The Far East was, indeed, quiescent. Japan was trying to digest her acquisitions, and China was making great efforts for the pacification of her country and its internal reform, with the help of League advisers. But Japanese ambition was not sated. She was waiting her opportunity to resume her conquest of China, and there was no sign that the United Kingdom or America were prepared effectively to go to the assistance of that country. It was symptomatic of the situation that the attempts of the Chinese Government to extirpate the curse of opium-smoking and similar drug addiction were deliberately hampered by the encouragement of poppy-growing in the parts of China occupied by Japan.

As to disarmament, the British Government still expressed

the hope that the Conference, maimed by the withdrawal of Germany, would nevertheless succeed. There were a number of private meetings of two or three Powers, which led to nothing, and occasionally the General Committee of the Conference was summoned and adjourned. The fundamental difficulty remained that France would not agree to German equality unless she were assured of security, while the British Government steadily reiterated its refusal to extend, or even to reaffirm its commitments.

In the course of the summer, Mr. MacDonald's Government announced an increase of air armaments while still asserting that it believed in the possibility of general disarmament. To European opinion the two propositions seemed incompatible and Europe made up its mind, rightly, that an armaments race would follow. War had become appreciably nearer and indeed seemed to me inevitable unless our support of the League became real and not only rhetorical.

The Austrian question began to be acute. Hitler, an Austrian by birth, always passionately desired the Anschluss. On the other hand, Mussolini had no wish for Germany as a next neighbour. Italy was therefore ready to support Austrian independence; but on one condition — the elimination of Austrian Social Democrats as a political force. Unfortunately for this policy, it was precisely the Social Democrat Party which was the chief obstacle to the spread of Nazi power. In these circumstances the Austrian Government suggested the reference of the question to the League. It was a reasonable proposal since, by the Paris Treaty, the Anschluss was forbidden unless the League agreed. But the British Government were opposed to this and I believe Monsieur Barthou, with his genius for being wrong, agreed with them. One of those futile diplomatic formulae was prepared. The two Governments declared that they regarded the preservation of Austrian independence as important for peace — and another blow had been struck at the authority of the League. The Nazis pursued their path. They arranged for a disturbance in Vienna and the murder of Dr. Dollfuss who, in his effort to conciliate Italy, had massacred the Socialists. From that time forward it was evident that unless the Western Powers intervened, the absorption of Austria by Hitler was certain.

No doubt the position had become exceedingly difficult. The Germans were more or less secretly re-arming under what was in fact a revolutionary government inspired by an extreme nationalistic faith. The power of the League had been allowed to wane. Britain and France seemed to have no very definite policy. In words they supported the League: in practice the British Government seemed to regard it as an excrescence, useful perhaps for regulating the manufacture and sale of opium and things like that, but of no use for dealing with great questions of peace and war; and France was in favour of the League so far and only so far as her immediate safety was concerned. There were two possible policies for the Western Powers. One was to throw their whole strength into support of the League. The other was in effect, to abandon it and devote all their resources to re-armament. They were not prepared to take the first course, and public opinion believed (as I think, rightly) that an enduring peace could not be achieved by the second. In any case, no vigorous attempt was made either to stop German armaments or to increase our own.

In February I went to Brussels, partly to deliver a lecture at the University on the League in Belgium, and partly to attend a conference of League of Nations Societies. The lecture went off very well and the conference showed that there was a much more active feeling for the League than some of the citizens of Brussels had believed. My Belgian friends took a very gloomy view of the European situation, especially about Austria.

On my return I went over to Ireland and spoke both at Belfast and Dublin. The latter was interesting because the politicians believed I had come over on a mission. Mr. de Valera, who came to the meeting (as well as Mr. Fitzgerald of the Opposition) evidently expected I might say something to him. But having nothing to say, I kept silence except for normal civilities.

On my return to London we felt, in the League of Nations Union, that with the Disarmament Conference evidently moribund and the power of the League diminishing, we ought to exert ourselves to convince the Government that if they would pursue a really vigorous League policy they would be supported by British opinion. It had often been suggested that some kind of consultation of the people might be arranged to enable them to express their views on the League, and at Ilford an experiment had been tried by the local branch of the Union, headed by Mr. Boorman. The result had been striking. With the help of the local paper, the *Ilford Recorder*, certain questions were submitted to the adult population on which they were asked to express their opinions. The questions dealt with the general policy of the League, Disarmament, the Locarno Treaties, and the arms trade. The Union and other societies interested in peace took the plan up. A larger number of persons 'voted' than had ever voted in any of the local elections, and there was a great majority in favour of the League. On only one of the questions did the vote go the other way and that was about Locarno. There, the voters expressed their disapproval of that policy, which the Union had always supported, and I was told that there was a feeling that it was too much mixed up with particular countries and that if it had been a general proposal it would have been upheld. I mention this because it showed that the voting was not mere unthinking compliance with the request of persistent canvassers, but expressed real though in this case mistaken opinion. This view was confirmed by the fact that an attempt by opponents of the League to obtain votes against it in Bristol, Hull and Lincoln failed.

To me these seemed most promising events. If we could organize a 'nation wide' vote of the same kind, the result might be a great spur to what we regarded as a lethargic Foreign Policy. Accordingly, after much consideration and debate, a Committee was formed in the autumn of 1934 representing not only the League of Nations Union but a number of other societies which took an interest in peace. In particular, all the chief religious bodies supported the movement. So did many of the Women's Societies and the industrial bodies. We asked for the help of all three political parties. The Labour and Liberal Parties responded warmly. But the Conservative Party and its allies declined, though many of its local branches and some leading Conservatives like Lord Caldecote assisted us. The League of Nations Union endorsed the movement both in its Executive Committee and in a meeting of the Council at Bournemouth in June. The plan laid before the Council was that a questionnaire should be submitted as far as possible to every adult inhabitant of the United Kingdom over eighteen years of age. It contained the following questions: —

1. Should Great Britain remain a member of the League of Nations?

2. Are you in favour of an all-round reduction of armaments by international agreement?

3. Are you in favour of the all-round abolition of national military and naval aircraft by international agreement?

4. Should the manufacture and sale of armaments for private profit be prohibited by international agreement?

5. Do you consider that, if a nation insists on attacking another, the other nations should combine to compel it to stop, by
    (a) economic and non-military measures;
    (b) if necessary, military measures?

It was explained that the answers to these questions would constitute a National Declaration, and the Resolution adopted by the Council recorded its approval of 'the plan for a National Declaration on the League of Nations and Armaments'. It is not necessary to set forth all the details of what came to be called the Peace Ballot. Its success greatly exceeded all our anticipations. I remember discussing it in the summer of 1934 with a number of journalists who were doubtful of its feasibility. And when I said that I hoped for a vote of 5,000,000 I was regarded as a wild optimist. As a fact, upwards of eleven and a half million persons voted! This astonishing result was obtained mainly by the help of 500,000 volunteer workers — in itself a proof of the interest excited. There were also a number of meetings and much support from the churches. The Labour and Liberal parties co-operated warmly. We were very much attacked. The isolationist press was very bitter, describing the movement as the Blood Ballot. That gave us an excellent advertisement. One incident surprised me very much. The Foreign Secretary, Sir John Simon, in a debate in the House of Commons on private manufacture of arms, went out of his way to denounce the National Declaration, singling out especially the fourth question as most unfair. Still more surprisingly, he was joined by Sir Austen Chamberlain who used very vigorous language on the subject. It is only right to say that both right honour-able gentlemen afterwards withdrew their intemperate words and I only refer to the matter because I am still in the dark as to why they and others like them were so excited on the subject. The questions were almost all merely paraphrases of the Covenant which the Government officially advocated. The one exception was this fourth question. The Covenant says that the private manufacture of armaments is open to grave objection. Our question introduced expressly the topic of private profit. No doubt those who, on national or local grounds favoured the private manufacture of arms, might reasonably dislike a question which drew attention to one of its chief objections. But there was nothing unfair in our doing so. However, though the attacks were annoying to the organizers of the ballot, they did nothing to hinder its success. The most common criticism of the whole enterprise was that those who voted did so without thinking. I can only say that my small personal experience in canvassing was quite inconsistent with this view. Those I asked were usually much interested. They read the questions carefully and gave their answers in writing. In a certain number of cases, qualifications were added to a negative or affirmative answer. Generally a choice between the different questions was exercised, the result being that whereas in answer to questions 1, 2, 4, and 5a, over 90 per cent of the replies were affirmative, in the answers to 5b which deals with military sanctions, the percentage fell to something over 70 per cent. In the answers to question 3 which refers to air armament, the affirmatives were only 80 per cent. The reason for this lower percentage about the air was believed to be that we had not properly explained what was to be done as to civilian aircraft. It is also noticeable that though the size of the total votes varied a good deal in different parts of the country, the percentage of ayes and noes was broadly constant.

The collection of the votes began in the autumn of 1934 and was completed in the early summer of 1935. The result was announced at an Albert Hall meeting. It was formally communicated to the Government, and Lord Baldwin, who had become Prime Minister, spoke of the ballot as having been of very great value — a great change in the Ministerial attitude. I have no doubt it influenced their policy for the time, but not permanently or, from my point of view, sufficiently. Nevertheless, I think we were right to make the attempt. We believed that the situation in Europe was deteriorating and would lead to war unless a very strong and courageous League policy were pursued. We thought that some of the Ministers at any rate were inclined to agree with us on that point, but were afraid that such a policy would not secure the support of the electorate. We hoped that the ballot would have convinced them that their fears were unjustified. I do not know what in fact went on in the Cabinet, but events showed, as I think, that on the general questions of policy we were right.

While the Ballot was getting under weigh, the so called 'Blood Bath' took place in Germany. A large number of alleged opponents of the Hitler regime were suddenly put to death without any judicial examination or trial. No serious resentment seemed to be caused in Germany by these events. Indeed, the docility of the German people throughout the Nazi regime shows how centuries of the drill sergeant have sapped their individuality.

In other quarters some encouraging things happened. I have already mentioned that in 1933 a beginning was made of the settlement of the Letitia question between Peru and Colombia. That was finally completed in 1934. In the Chaco affair, the British representative on the League Council urged an embargo on the supply of munitions to both combatants. A League commission had been sent out to enquire into the position and had reported, among other things, that the war was carried on by means of weapons sold to the combatants by armament firms in Europe and America. The threat of an embargo was therefore a very powerful argument and the parties became more amenable to pacification. Even so, the negotiations were long drawn out, but peace was at last reached in 1935. In both these South American cases it was again shown that remonstrances backed by practical measures of coercion may, if properly handled, lead to peace. Without such measures the most eloquent appeals are useless.

Another incident pointing in the same direction was the organization of the vote in the Saar district as to whether or no the population desired to return to Germany, which was directed by the Treaty of Versailles to take place. A good deal of anxiety was felt about the danger of a clash between French and German interests on and near the day of the poll. In the year we are discussing, all arrangements were made for the poll to be taken in the following year under international supervision, including provision for the presence of an international force to keep order. The poll in consequence was held in 1935 in complete calm and voting resulted in a large majority in favour of a return to Germany of this eminently German district.

Early in July, the French Foreign Minister, Monsieur Barthou, tried to organize a pact of mutual assistance to be entered into by France, Russia, Germany and some of the Central European States. Our Government expressed approval, provided we were not expected to do anything to help. The plan failed. It is worth notice that attempts at European pacification outside the League were not encouraging. This particular effort was still pending when Monsieur Barthou was assassinated at Marseilles at the same time as the King of Jugoslavia, just after the Nazi murder of Dr. Dollfuss in Vienna. For a time there was a danger that Serbian indignation over the death of their King might take the form of an attack on Hungary, where the crime was said to have been planned. Fortunately, the question between the two States was rapidly settled by the Council of the League, on the initiative of Mr. Eden, the British representative.

The various matters referred to above in which the League machinery succeeded were treated by the Council. The Assembly was less fruitful. The outstanding event was the admission of Russia to the League. Some excellent people were shocked because they disapproved of the religious and economic views of the Russian Government. But the League was not founded as an international club but as an instrument for the preservation of peace, and for that purpose I could not doubt that it was better to have Russia inside than outside. It is only fair to say that until her monstrous invasion of Finland, she co-operated loyally with the other members of the League who strove for the maintenance of peace.

Beyond this, useful work of a non-contentious kind was done by the Assembly, particularly with regard to opium, where the international machinery for controlling illegitimate consumption was set in motion, intellectual co-operation, where the Committee pursued its valuable way under the Chairmanship of Professor Murray, and other matters such as international action to prevent the destruction of birds by the oil pollution of the sea. There was also a certain number of speeches by distinguished statesmen. But the general feeling was that nothing had been done to arrest the weakening of the League in spite of all the danger of that process to European peace. Disarmament was failing, Japan was still in occupation of the four Northern Provinces in China and was preparing a fresh onslaught on that unhappy country.

(VI) 1935 AND 1936: ABYSSINIA AND SPAIN

At the beginning of 1935, therefore, the League was in a critical position. The first decade of success, in its achievements and growth of its authority, had come to an end, in 1931. It had been followed by a period of world economic confusion which led to a recrudescence of economic nationalism. At the same time, and partly in consequence of these economic difficulties, a wave of political nationalism swept over many European countries. Totalitarianism with its insistence on racialism and armed force greatly increased this tendency. One of the first of its manifestations was the Japanese Manchurian adventure, disapproved but unchecked by the League of Nations. Then came the long drawn out tragedy of the Disarmament Conference, which was also a serious blow to the ideas of Geneva. The result was a considerable diminution in the influence of the League. Nevertheless, there were many signs of its vitality. It was still able to adjust international difficulties, as in the Saar and in South America, and the result of the Peace Ballot showed that it still enjoyed a large measure of popular support in this country. Had 1935 proved favourable to the League, there is no reason to doubt that it would have recovered a great part if not the whole of its strength and usefulness. Whether that was to be so or not depended, as always, on the action of its members and particularly of France and the United Kingdom, its natural leaders. As events turned out, the test was searching and the result disastrous.

Abyssinia had been admitted in 1923 to the League on the earnest advocacy of France and Italy, reluctantly acquiesced in by Britain who had doubts about her suitability as a member, particularly in view of her continued toleration of slavery. After her election her Government, under the inspiration of the Emperor Haile Salassie, made a genuine and not unsuccessful effort to improve her social and political conditions. Certainly, if she was entitled to the rights of membership in 1923, she had done nothing to forfeit them in 1934-36. Unfortunately for her, the Fascist Government of Italy was anxious to increase the international importance of that country and believed that a Colonial Empire would greatly assist that object. In looking round for territory which could be turned to this use, Signor Mussolini noted that Abyssinia was still independent. His Government was well aware of this fact since it had more than once guaranteed this independence. He therefore, in spite of these guarantees and of Italy's obligations to the members of the League of Nations under the Covenant, determined to conquer the Ethiopian State. Italian intentions were the subject of common talk in Rome at least as early as the summer of 1934.[1] A distinguished English visitor to Rome at that time was so much impressed by what he heard that on his return to this country he thought it right to inform our Foreign Office which, however, took no action. In the course of the autumn, a dispute arose between Italy and Abyssinia as to the sovereignty of a place of no great importance called Walwal. It was near the boundary of Italian Somaliland and, by most of the maps then existing, it was well within the Ethiopian territory. There was, however, no properly marked boundary and, as there seemed to be no desire to settle the incident peacefully, it got worse, involving a skirmish with thirty Italian casualties and about a hundred Abyssinian. Demands for reparation were made by Italy, and on December 6th, Abyssinia asked for arbitration under the treaty of 1928 with Italy, which was refused. Other minor incidents took place, and on January 3rd, 1935, Abyssinia appealed to the Council of the League under Article 11 of the Covenant, which gives

[1] Marshal de Bono, in his *Anno XIIII*, states that as early as 1932 he and the Duce were agreed that Italy must prepare for military action in East Africa.

members of the League the 'friendly right' to call its attention to any circumstance which threatens to disturb the good understanding between nations. Just at this time, Monsieur Laval, on behalf of France, was negotiating at Rome, with Mussolini in order to improve the relations between the two countries. They came to an agreement on a number of matters. Whether Ethiopia was mentioned is not clear. The terms of the agreement have not been published. But somehow or other, the Duce arrived at the conclusion, either then or soon after, that the French Government did not propose seriously to interfere with his Abyssinian adventure. In the result, this first appeal of Abyssinia to the League was postponed.

In February, an agreement was made in London between England and France, which turned out to be completely valueless. It provided for consultation if the integrity of Austria were threatened, it suggested a special pact for mutual assistance against air attack between the Great Powers — which came to nothing — and it laid it down that Germany could not by her own arbitrary action free herself from treaties by which she had entered into obligations to the other parties to them — a declaration which Germany almost immediately defied by introducing conscription and has continued to ignore in various ways ever since.

In March, the British Government announced in a White Paper that, in effect, they had abandoned all hope of international disarmament and intended to start what has since been called re-armament. Incidentally, Mr. Baldwin intimated that he had no hope of collective security under the League. If this was to be so, a much more vigorous policy of re-armament, however unsatisfactory, was essential. But the Government insisted that they were not going to increase armaments but only to modernize them. Within five days, on March 16th, Germany re-introduced conscription. There was the usual protest from our Foreign Office, followed by the acceptance of an invitation for the Foreign Secretary, Sir John Simon, to go to Berlin to discuss the matter. Hitler rejected all British proposals and utterly refused to withdraw his conscription order. Sir John thereupon returned to London and Mr. Eden, in pursuance of this system of visits to foreign statesmen, instead of open discussions at Geneva, went on to Moscow. Monsieur Stalin expressed himself as favourable to the collective peace system! Mr. Eden then went to Warsaw where the Poles rejected an Eastern Pact, and to Prague, and returned very unwell from the consequences of an exceedingly stormy journey.

Meanwhile, Abyssinia had, on March 17th, made a further appeal to the League, this time under Article 15 which deals with international disputes likely to lead to a rupture, the attitude of Italy having grown more threatening. There was to be a special meeting of the Council to consider German armaments, and the Ethiopian Government asked for its appeal to be considered then. But again, at the instance of the British and French Governments, it was postponed.

Meanwhile, at Stresa the head of the Governments of France and Italy, and their Foreign Ministers, had met the British Prime Minister, Mr. MacDonald, and his Foreign Secretary, Sir John Simon, to discuss the European situation and the rearmament of Germany. Nothing was said about Abyssinia, though we now know that the representatives of Italy anticipated that if the Western Powers had objected to the African enterprise they would have said so. But the British Ministers reiterated their statement that they would in no case undertake further responsibility for peace. If the object of the British Government at this stage had been to encourage Mussolini and discredit the League it is difficult to see how that could have been done more effectually. A futile protest against German re-armament was also made, which the Council of the League was induced to endorse.

Meanwhile, the Italian and Abyssinian Governments were negotiating about a Conciliation Committee which, after a further appeal by Abyssinia — the third — was agreed to at the ordinary meeting of the Council of the League in May. A limit of time was imposed on the Committee, which was to deal with the incidents at Walwal but not with the boundary question. It was decided that if no settlement had been reached by the end of July, the matter should again come before the Council in August. This suited the Italians perfectly. During the intervening rainy season, no military movements were possible and meanwhile their preparations for invasion could continue. It was said that both sides were arming. But Ethiopia had few resources and almost no modern arms. I believe she had actually two ill-equipped aeroplanes when war broke out, to meet large numbers of Italian bombers, so that there was nothing to interfere with the enjoyment of Signor Vittorio Mussolini, an Italian flying officer, as described in his book, *Voli sulle Ambe* — 'I dropped an aerial torpedo in the centre of the group [of Ethiopian horsemen] and the group spread out like a flowering rose. It was most entertaining', and: 'About fifty brigands had a taste of our splinters. It was most entertaining work and had a tragic but beautiful effect.'

We were absorbed, in England, by the Silver Jubilee, and as soon as the celebrations were over Mr. MacDonald resigned the Prime Ministership and was succeeded by Mr. Baldwin. At the same time, Sir Samuel Hoare became Foreign Minister in the place of Sir John Simon. Both of the outgoing Ministers remained in the Cabinet. This was on June 6th, and on June 20th the Ethiopian Government made their fourth appeal to the League, on the ground that aggression by Italy was imminent.

It must have been about this time that the British Government, as it is said, urged Haile Selassie not to attack Italy but to trust to the protection of the League. If so, it may have been due to the announcement of the figures of the Peace Ballot which was made on June 27th. In any case, the Ethiopian Government, in its fourth appeal and on other occasions, professed its readiness to submit all its disputes and difficulties with Italy to international arbitration, to which the Italian reply was to say that Italy was engaged in a conflict which they would carry on to the bitter end. In other words, the controversy expressly raised the issue of whether international disputes were to be settled by force or, as provided by the Covenant, by submission to arbitration or some form of pacific settlement. On the outcome of this issue depended the peace of Europe and of the world. For no country was it more important than for the British Empire. Nevertheless, large numbers of highly placed Conservative politicians could not be induced to accept this point of view, with results which are now manifest.

There were other events before the tragedy was played out. In August, a desperate attempt was made in which Mr. Eden for Britain was the chief mover to set up again the Italo-Abyssinian Conciliation Committee. Ultimately it failed, in spite of more than one suggestion of settlement accepted by Abyssinia and rejected by Italy.

Meanwhile, Britain had imposed a strict embargo on arms for both parties. As Italy was fully armed and Abyssinia very much the reverse, it was very far from a just measure. Debates in Parliament elicited promises from the new Foreign Minister that we would stand by the League of Nations.

In this situation, the Council and the Assembly met early in September at Geneva. It was obvious that grave decisions would be considered, and in order to strengthen the hands of the British Government, a number of individuals, including myself, were consulted by the Foreign Office as to whether we would support them in a strong League policy. I, of course, gave the required assurance. What others may have said I do not know. On the next day the Cabinet met and decided to support the League. When, therefore, the Geneva meetings took place, it may be assumed that the Government knew that in resisting Italian aggression they could count on the approval of the British public opinion.

On September 4th, Mr. Eden made a strong speech to the Council urging that they must use all the machinery of the League to protect Abyssinia, and on September 11th Sir Samuel Hoare reinforced this declaration by his celebrated speech to the Assembly. It is unnecessary to quote it in detail. The speaker made it perfectly clear that the British Government believed in collective security through the League of Nations and, with what was understood to be an allusion to the recently announced results of the Peace Ballot, he declared that British public opinion was as much in favour of the policy as the Government. He emphasized that Britain's action must be conditional on other members of the League doing their share. He concluded by repudiating the idea that Britain's fidelity to the League could not be relied on, and declared that such an opinion was a dangerous delusion. Altogether, it was understood to be an uncompromising statement that unless Italy abandoned her invasion of Abyssinia, Britain was prepared to co-operate with the other nations in forcing her to do so by collective action. A particular sentence may be quoted: — 'In conformity with its precise and explicit obligations, the League stands, and my country stands with it, for the collective maintenance of the Covenant in its entirety and particularly for steady and collective resistance to all acts of unprovoked aggression.' Other speeches on the same lines were made both by Sir Samuel and Mr. Eden. A broadcast by the latter was particularly definite. I am sure that both speakers would have indignantly rejected any suggestion that their language had been influenced by the near approach of the General Election, though in fact after the election was safely over the policy was destroyed by the Hoare-Laval agreement.

At the same time as these declarations of policy were made, the French and British Governments interchanged views on the position. The French were assured that the policy announced would apply to all cases of aggression and not only to the Ethiopian case, and the British were told that in case Italy attacked them France would fulfil up to the hilt her obligation under the Covenant to give them support.

The next step was the formulation by a committee of the Assembly of a far-reaching scheme for the reform of the Abyssinian Government under the supervision of foreign specialists, together with a recognition of the special interests of Italy. She nevertheless refused to consider any such proposal and on October 2nd began her invasion. On October 11th, the Assembly, by fifty votes to four, pronounced that Italy was the aggressor, three of the four being Powers dependent on Italy. So far the action of the League, under British leadership and with the acquiescence of France and all other important members of the League, had been not unsatisfactory. Thenceforward it was not so good.

The obvious next step indicated in Article 16 of the Covenant and still more in the resolutions on the subject by the Assembly of 1921, would have been to have broken off diplomatic relations between the League States and Italy. That would have amounted to an impressive international condemnation of Italian policy and would have publicly committed those who took part in it to coercive action. Moreover, it would have been directed against the really guilty party — the Italian Government — as distinguished from its subjects. Unfortunately, just the opposite course was taken. A gradual, almost tentative, application of economic sanctions was resolved on which directly affected the Italians and only indirectly their Government. This was coupled with repeated assurances that they implied no hostility to Italy and were only imposed by the League Powers from an apparently reluctant loyalty to the principles of the Covenant. Indeed, it was freely said that the French Government went further and assured the Duce that no action which would lead to war would be taken against Italy. It is to be hoped that this assurance was given without the connivance of any British Minister. It is difficult to imagine a more futile or dishonest proceeding. While with one hand the League Powers were causing grave hardship to the people of Italy, with the other messages were being sent to the Italian Government by one of the League's most important members, that nothing would be done effectively to arrest their criminal aggression. Had the League members first withdrawn their Ambassadors from Rome and then gone on to inform the

Italian Government that unless the invasion was stopped communication between Italy and Africa would be interrupted, the invasion must have been abandoned. Nor was Italy in a position to make any effective reply. I know that hints were later thrown out that she might have made an air attack on Malta. Considering the possible retaliation against Italy, such action was most unlikely. It was also said, contrary to the openly expressed opinion of the Admiral commanding in the Mediterranean, that our fleet was not strong enough to resist an attack by Italian ships. I cannot believe that any British authority endorsed such nonsense. Unfortunately, it was commonly credited on the Continent and greatly reduced our international influence. Then it was whispered that other Powers might join in Italy's defence or at least hamper League action. At an early stage the United States repudiated the suggestion as far as they were concerned, and it was known that Germany was not then prepared for war. It was before the days of the Axis.

No! The feebleness of the action from the start and the subsequent abandonment of resistance to aggression was not due to any reasonable fear of the consequences to us and France of League action against Italy. It was the result of the view held at that time vigorously in France and actually, though not explicitly, in Britain, that to regard prevention of war, by force if necessary, as our highest interest and duty was a piece of visionary nonsense, and that nothing of that kind should be attempted unless some fragment of national territory or a section of national trade was also threatened. There was a further desire to 'buy' Italy — which will certainly never be achieved by showing we are afraid of her. The sequel of the Abyssinian question and its later results are the deplorable commentary on our action at this time.

Meanwhile, in June, 1935, a naval agreement had been made by Britain with Germany which greatly increased the anxiety of France. Germany agreed that for the future her fleet, compared with ours, should not exceed a ratio of seven to twenty. The agreement was made without any proper consultation with France, and when it was published she and Italy protested vehemently not so much against its actual terms as against the way in which they had been negotiated. It was said that, in view of the fact that the Stresa Powers had recently condemned Germany for her repudiation of the disarmament clauses of the Treaty of Versailles, it was scarcely consistent with good faith that one of them, behind the backs of the other two, should make an agreement with the treaty-breaker which by implication condoned her action provided she did not challenge our naval superiority. Unquestionably, this very clumsy piece of diplomacy made loyal working with France in the Ethiopian question more difficult. In spite of this, the preparation for sanctions went on smoothly if slowly. Almost every country joined in the necessary action. Even Japan was favourable to Abyssinia though not taking part in the sanctions. At Geneva, Monsieur Laval, the French Prime Minister, grudgingly but decisively pledged himself in support of sanctions and there was a chorus of the smaller nations on the same side.

At home, the Trades Unions, the Labour Party and the Liberals pledged their support for any action taken to uphold the authority of the League. The Conservatives were less explicit but Mr. Baldwin, in his speech to the annual meeting of the Party, strongly endorsed the League policy hitherto pursued by Britain as being in accordance both with her vital interests and her international obligations. The arrest of the Italian aggression was, in fact, very popular and the promise of it largely removed the doubts about the Government of the millions who, as the Peace Ballot had shown, were strongly in favour of the League. Electioneeringly, therefore, the Government felt themselves in a strong position and determined to make the most of it by having an election in November.

Accordingly, on October 27th, the Government issued their election programme. In it they said the League of Nations would remain the keystone of their foreign policy and that there would be no wavering with regard to the dispute between Italy and Abyssinia. In their speeches the leading members of the Government took the same line, the Chancellor of the Exchequer (Mr. Neville Chamberlain) being particularly explicit. The result was eminently successful. The Government came back with a majority of 428 members as against 184 of the Opposition. It is safe to say that if the country had known what was to happen in a few weeks' time, the Ministerial majority would have been greatly diminished if, indeed, it had not altogether disappeared.

While the election was still in progress, on October 29th, the imposition of sanctions began in this country by an Order in Council which, however, only affected a very small number of articles. On November 4th the League fixed November 18th for the general application of sanctions. Sir Samuel Hoare, who was present, expressed great regret at the necessity for the sanctions. On November 22nd the British Government, in answer to a complaint from Italy, warmly defended sanctions, and on December 3rd the King's Speech at the opening of Parliament reiterated the intention of the Government to fulfil its obligations under the Covenant and, at the same time, to work for the preservation of peace. In the debate, Mr. Baldwin's speech gave the first indication of faltering. But three days later Sir Samuel Hoare assured the House that the machinery for sanctions was working well and that on the whole the Member States were playing their part. The question of cutting off oil — so absolutely vital for the conduct of modern war — was to be immediately considered.

Meanwhile, a Foreign Office official, Mr. Peterson, now Sir Maurice Peterson, had been in Paris since the last days of November to discuss possible readjustments of territory between Italy and Ethiopia. No conclusion had been reached, and on December 6th Sir Samuel Hoare, on his way to Switzerland for a holiday, stopped for a day or two in Paris and there elaborated with Monsieur Laval proposals for a partition of Abyssinia which involved its practical dismemberment. The proposals were to be secret until they had been presented to Abyssinia, and the British Minister in Addis Ababa was instructed to press their acceptance on the Emperor. As usually happens, especially with negotiations in Paris, the terms were in fact published almost immediately. The Cabinet met on December 9th. It then appeared that these very important proposals had been made without the knowledge of the Cabinet or, it was said, of the Prime Minister. I confess I find it very difficult to credit this last statement. A Foreign Minister abroad would never have agreed to such proposals without at least telegraphing or telephoning to his Chief. It is of course possible that a telegram was sent but was never read by Mr. Baldwin. But if so, the methods of the Administration must have been inconceivably casual. In any case, the Cabinet — still, by all accounts, more or less in the dark as to the nature of the transaction — approved it. Immediately the public heard of it there was one of those uprisings of public opinion which from time to time take place in England, and it became politically impossible to go on with the proposal. The House met to consider the matter on December 19th, and Sir Samuel, who had returned to England, defended himself on the ground that the agreement was the only alternative to military sanctions which he was not prepared to advocate. He recognized, however, that the opinion of the country was against him and he had resigned the previous day. Mr. Baldwin admitted, apparently, that he had agreed to the proposals and that he was in error in doing so. But, very surprisingly, he did not resign. It would have been far better if he had done so. His successor, whoever he might have been, would have come into office unfettered by these events and might perhaps have minimized their deplorable effect at home and abroad. Though he re-asserted the sentence in the Government programme at the election that 'the League of Nations will remain as heretofore the keystone of our foreign policy', in fact the League has never recovered from the blow then struck at it.

By the Covenant, the members of the League undertake

'to respect and preserve as against external aggression the territorial integrity and existing political independence of all members of the League', and here were the two most important members of the League agreed in trying to force another member to yield more than half her territory to the country which the League had declared to be an aggressor. It was the first clear example — for in the Manchurian question other motives came in — of what came to be called the policy of appeasement, that is, a policy of placating your enemies by sacrificing your friends. It is a policy equally indefensible on moral as on political grounds. The strange thing is that the section of British opinion which in effect condoned this proposed transaction had been outraged when it had been suggested that, in order to secure peace, we might cede to Italy a very small bit of British territory!

Mr. Eden succeeded Sir Samuel Hoare and other less important changes were made in the Government. Sir Samuel remained out of office for a few months and was then restored to the Cabinet by Mr. Baldwin.

The Abyssinian struggle went on. It had already become clear that in anything like a battle, the Ethiopians had no chance. They had little or no defence against the equipment of a modern army and the Italians could and did gas them and bomb them at their pleasure. The only hope for Abyssinia lay in guerrilla warfare. Possibly if the League Powers had rigidly enforced the oil sanction — that is, deprived Italy of all imported oil — the contest might have become more equal. But it would have been difficult to do this without the acquiescence of the American exporters. Before the Hoare-Laval agreement, there seemed a good chance of securing such acquiescence. But when it became clear to American opinion that the League Powers were not in earnest, that they were probably engaged in some obscure international intrigue, the chance of American assent to an oil sanction vanished. The oil sanction, therefore, though often discussed, was never imposed. The Italian attack was pressed with increased vigour and, though the effect of the sanctions actually imposed was not even then negligible, it was not formidable enough to stop an aggression immediately, in the full tide of victory.

For the time, our Government remained apparently firm in support of the League. In the early months of 1936 the new Foreign Secretary made several speeches reiterating our support of the League against Italian aggression.

On January 17th, when Italian difficulties still seemed considerable, he declared that aggression ought not to be allowed to succeed and that Britain would always be found arrayed on the side of the collective system. I was still hopeful. I remember a conversation at the end of January with Mr. Winston Churchill in which he delighted me by praising the Peace Ballot and warmly supporting a policy of rearmament and the League. But on February 18th, Lord Phillimore in the House of Lords, with the apparent approval of most of the Conservative Peers, called on the Government to avoid the risk of war save where the immediate and direct interests of the British Empire were concerned. By this he meant the exact opposite of what Mr. Eden had laid down a month earlier. To him and those who agreed with him, it was not 'an immediate and direct interest of the British Empire' that 'aggression should not be allowed to succeed'. It was because Mr. Neville Chamberlain came to accept this view that we are now again plunged into European war. But for the moment the Eden policy was still dominant.

On March 3rd the Government definitely began its rearmament policy. It issued a White Paper in which it reaffirmed its belief in the League and in Collective Security, and declared that, for that reason, we must increase our armaments, since sanctions without military backing were not sufficient to prevent war. I have no doubt that the proposition so laid down is broadly true. But it does not explain why the British Government did not act with greater vigour in the early stages of the Abyssinian affair, for our naval strength was undoubtedly sufficient to coerce Italy. Moreover, unless the League was kept in full vigour, that is to say, if we were to trust to our own armaments alone to preserve peace in Europe, the re-armament proposed in the White Paper was insufficient.

If the policy of the White Paper was one consequence of the approaching Italian victory over the League, the breakdown of the Naval Conference at the end of March was another. The object of the Conference had been to prolong the Washington Naval Treaty and the London Naval Treaty of 1930. After weeks of discussion the Japanese declined to go on with the negotiation and resumed their freedom of action.

Germany furnished another practical commentary on our policy. In answer to a suggestion that we should resume discussion of a pact to limit air forces, she announced that she would no longer be bound by the Versailles provisions for a demilitarized zone on her western frontier, and marched troops into the zone. This was a breach not only of the Versailles Treaty but of the Locarno Treaty also, which Hitler had personally confirmed. But it could scarcely be called a 'resort to war' forbidden by the Covenant, for the zone was German territory. The French were certainly entitled to resist the occupation, and had they done so and had Germany replied by hostilities, we should have been bound both by Treaty and by policy to go to the assistance of France. But British opinion was not enthusiastic for resisting the German move, partly because a demilitarized zone exclusively on the German side of the frontier did not seem a very fair arrangement, and partly because there was considerable feeling that if the French had been unwilling to uphold the Covenant as against Italy, it was unreasonable of her to take a rigid attitude in the much less clear case of the Rhineland zone. The result was the usual spate of remonstrances and reproofs, first by France and Britain, then by the Powers parties to the Locarno Treaties, and finally, at a meeting of the Council of the League held in London — to all of which the Nazi Government paid not the smallest attention.

Meanwhile, the Italian advance in Africa went on and

what may be called the pro-Phillimore wing of the Government became more insistent against the maintenance of sanctions. While the Foreign Minister still urged their continuance, the Chancellor of the Exchequer and the Prime Minister began to say they were useless without military backing and that might lead to war!

On May 5th Italy occupied Addis Ababa, the Ethiopian capital, and though we of the League of Nations Union, with the support of Mr. Attlee, the Leader of the Labour Party, and Sir Archibald Sinclair, the Leader of the Liberals, insisted that we should not yet give up the struggle against aggression, it was evident that the Cabinet had resolved to surrender and, as a symbol of its decision, Sir Samuel Hoare was again given office.

That was on June 5th, and on June 10th Mr. Neville Chamberlain declared that to advocate the maintenance of sanctions — the policy which was still, in public, that of the Foreign Secretary — was midsummer-madness. On June 18th Mr. Eden announced the dropping of sanctions and, in a debate in the House of Commons on June 23rd, Sir John Simon warmly defended the new policy, saying that he 'was not prepared to risk a single ship to preserve Abyssinian independence'. The phrase was very illuminating. It breathed the essential spirit of 'appeasement'. For, after all, we were quite expressly bound by our own undertaking in the Covenant 'to respect and preserve the territorial integrity and political independence' of Abyssinia. We had over and over again admitted the existence of this obligation and had encouraged Abyssinia to rely on it. To say now that we would not risk a single ship to carry out our pledged word was an advertisement to the aggressive powers and to the 'neutrals' that the Covenant meant nothing to us. It was the deathblow to collective security and indeed to the League as a guarantee of peace. If it had been followed by our withdrawal from the League or even by a demand for the abrogation of those Articles in the Covenant designed forcibly to prevent resort to war in international disputes, our position

would have been clear both abroad and at home. But the
members of the Government, on the contrary, persisted in
their verbal support of the League, ignored its application
to the Italian aggression and claimed to the electors here
that they had 'kept us out of war'. Thus Mr. Baldwin, on
July 2nd, said sanctions had to be raised because if persisted
in they might lead us into war and he was determined by
every means in his power to keep us out of war. By this
policy at the best we gained an uneasy respite which lasted
rather more than three years, and for that, sacrificed the
interests of other nations and our own reputation. At the
worst we missed the chance of destroying war.

That was the end of the Abyssinian question — at least
for the time being. There were speeches at Geneva — protests, from the smaller Powers, from some of our Dominions
and from Russia — and there was a humiliating set of
manœuvres designed to exclude the Abyssinian Negus from
the Assembly, which fortunately failed. For some two years
more we had the grace to refuse to recognize the Italian
conquest, in accordance with previous decisions of the Assembly not to recognize such lawless acts. But even at the
cost of Mr. Eden's resignation in the spring of 1938, that
concession to legality was abandoned and our humiliation
was complete when the Prime Minister, Mr. Neville Chamberlain, and the Foreign Secretary, Lord Halifax, attended a
banquet at Rome in January 1939 and drank to the Italian
Emperor of Abyssinia. The only result of this policy in our
relations with Italy was that she, having become the
collaborator with Germany in the 'Axis', helped her partner
to deceive our Prime Minister at Munich.

Before proceeding to the next chapter of our international
misfortunes, the revolt in Spain, I must say a word about the
regular meetings of the League Assembly in 1935 and 1936.

In 1935, the Assembly was mainly interested in the
Abyssinian crisis, but in other matters useful work was done.
A discussion arose on the problem of the nationality of

women and their social and political status. But nothing concrete resulted. The first steps were taken in the effort to improve nutrition; the limitation of the production of opium to the amount needed for medicinal purposes was begun; and an attempt was made to help the miserable condition of stateless women, especially in the Far East — an attempt foiled by the senseless clamour about economy. For that folly we, as an Empire, are largely responsible. But this year the cause was taken up by Monsieur Laval who, no doubt from hostility to the League, was glad to demand a ten per cent reduction in its budget. There were, further, the usual debates about refugees, mandates, slavery, and such subjects as penal reform.

The Assembly of 1936 was oppressed by the Abyssinian defeat. It gloomily endorsed the stoppage of sanctions. The prevalent feeling on the subject was well expressed by the representative of South Africa, Mr. te Water: — 'Fifty nations, led by three of the most powerful nations in the world, are about to declare their powerlessness to protect the weakest in their midst from destruction.' That was done in the Special Assembly of July.

The regular September Assembly discussed the possibility or usefulness of amending the Covenant, and referred it to a special meeting to be held in December, at which, in effect, nothing was done. Mr. Bruce of Australia stated the problem on September 25th: — 'Two questions have to be considered. The first is whether, if fully implemented, there is a defect in the system of collective action contemplated by the Covenant. The second is, if no such defect exists, why has the system failed in operation? The answer to the first question would appear to be that there is no defect in the system embodied in the Covenant if it is fully implemented.' But, he went on: — 'However perfect the machinery may be in theory, its efficacy has to be qualified in practice by taking into account the human element. The human element is that, despite their devotion to the principles of the League, nations are not prepared to commit their peoples to war for a cause which does not vitally concern their immediate national interests.' He then went on to explain that economic sanctions, properly applied, would succeed, but only if they were backed by a readiness to resist retaliatory military measures. Except that I should substitute for the expression 'the human element' some such phrase as 'age-long tradition', I agree with Mr. Bruce's analysis of the position. In other words, it is vital to recognize that 'peace is indivisible' if we really mean to get rid of war, and that is why the 'keep-out-of-war' attitude was, in reality, the surest way to bring war upon us.

For the rest, the Assembly of 1936 worked at its usual subjects — finance, health, child welfare, traffic in women, opium, refugees, mandates, intellectual co-operation; and set up again a committee to consider disarmament.

The International Labour Office also was active in trying to improve industrial conditions. The League's continual activities in these respects showed two things. One, that there is a vast mass of common interests among the nations of the world which, if properly handled, could help to bring the nations closer together; and second, that no operations of this kind will, by themselves, be sufficient to maintain international peace. On the contrary, unless some efficient way of getting rid of war can be found, all other forms of international progress will be precarious if not ephemeral.

The consideration of one other subject destined to add gravely to international troubles was begun — the revolt in Spain. I do not propose to examine the intrinsic merits of this controversy. Probably the actual Government in power in Spain was not a good one. But I have some difficulty in believing that its evils were greater than the wholesale slaughter and destruction resulting from the civil war. That, however, was a matter for the Spaniards to determine for themselves. We and other peace-loving nations were only concerned in preventing outside nations from creating a likelihood of war by using the Spanish troubles to advance their national or international policy, as they unquestionably did. When, therefore, the British Government announced that their aim was to secure non-intervention by any country, many of us were disposed to accept that policy. Unfortunately it was never carried out. An international committee was set up, consisting of all the interested powers, in London, which had lengthy discussions in private and passed voluminous resolutions declaring that there should be no interference by any government in Spain and that the Spanish factions should be left to fight it out by themselves. In fact Germany and Italy on one side and Russia and — to some extent — France on the other, furnished men and materials in increasing quantities. It was a sordid and discreditable business. Had the Committee met at Geneva under the auspices of the League and with the assistance of League machinery, it might have been better. It could hardly have been worse. In the result the German and Italian assistance ensured victory for the Franco party and was openly celebrated in Rome and Berlin as another triumph for dictatorships over democracy. It was during the progress of the struggle that the then Spanish government made repeated appeals to the League on the grounds that the Italians and Germans were, in effect, making aggressions on Spain. The first of such appeals was made in this year, 1936, at the Assembly, in a speech by Señor del Vayo, the Foreign Minister in Spain, and was more formally renewed at a special Council in December. The Council was very poorly attended. Indeed, from this time forward the tendency of our Government to avoid bringing to the League any important international question was accentuated on the ground that in the absence of Germany, Italy and Japan no vigorous action by the League could be looked for. The contention was, no doubt, plausible.

It will be remembered that Japan had given notice of withdrawal from the League in March, 1933, on the ground that the League had unjustly condemned her action in the Manchurian question. Germany had given a similar notice in October 1933, alleging her dissatisfaction with the Disarmament Conference. Italy had followed suit in December, 1937, after her defiance of the League and its sanctions over Abyssinia, and had at the same time proclaimed her determination to act with Germany in the so-called 'Axis'. The pretexts given for their withdrawal by the three militarist powers were not their real reasons. Their objections to the League were much more fundamental. The whole purpose of the Covenant was to limit and gradually abolish the right of nations to resort to war as a remedy for their grievances against other nations. The contention of the militarist powers was that every sovereign state had an absolute right to go to war whenever it thought it desirable to do so, and that it was not amenable to any international authority as to the justice of its action. In consequence, they were opposed to the whole conception of the League and not only did they withdraw from it but they carried on a vigorous campaign for its destruction. Germany went so far as to refuse to take part in any international activity such as the International Labour Office, or even in the efforts to bring about a reunion of Christendom, lest the uncontrolled sovereignty of the Reich should be impaired. It is therefore a complete misunderstanding of the position to suggest that if this or that had been done to avoid the actual occasion of withdrawal by any of the three powers they would have settled down to work with the rest of the world for the establishment of international peace based on respect for the freedom and independence of other nations. Hitler demands the dominion of Europe at least; Mussolini hopes for the re-establishment of the Roman Empire; the Japanese army claims the leadership of Asia. With those ambitions, membership of the League is and was incompatible. The actual occasion for separation was of little importance. The real ground for the rejection of the League was that it stood for organized peace, and the degree of hostility to it of the militarist Governments was in direct ratio to its energy and success.

To say that no international question of importance should

be brought before the League in the absence of the militarist Powers was, therefore, to condemn it to impotence. Nor was any alternative policy effectively pursued. It ought to have been clear that if the League was to be eliminated, the danger of war was greatly increased and every nerve should have been strained to prepare for it both in England and France.

Meanwhile, some of my French friends who accepted the League had proposed in the spring of 1936 that a new international society should be started in its support. There was a meeting in my house in London at which the general lines of the movement were agreed upon. The case for it was that, though there was considerable support for the League in many foreign countries, there were very few national League of Nations societies with any large numerical membership. Indeed, I remember Monsieur Bourgeois being rather shocked when I suggested, early in the League's history, a democratic League Society in France! On the other hand, there were in France and in several other countries a considerable number of societies whose primary business was to advocate social and philanthropic causes, who were yet in favour of the League. The proposal, therefore was to have an organization which should not have any individual members, apart from a few exceptional personalities, but should consist of representatives of other societies who were in agreement with the fundamental tenets of the new body. Accordingly, four principles were laid down, acceptance of which was to be the test for membership. They were: —

1. Recognition of the sanctity of Treaty Obligations.

2. Reduction and limitation of armaments by international agreement and the suppression of profit from the manufacture of and trade in arms.

3. Strengthening of the League of Nations for the prevention, and stopping of war by the organization of Collective Security and Mutual Assistance.

4. Establishment within the framework of the League of Nations of effective machinery for remedying international conditions which might lead to war.

There were to be National Committees in as many countries as possible, which were to elect an International Committee to be established at Geneva. The French name chosen for the organization was *Rassemblement Universel pour la Paix*, which indicated that provided we were satisfied that any society genuinely accepted the Four Principles, it would not be excluded because it held any political beliefs on the Right or the Left. We could find no satisfactory translation of the French name and fell back on the rather colourless 'International Peace Campaign'.

From the outset we were charged with being a Communistic body. Where this charge originally came from we never ascertained, but we strongly suspected the ubiquitous manufactory of falsehood directed by Dr. Goebbels. Essentially it was quite untrue. None of the chief officers were Communists, and the overwhelming majority of the headquarters Council were not of that persuasion. There were, however, one or two Communists among them, notably Monsieur Cachin. And one of our Secretaries, a very loyal and exceedingly able young man, had once held communist economic opinions, though he had never been a member of the Communist Party. It was also true that public meetings held in connection with the organization were often attended by considerable numbers of persons who were certainly far to the Left and did not hide their light under a bushel! But never did the organization take any political action in support of communist opinions and such feeble attempts to use its machinery for that purpose as were made were easily suppressed. At the same time, experience of what some Communists and their friends think fair and loyal has led me to the conviction that any political co-operation with them, even for peace, is exceedingly difficult and may even be dangerous.

The first big demonstration of the International Peace Campaign was held at Brussels in September 1936. It was certainly a very remarkable gathering, showing genuine enthusiasm for peace on the basis of our Four Principles. Repeated large meetings were held and a number of resolutions and reports were agreed to. On the whole they were innocent enough, as were the speeches made. There was an attempt to use the gathering for a pronouncement in favour of the Spanish Republican Government, but this was prevented. No doubt at least half of those present belonged to the extreme Left. To me it seemed, at that time, that so long as they confined themselves to advocacy of the Four Principles, they could not be better or more harmlessly employed.

I do not propose to examine in detail the activities of the International Peace Campaign or the controversies in which it was engaged. On the whole it did useful work for peace. It naturally suffered when the present war began, particularly in its finance. But it is still an active force in England and in some other countries, notably Sweden and China. When the terms of peace are discussed, I trust it will prove of essential service.

There was an outstanding domestic event in the autumn of 1936 which had only an indirect bearing on the subject of this book, namely, the abdication of King Edward VIII. At first it caused doubts abroad about the solidity of the British State. These quickly passed, owing partly to the remarkable skill and success with which Mr. Baldwin, as Prime Minister, dealt with an extremely delicate and difficult personal issue; and partly to the wonderful political judgement of the English people.

But the European position showed no signs of improvement. The Spanish War created a fresh danger spot, though perhaps it also acted as a kind of safety valve through which the aggressive energy of the Dictators might, for the time, escape. In any case it was clear that the re-occupation of the Rhineland was merely a stage in German expansion.

In November, the Duce proclaimed the Italo-German Axis. Japan made an anti-Comintern Alliance with Germany in the following month, and definitely freed herself from all naval limitation. These were the results of a militarist effervescence there, which also showed itself in the murder of several distinguished statesmen, including the veteran Admiral Saito.

Meanwhile, in England the anti-League movement took on a new phase. Its manifestations, which I watched in the Foreign Policy debates in the House of Lords, were remarkable. There was a kind of coalition between extreme pacifists, reactionaries and ex-diplomats. They were agreed on only one point — their distrust and dislike of the League as an instrument of peace. Beyond that, they differed on almost every question. The pacifists wanted British disarmament irrespective of what other nations did; the reactionaries wanted increased armaments and no alliance, and no reduction of our Empire responsibilities. In this line of thought the Conservative caucus passed a resolution saying that any cession of British territory was not discussable. The main attitude of the diplomats was that the League was a new-fangled instrument and therefore to be avoided. In a word, they took the usual professional attitude which made the doctors resist antiseptic surgery and the lawyers the abolition of Fines and Recoveries. To all three sections the Government slogan 'We've kept you out of war' was a godsend. It gave them a popular appeal and enabled them to accuse the Opposition and people like myself of being war-mongers! Unfortunately, the end was not yet.

There was another development which did much harm. A number of persons, many of them of considerable ability and all of impeccable intentions, accepted suggestions from Berlin that much good could be done by personal contacts with Hitler. Accordingly, they went over for a day or two, had interviews with Hitler and some of his chief Ministers, and came back to assure us that Hitler was a much misunderstood man, that his lurid utterances in *Mein Kampf* and elsewhere must not be taken seriously, and that he really was a convinced advocate of peace. It was this illusion which formed one of the foundations of the policy of appeasement. Its earlier effect was to induce its advocates, even where they were supporters of the League, to keep it as much as possible in the background for fear of offending the Dictators.

One other incident of this period should be mentioned. It will be remembered that the voters in the Peace Ballot by a very large majority urged the abolition of private profit in the manufacture of arms. There was a very strong feeling in the country on this point. To meet it, the Government appointed a Royal Commission of eminent persons, presided over by a distinguished judge. The League of Nations Union gave evidence in support of the Peace Ballot view, and urged that the business of arming the country should be taken over completely by the Government. Evidence on the other side of a weighty character was also heard. In the result, the Commission recommended not that the arms manufacture should be taken over but that it should be controlled by the Government. Nothing effective, however, was done in this direction, though of course as soon as war was declared control became essential, which has become progressively more severe.

(VII) 1937

The close of 1936 showed a continued advance towards war. Germany was obviously the centre of the impulse in that direction. Her Government accepted the traditional Prussian belief in force, the Bismarckian gospel of blood and iron, which was at least as old as Frederick the Great. Its modern version, Hitler's *Mein Kampf*, written in the turgid and verbose style which seems characteristic of much revolutionary literature, was at least plain in its acceptance of the doctrine that in international affairs might is right. To meet this, the steps taken by the Western Democracies were inadequate. Britain and France did make some effort at re-armament. They did draw closer together. Our Government did reassert its obligation to defend France's eastern frontier. But they coupled these tentative steps with two fatal mistakes. They continually, after solemnly condemning some aggression by the Dictators, acquiesced in its results and they, partly to conciliate the Dictators, allowed the League of Nations to sink lower and lower in power and authority. It was with this last, as part of the British policy, that I was most intimately concerned. If the League went, nothing but armaments and alliances remained to save us from the threats of Hitler and Mussolini and, in my view, even militarist expedients of this kind were terribly costly and could not by themselves be relied on to secure peace. In the hope of converting our Government to this point of view, we issued a very influentially signed Declaration at the beginning of 1937. It was in the following terms: —

SAVE THE LEAGUE: SAVE PEACE.

In every cuontry there is talk of war, and in some countries attacks have openly been made upon the League of Nations and the principle of collective security.

We, the undersigned, declare that war can be averted and a stable peace permanently maintained if the nations which are members of the League will now make plain their determination to fulfil their obligations under the Covenant and to take any measures required for the prevention or repression of aggression, including, if necessary, military action. Only so will the peaceful settlement of international disputes become possible.

We affirm that, if the members of the League are united in this policy, their joint strength will be so overwhelming that no intending aggressor will venture to refuse the settlement of disputes or other outstanding questions by peaceful means. We accordingly urge that in any reform of the Covenant which may be undertaken nothing shall be done to weaken its provisions in this respect, but that, on the contrary, the system of the League shall be strengthened for the prevention of war.

We also urge the importance of establishing within the framework of the League of Nations effective machinery for remedying by peaceful means international conditions which might lead to war.

No attempt was made to obtain a large number of signatures. They were confined to three leaders of the Labour Party, Messrs. Attlee, Dalton and Noel Baker; three leaders of the Liberals, Mr. Lloyd George, Sir Archibald Sinclair and Mrs. Corbett Ashby; three unofficial Conservatives (evidently members of the Government could not sign), Mr. Winston Churchill, Lord Lytton and the Duchess of Atholl; and three persons not prominently connected with party politics, the Archbishop of Canterbury, Professor Gilbert Murray, and myself.

The Declaration was published in the press, but unfortunately produced no visible effect on Government policy. I remember we were told by an influential Ministerial organ that our action was ill-timed! This no doubt meant that it would hamper the British peace efforts, which were based on appeals to the reason and moderation of the German Government. The advocates of this policy, perhaps misled by the reports of the Berlin visitors to whom I have referred, chose to disregard both the traditional policy of Prussia and the explicit declarations of Hitler and his associates. Even Hitler's hostility to the League ought to have warned them of the truth. For, as I have said, he and the other militarists undoubtedly hated the League not because of its connection with the Treaty of Versailles — evidently a trivial matter — or because of the baseless charges of its unfairness to Germany, but simply and solely because as long as it remained as influential as it was in 1931, it was a serious obstacle to aggression.

Running as an accompaniment to all other international events of this year was the imbroglio in Spain. I shall not attempt to recount the various incidents. Indeed, there was a terrible sameness about their repetition. At intervals representatives of Spain went to Geneva and complained of acts by Italy and Germany which, on their showing, amounted to invasions of her territory. On the other hand, the French and British Governments treated the Spanish fighting as an internal matter and accepted the view that German and Italian help to the Spanish rebellion was the work of volunteers, just as French and Russian and even, to a very minor degree, British volunteers were helping the Spanish Government. The result was that the League urged non-intervention and expressed hopes that the efforts in this direction of the Committee which had been set up in London would be successful. This was all very well on paper, but as time went on it became more and more clear that men and munitions were being sent by the two Dictatorship Governments, as ultimately was frankly admitted. It was then said even by those who, like myself, had supported non-intervention, that at least it must be impartially applied to both sides, and if not, it should be abandoned. The answer made, that if that were done the war might spread far beyond the Spanish borders, was not very convincing. It seemed to mean that we were to take action clearly unfair to one party in Spain in the name of non-intervention — a policy unpleasantly like what was afterwards called 'appeasement'. Some of us, therefore, urged that the whole dispute should be referred to Geneva, believing that the machinery of the League would be much more likely to produce non-intervention than the secret discussions of the Committee in London. This, however, was refused on the ground that Germany and Italy would not go to Geneva — a fatal attitude to take from a League point of view.

One step, however, of an effective kind was taken in the summer. Submarines — universally believed to be Italian — began to torpedo ships trading with Government Spain, including British ships. Thereupon the British and French Governments summoned a meeting of all the interested Powers to stop these proceedings, which were so illegal that they were popularly described as 'piracy'. The meeting was held at Nyon and not at Geneva, out of deference to Italy and Germany, but in fact it was a League meeting, staffed by the League Secretariat. Neither Germany nor Italy attended the first meeting, with the result that the proceedings were very short. In four days it was agreed that Britain and France, with the assistance of the smaller Mediterranean Powers, would patrol that sea and destroy any submarines that attempted illegally to torpedo merchant ships. An acknowledgement of the courageous support given by the smaller Powers to League principles, so long as the Great Powers stood by them, should be made. Thereupon, Italy asked to be allowed to join — and was allowed to do so. The protection was not extended to Spanish ships. But in fact submarine attacks were abandoned thenceforward. Undoubtedly, similarly vigorous procedure could have stopped the Spanish war and, indeed, could have called a halt to the whole policy of aggression by Germany and her imitators. Once again it was shown that collective action for peace backed by force is effective: collective remonstrances are not. The lesson was, however, thrown away on those who believed that the only way to 'keep out of war' was by concession to the aggressors.

Nevertheless, the League was still alive. Not only did it contrive to deal with social, industrial and economic questions, at least by discussion, but even in political questions it was able to do valuable work. Thus, in the early part of the year it took steps to settle a controversy between Turkey and France about the status of the Sanjak of Alexandretta. The Foreign Ministers of both countries expressed their obligation for the way in which the question had been dealt with.

In May of this year, 1937, King George VI was crowned with all the ancient ceremonies in Westminster Abbey. Mr. Baldwin had only retained office until the new reign was well-established, and he then resigned on May 28th. His great personal charm and cultivation and his personal kindness to myself make it impossible for me to attempt any estimate of his character and abilities. That we did not — particularly in the years after 1931 — see eye to eye on matters of foreign and fiscal policy is unfortunately true. But I hope I may say that that fact has made no difference in our personal friendship. He was succeeded by Mr. Neville Chamberlain; Sir John Simon became Chancellor of the Exchequer; and Sir Samuel Hoare Home Secretary. Another event which may have had a very serious effect on the course of foreign affairs was the death, a month or two earlier, of Sir Austen Chamberlain. His great official experience, his position as an elder statesman and the sobriety of his judgement made his convinced support of the League and all it stood for of great value, especially in reference to Conservative opinion.

As many representatives of the Dominions had come over here to be present at the Coronation, it was decided to hold a meeting of the Imperial Conference. The meeting was, I believe, very successful. Its only bearing on the subject-matter of this book is that those who were beset with the idea that peace could be kept by promoting 'contacts' with the Dictators, instead of using and supporting the League, made considerable efforts to induce the Conference to make a declaration in their sense. Some of the Dominion statesmen, however, took a different view, as did some of our own ministers, and no such declaration was made. In view of what has since happened it is fortunate that this crowning mistake was not committed.

Meanwhile, serious events were taking place in the Far East which were brought before the League with results which were far from satisfactory. In July, Japan renewed her invasion of China, this time up the Yangtse valley. The occasion for this attack was a disturbance near Peiping occasioned by a review of Japanese troops to which the Chinese authorities strongly and not unreasonably objected, since the site of the review was admittedly in Chinese territory. There can be little doubt that the Peiping incident was not the real cause of what has since developed into a war involving terrible slaughter and destruction. It was beyond all doubt a fresh step in the long-range Japanese policy which aims first at the conquest of China and afterwards at the domination of Asia The whole procedure bears a great resemblance to German policy in Europe which may be due to the fact that Japan has recently been ruled by a military faction. As is well known, the Japanese army is constitutionally independent of her parliament and has been largely trained and inspired by German officers. Be that as it may, heavy fighting took place at and near Shanghai, from whence the Japanese forces advanced up the Yangtse and captured and sacked the Chinese capital at Nanking with every circumstance of horror and cruelty. The position was brought before the Assembly in September by Dr. Wellington Koo, with great force and moderation. France and Britain said as little as they could and it was left to Mr. Bruce of Australia to recite the usual reasons why the League could not take any effective action, and to suggest that the whole question should be relegated to a Committee of interested Powers which should meet at Brussels with a view to obtaining a settlement. Meanwhile, Japan continued in her course, bombing open towns, raping the women and slaughtering the peaceful inhabitants of China. This was too much for the Assembly, which responded to the violent indignation excited in many countries by Japanese actions. Accordingly, the Committee which had been set up to consider the Manchurian question and which had been called into activity again to deal with this new aggression, met and passed resolutions condemning the bombing of open towns and the slaughter of women and children. It also presented two reports to the Assembly. In the first it expressed no opinion about the original Peiping incident, but pointed out the large military and naval measures taken by Japan which amounted to invasion and for which there was no justification. In the second report it agreed to the summoning of a Conference outside the League of Powers interested in the Far East. No doubt this was due to the policy of 'appeasing' the non-League

Powers by sacrificing the League. The Assembly adopted the reports by a resolution which expressed its moral support for China and recommended all Powers to do nothing to weaken her resistance or increase her difficulties, and to consider how far they could individually extend aid to her. No country opposed this resolution, but Siam and Poland (!) abstained from voting.

That was on October 6th. It was a feeble and wholly inadequate attitude. But in the absence of a more vigorous lead by the Great Powers it was all that could be expected. The Assembly had before it the strong speech made by President Roosevelt on October 5th in Chicago, in which he denounced the ruthless murder of civilians and said that 'the peace-loving nations must make a concerted effort in opposition to those violations of treaties, those ignorings of human instinct'. Mr. Cordell Hull telegraphed to Geneva that he was in general accord with the Assembly's findings. But these two American statesmen received little encouragement from the 'peace-loving' Powers to which they had appealed.

During the concluding months of the Baldwin Ministry there had been the usual speeches which may be not unfairly summarized by saying that they approved of the League provided that it did nothing vigorous to safeguard peace. There was a little vague talk about the desirability of regional pacts. The main purpose of the talk appeared to be to furnish a plausible reason for taking no action through the League itself. There was also some suggestion of a movement towards freer trade which had equally little result.

On October 26th, 1937, Parliament met with the Chamberlain Government in office. The King's speech, for the first time for very many years, made no mention of the League of Nations. On November 16th Lord Halifax, a member of the Cabinet, went to Berlin, nominally to visit some kind of hunting exhibition. While there, he saw Hitler. No account of what passed has ever been published, but we were at least spared the futile assurances of the Führer's peaceful intentions! In November the Conference on the Far East met at Brussels. A representative of the United States was present. Italy attended and did her utmost to prevent anything being done, in which she entirely succeeded. Japan refused to attend, so that the effort to induce the aggressive Powers to take action against aggression by ignoring Geneva had its usual failure, which was followed, on December 11th, by the resignation of Italy from the League.

On December 21st the new Prime Minister, Mr. Chamberlain, made a speech in which he declared that the League of Nations in its present condition was 'unable to discharge some of the functions with which it was invested when it was first created'. He said that the method of the Government was to work for a general settlement by means of personal contacts and friendly and frank discussions. This policy, which soon afterwards developed into the much less defensible policy of appeasement and, as I think, directly led to the Polish war, was based on an entire misconception of the point of view of the Nazi Government. Friendly and frank discussions can only be useful if there is a basis of agreement between the parties. The basis did not exist. That we should think our conception of international relations right is reasonable enough. It is not unreasonable that we should believe that in this matter our view is superior to that held in Germany. But it is simply foolish to ignore that on both points the Nazi Government and large numbers of Germans disagree with us. We hold that there are certain fundamental principles of justice and morality which have a claim on our loyalty, superior even to the maintenance of national interests. The Nazis emphatically reject this attitude. To them the slogan 'Germany before everything' is literally true. The other day, a German Minister cited as proof of our degeneracy that we no longer approved of the attitude of Hotspur in the first part of Henry IV. The answer is: we never did. It is obvious that general discussions between disputants one of whom bases his contentions on justice and the other on national interests is very unlikely to lead to an agreement, unless, indeed, the advocate of justice has behind him some international authority which will compel concessions to his view. Unhappily events were to show in the course of a very few months that, in the absence of such an authority, the Anglo-German controversy could only lead to war.

While these events were taking place, my wife and I had gone on a visit to America. The main purpose of the visit was to enable me to discharge an engagement I had made to speak at Boston on the international situation, to a gathering arranged by one of the great religious organizations of the United States.

We sailed from Southampton in that very delightful vessel, the *Empress of Britain*, on October 30th, and reached Quebec on December 5th a little late owing to bad weather off Newfoundland. We thereby missed our train connection, but, with hospitality characteristic of the American continent, Mr. S. J. Hungerford, the Canadian railway magnate, who happened to be on board and heard of our difficulty, placed at our disposal a private car which took us without change to Ottawa. There, we had the honour of staying with the late Lord Tweedsmuir — a very old friend of mine — who made our two days' visit both interesting and very comfortable. I had some conversation both with him and with the Canadian Prime Minister, Mr. Mackenzie King, who had been much infected with what seemed to me the dangerous views of the British Government. Thence we went to Toronto, where we had a most delightful visit to Dr. Bruce, still Lieutenant Governor of Ontario. Both at Ottawa and Toronto there were very successful meetings which showed that Canadian interest in the League and International Affairs was very much alive. We went on to Boston, where there were also interesting meetings, and from there we went through New York to Washington.

The President had been good enough, some months earlier, to ask me to stay with him if I ever again came to America, and so I ventured to propose ourselves and we were invited for a week-end. We both enjoyed it immensely. Indeed, I have never enjoyed two days more.

We reached Washington in the afternoon of November 13th and drove to the White House. When we had been shown our rooms we were told that the President would receive us at tea, to which we went. It was a small and delightful family party, though, to our very great regret, Mrs. Roosevelt was away. There was no kind of stiffness. The President is a brilliant conversationalist. He not only talks well but he has the gift, as a listener, of making what is said to him, however banal and commonplace it may be, appear to be full of point and interest. The late Lord Balfour had the same power. After some time, his secretaries came in and we withdrew. My wife went to dine at the British Embassy, but I went with the President to the annual dinner of the Washington Press Club. There were songs and speeches, including a speech from the President. As these gatherings are strictly confidential I will only say that no one could listen to him without appreciating how deeply he cared for peace. When he went away we found a crowd waiting in the street, as seemed to be the case whenever and wherever he moved. Indeed, the impression of his popularity was very great. It had a note of personal affection and esteem which was very striking and made a curious contrast to the way he was regarded by some of the richer people whom I met in New York.

Next day, being Sunday, we went to church with the President and again I was struck with the simplicity and want of ceremony. In the afternoon he was good enough to take us for a drive to see the principal buildings in that beautiful city. It was a glorious early autumn afternoon and there were numbers of people in the street who did not fail to greet Mr. Roosevelt with affectionate admiration. In the evening we had the chance of hearing the President give one of his celebrated 'fire-side' radio talks. The subject of it was quite uncontroversial and of no special importance. But the technique was deeply interesting. His voice is perfect for the

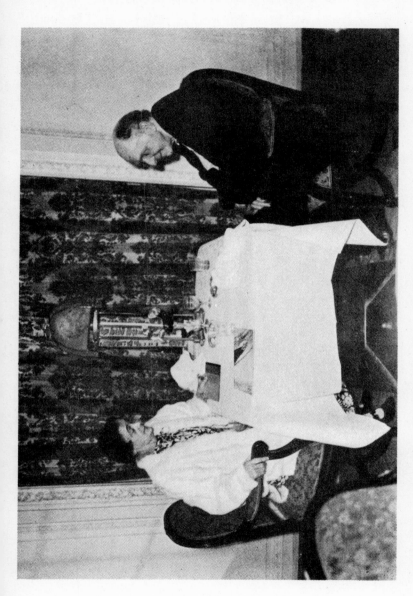

LORD AND LADY CECIL ON R.M.S. 'BERENGARIA', COMING HOME, 1937

purpose and one felt the kind of intimate tone he was able to infuse into what he said, which must be immensely effective. We were told that not only are there a very large number of direct listeners, but it is a custom in many parts for those who have receiving sets to ask their neighbours who have not to come in and listen when the President is speaking. By these means he is able to get into personal touch with many millions of his fellow-countrymen. It is not for me to make any estimate of the political value of this novel method of communication.

Next day we went away and I can only record my own feeling that I had been for two days in company with a very great man. His courage, physical and moral, is unbounded. I believe him to be essentially sincere and patriotic in the best sense. He wants what is right and no personal consideration will deter him from pursuing it. If I may say so, I can imagine no better companion for tiger shooting, and the larger and fiercer the tiger the more confidence would one feel in his courage and resource.

We returned to New York, and while we were there it was announced that I had received the Nobel Prize for peace work. The information happened to reach me at the moment when President Nicholas Murray Butler was giving me an Honorary Degree at Columbia University. The coincidence was seized upon by my friends in the press, so that for the moment I became 'news'.

A few days later we sailed for Europe. We had enjoyed ourselves greatly. American kindness and hospitality had been as wonderful as ever. But the international outlook of our friends in New York was less sympathetic to our ideas than it had been in earlier visits, partly owing to a wave of isolationism and partly because British and French policy was regarded as mainly self-seeking and therefore of little interest to America. A recently published book entitled *England Expects that Every American will do his Duty* had had considerable success and though my American audiences were far too courteous to say so, they felt that advocacy of the

League as an impartial peace keeping instrument was incompatible with actual British policy. It was not that Americans blamed us for looking after our own interests. But they thought that it was our business and not theirs. When I got back I pressed this point as strongly as I could, both at meetings and in Parliament, but without effect. Ministers continued to declare that they were in favour of the Covenant ideas, but added that they were not prepared to take any risk in their support unless British subjects or British property were threatened. That is why neutrals have, in the Polish war, taken very much the same line as I found prevailing in the United States.

(VIII) 1938—TO THE OCCUPATION OF PRAGUE

The speech of the Prime Minister, Mr. Chamberlain, made on December 21st, 1937, had marked — and was no doubt intended to mark — a definite change in the Foreign Policy of the country. Thenceforth no attempt was to be made forcibly to stop aggression by utilizing the machinery of the League, but reliance was to be placed on personal contacts and appeals to the reason and moderation of the aggressive Governments. In 1938 this policy was tried out. The first experiment was made with regard to the Spanish question. It may be fairly said that till the beginning of this year, neither the Government nor the insurgents in Spain had obtained any marked advantage. Indeed, in the early days of the year the Government captured Teruel, and, though this was re-taken after a few weeks, the incident induced General Franco — or, more probably, his Italian and German advisers — to increase the severity of the bombing of Government towns, with the consequence that several British merchant vessels in harbours were hit. That was the first reply to the announcement of a new British policy. There were the usual protests, but Mr. Eden, who was still Foreign Secretary, was not content with these. The Spanish Insurgents were told that if such action was repeated, retaliatory action would be taken. Meanwhile, the Non-Intervention Committee was devising elaborate schemes to secure the withdrawal of foreign troops from both sides. The Italian and German representatives indulged in the parliamentary device of obstruction, not by any means for the first time. Nevertheless, the Italian Government, anxious to obtain a free hand in the Spanish war so that they could finish it off quickly without the danger of interference from the Western democracies, proposed that there should be a general settlement of Anglo-Italian differences. To this, Mr. Eden, in substance, replied that he was not prepared to have fresh Anglo-Italian discussions until the Italian Government had shown its good faith by carrying out its promises to withdraw its troops from Spain. The Prime Minister took a different view. He did not seem to attach much importance to the charge of breach of faith by the Italian Government. He was, no doubt, personally more sympathetic to Fascism than to what he regarded as the Reds of Spain, and above all, he was anxious to take this opportunity of launching his new policy. The relations between the Prime Minister and his Foreign Secretary had for long been difficult, and this was the last straw. Mr. Eden resigned. He had, a few days before, made at Geneva a re-affirmation of his belief in the League, and he cannot have felt that, on that point either, Mr. Chamberlain and he were in real agreement. Moreover, both he and his Under-Secretary, Lord Cranborne, who also resigned, regarded the language used by the Italian Ambassador in suggesting an understanding, as, in effect, a threat. They protested against what they regarded as a surrender to blackmail.

The new Foreign Secretary was Lord Halifax, and Mr. R. A. Butler took Lord Cranborne's place.

Mr. Eden in his speech explaining his resignation, put it on very broad grounds. He said that if he had not resigned he would have had to tell the House that he believed the Prime Minister's policy would succeed and would, in the end, contribute to European appeasement; whereas he believed exactly the opposite. The Prime Minister denied the charge of blackmail and reiterated his belief in the usefulness of negotiations, even without any action by Italy in fulfilment of promises to withdraw her troops. The issues between Mr. Eden and his chief were evidently of considerable importance. One was as to the 'scrupulous respect for all treaty obligations in the dealings of organized peoples with one another', declared to be fundamental to the Covenant. It is no doubt true that treaties in time grow old like other things and may become obsolete either for that reason or because the circumstances in which they were made have completely changed. But even in such cases, under the League system they should not be disregarded by one party to them until at least they have been reconsidered by the members of the League under Article 19. In this case no question of that kind could arise. The powers represented on the Non-Intervention Committee had long agreed that foreign troops should, in principle, be withdrawn from Spain and that, as a first step, no fresh troops or munitions should be sent to help either of the parties. It was notorious that Italy had sent a considerable amount of assistance of this kind to the Insurgents and was, in fact, resolved to send still more. To condone this conduct by making a fresh agreement with her was to increase the tendency to ignore treaty obligations which has since become a disastrous commonplace of totalitarian diplomacy. It was further to put the government of Spain at a clear disadvantage in their struggle with the Insurgents, since they were by this time receiving no aid from any foreign Power. All this was done in order to induce the Italians to make a friendly arrangement with us.

Immediately, negotiations for an Anglo-Italian understanding were set on foot. That by itself secured to the Fascist Government one of its chief objects. It enabled Italy to give to General Franco the means of developing his attack on the Government position partly by direct operations against the Government forces and partly by greatly increasing his bombardment of Barcelona and other towns from the air. There was no serious claim that these bombardments were confined to military objectives. Their purpose was simply to strike terror into Government adherents by indiscriminate bombing. Again, under pressure of opinion, the Western Democracies made futile protests to the Insurgent Government. Meanwhile, these events had been the subject of several debates in Parliament, and in the course of one of them the Prime Minister had declared that collective security was an illusion and that they ought not to delude small, weak nations into thinking they could be protected by the League of Nations. When reminded that he had stated the exact opposite before the General Election and that it was on that basis that the Government had obtained a majority, he merely replied that he had changed his opinion. There used to be an old constitutional understanding that if, on a matter of first-rate importance, ministers are no longer able to carry out the pledges on the faith of which they obtained power, they should either resign or a fresh opportunity should be given to the electors to say whether they still had confidence in the Government.

The negotiations with Italy proceeded, and in order to make things easier for the re-constituted British Government, Mussolini expressed his agreement with the latest proposal of the Non-Intervention Committee for withdrawing foreign troops. It was a perfectly safe move because the proposals could not come into force without General Franco's assent, which was duly withheld a few weeks later.

Early in April, information reached this country that the Italians were increasing their military assistance to the Insurgents. At first the Prime Minister disbelieved the report and declared that, in any case, British interests were not affected — the fundamental fallacy of British policy at this time. When, a little later, Italian increased intervention could not be denied, it was on some ground or other condoned.

On April 16th it was announced that the Anglo-Italian agreement had been concluded. It contained a number of assurances that in accordance with already existing understandings, the two Powers would not interfere with one another in various places in and near the Mediterranean. To it were attached certain exchanges of Notes by which the Italian Government promised, in the first place, to withdraw its troops in Libya at the rate of 1,000 a week, till they were no more than one half of what they had been at the commencement of negotiations. This was carried out for a few weeks and afterwards the troops were again increased. In the next place, there was a promise to withdraw troops from Spain in accordance with whatever should be determined by the Non-Intervention Committee. As General Franco could not agree, no such determination was made. It was added that, in any case, the troops and material would be withdrawn at the end of the war and that Italy would not seek any political, economic or territorial advantages in Spain or her dependencies. Finally, Italy acceded to the Naval Disarmament Treaty of 1936.

In themselves, though the provisions of the agreement were not of very great importance, yet, as far as they went, they were beneficial to this country provided they were carried out. That proviso must be added because one of the assurances that neither party would engage in propaganda against the other has been almost continuously disregarded by Italy ever since.

On the other hand, Italy, by the exchange of Notes, received two very important advantages. One was the virtual abandonment of any attempt to secure the withdrawal of Italian support of the Spanish Insurgents, until the end of the war — which in practice meant until General Franco had been enabled to win by Italian and German assistance. That was a concession of a vital interest to the Spanish Government in order to secure terms for ourselves! It may be argued that we were under no obligation to do anything for the Spanish Government. Still, we had continuously urged the withdrawal of foreign interference on both sides and had stood before the world as the protagonist of that view. The new arrangement was an advertisement to the world that we were not prepared to resist aggression by a strong Power on a weak one, whether through the League of Nations or otherwise. It must be remembered that throughout these months Señor del Vayo, the Foreign Minister of the Spanish Government, was continually making protests at Geneva against the action of the German and Italian Governments. The answer made to him by the British Government was that the League had nothing to do with civil wars, but in view of the Italian action that excuse must be admitted to have been a little thin.

The other sop given to the Italians was even less defensible. We promised, with a little diplomatic circumlocution, that we would secure the rescission of the resolution of the League of Nations over the Manchurian question not to recognize conquests inconsistent with the Covenant, so far as that applied to the Italian conquest of Abyssinia. Accordingly, on May 12th, the British representative at Geneva proposed that the League should admit the right of each member to decide for itself whether it would or would not recognize that Abyssinia had been conquered. He explained that this did not mean approval of Italian action or disapproval of what the League had done. But he said that to go on refusing recognition might cause discord and friction and be inimical to peace. In other words, he thought that, in order to improve the chances of peace, we were entitled to disregard our obligations to Abyssinia, who had made no submission to Italy and was still in arms in parts of its territory.

Opportunism in politics is inevitable. It is generally true that agreement in disputes can only be reached by compromise and that may involve the abandonment by each side of something to which it thinks it has a right. So long as the abandonment affects only a right belonging to the party making the agreement, the transaction may be legitimate enough. But when, as in the case of the Anglo-Italian agreement, the concession implies the disregard of an obligation to third parties, the position is very different. In the case of the Spanish Government, the obligation might be put in two ways. It was considered that Italian intervention had amounted to an invasion of Spain, then the Government which we recognized as the legitimate Government of Spain was entitled to our protection under the Covenant. If it was thought that Italian intervention was not by State action but the result of volunteer effort by Italian citizens — a proposition which it was not easy to square with the facts — even then we had undertaken, through the Non-Intervention Committee, to hold the balance fairly between the Government and the Insurgents in the matter of intervention. To permit Italy to help the Insurgents while forbidding British subjects to assist the Government was clearly not fair and was an injury to the interests of the Spanish Government. That is to say that, to promote a policy which we thought desirable, we were making a third and unwilling party pay the price.

The case of Abyssinia is simpler. We were under an admitted obligation to help her against the Italian invader. We had failed to do so effectively and we now undertook to please Italy by extinguishing, as far as we could, the last hopes of her victim. At the suggestion of the United States we had taken a different course in the case of Manchuria. We have never recognized the puppet State of Manchukuo; and I believe the United States have not recognized the occupation of Manchuria or the conquest of Abyssinia.

The British Government did not deny that, in the course they recommended, a wrong would be done, but they urged that if we had a duty to Abyssinia we also had a duty to encourage peace. That is to say, we recognized the Italian conquest of a friendly country in order to induce Italy not to make war or encourage others to make war. Such a policy is difficult to defend. Paying Danegeld is usually bad enough. But it is far worse if the funds required are taken from someone else.

However, my business at the moment is not so much with the moralities as with the wisdom of this transaction. I believe that the result of this new policy was bad, and it was perhaps made worse by the way in which it was done. We did not simply announce that we had come to the conclusion that recognition of the Italian Empire of Abyssinia must be made. We declared that we and all other members of the League had a right to do so if desired, but that for ourselves we would not do so till the end of the war in Spain. In other words, we openly treated the independence of Abyssinia as a bargaining counter in our negotiation with Italy. The effect on the minds of other European Governments can easily be imagined.

When this last consideration was put forward in any of these discussions, the opponents of the League system were accustomed to belittle the importance of the smaller countries and to say that it was only the Great Powers which counted. No one would say so now. But at the time it was a useful argument for those who contended that the withdrawal of Germany, Japan and — later — Italy destroyed the whole coercive power of the League. If that were true, it would mean that Germany, with the possible assistance of Italy, could successfully have defied all the remaining League Powers. Since then, the force at the command of the peace keeping Powers has been diminished by the loss of Poland, Czechoslovakia, Austria, Republican Spain and Russia, apart from Norway and Holland. We should evidently have been in a stronger position under the League system than we are now. Nor must we forget the effect which has been produced on what we now call neutrals by the long continued belittling of the League coupled with our attitude to the weaker nations, beginning with China and Abyssinia.

Before I pass to the case of Austria, it will be convenient to say here that the war in Spain continued without any marked change till about the end of the year. After that the Republicans fell to pieces. It was contended that this was largely the result of the continued bombing of their towns by German and Italian machines. Whatever the cause, the war came to an end with the complete victory of General Franco at the end of March 1939. The Italian Government openly took credit for the result and Italian troops led the

Insurgent entry into Barcelona. The German Government officially congratulated General Franco but for once were more reserved than their Italian colleagues.

Almost simultaneously with the resignation of Mr. Eden the Germans began their attack on Austria. Undoubtedly his presence in the Cabinet had exercised a measure of restraint on the Dictators, and they had accordingly been carrying on a violent press campaign against him. Perhaps they had been informed that his position in the Cabinet had become very precarious by the beginning of February and, accordingly, on the 11th of that month, eight days before Eden's resignation, Hitler summoned Dr. Schuschnigg, the Austrian Chancellor, to Berchtesgaden. It will be remembered that, under the Paris Treaties, the union of Austria to Germany was forbidden unless with the consent of the League of Nations. During the Weimar Government, Germany had been held strictly to this provision and, as I have already stated, a *Zollverein* between Austria and Germany was prevented. At that time, there is little doubt that the Austrians wished for the *Anschluss*. But when the Nazis came into power their dictatorial attitude and, in particular, their complicity in the murder of Dr. Dollfuss, produced a considerable change of feeling. Before the formation of the Axis, Italy was opposed to the *Anschluss*. She did not wish to have Germany for a neighbour and it was because Dollfuss was supported by Italy that the Germans murdered him. At one time, as we have seen, it was suggested that these difficulties should be submitted to the League. But the French and British, fearing perhaps that the League would recommend the *Anschluss*, persuaded the Austrian Government, very unwisely as I think, not to invoke Geneva. It was no doubt because Hitler perceived that Austria was slipping away from him that he decided to strike. When, therefore, Dr. Schuschnigg reached Berchtesgaden, it was to find an enraged tyrant who denounced him with the greatest insolence. He was told that he must reconstitute the Austrian Government by placing in power well-known partisans of Germany, or otherwise his country would be immediately invaded. If he complied with this demand, the Austrian Chancellor received a verbal pledge that Germany would respect Austria's independence. Hitler's orders were obeyed and a number of Austrian Nazis were given office. One of them, by name Seyss-Inquart, who openly sought and received instructions from Berlin, at the request of Schuschnigg broadcast a statement accepting Austrian independence. But a few days later he was, on further German instructions, fomenting disturbances in Austria. The end came when, on March 9th, Schuschnigg proposed to submit to a plebiscite whether or not the Austrian people desired the *Anschluss*. Further organized disorders took place, and on March 11th Hitler demanded first the withdrawal of the plebiscite and, when that had been agreed to, the resignation of Schuschnigg under threat of invasion. This also was agreed to, but none the less the invasion took place, and on March 13th Austria was declared to be part of Germany. Dr. Schuschnigg, who had only discharged his legitimate functions, was arrested and still remains in prison. The establishment of the usual Nazi tyranny followed, enforced by the infamous Gestapo and its Chief, Himmler.

By the Stresa agreement of 1935 — one of the earliest substitutes for the League — France, Italy and Britain agreed to maintain Austrian independence. When the German aggression began, the British Government declared that they were under no obligation, under this agreement, to act unless the other parties to it took action. Instead, the British Ambassador was instructed to make one of his usual futile protests to the German Government, which was repeated by British Ministers to the German Ambassador in London. The only result was a curt note from Baron von Neurath, still German Foreign Minister, saying that Austria was none of Britain's business. What is called, in Parliamentary circles, a 'strong' speech was made by the Prime Minister repudiating von Neurath's doctrine and deploring the German action. Some of us, including Mr. Winston Churchill and myself, pointed out the dangers which threatened Czechoslovakia. But we were asked to rely on the solemn assurances given by the German Government. We were further informed that material preparations were being made to deal with the situation and to restore the sanctity of International Law! All reference to the League was rejected on the ground that nothing could be done by it without war — the usual attitude. Nor would the Government give any pledge to defend Czechoslovakia. Hitler had once more caused might to triumph over right and prepared the way for further illustrations of that pernicious doctrine. Well-meaning persons, obsessed with appeasement, went so far as to rejoice that the occupation of Austria had been carried out without violence! When they saw, a few days later, the wholesale bestial torture and butchery of Jews and Austrian Liberals and pacifists, they realized how they had been deceived, not for the first or, unfortunately, the last time.

The danger to Czechoslovakia which was obvious in London had not been overlooked in Prague. The Czech Minister in Berlin was sent for by Goering on March 12th, while Austria was being invaded, and informed that if Czechoslovakia did not mobilize as a result of the Austrian business, he, Goering, promised on his word of honour as a Prussian officer that no territorial demands would ever be made against Czechoslovakia. At a second interview, while Hitler was in Vienna and Goering was acting head of the German Government, these promises were repeated and Goering 'several times stressed his Prussian word of honour'.[1] He also suggested that the Czech minister should ask von Neurath for a re-affirmation of the Arbitration Treaty of 1925 between the two countries, which was duly given. These assurances, repeated to the British Government, were those upon which we were invited to rely by the British Cabinet.[2]

The situation was very disquieting. The policy of 'contacts' with Berlin and Rome, and appeals to the reasonable-

[1] See letter published in the *Daily Telegraph* of April 13th, 1940, by M. Jan Masaryk.
[2] For the whole of the Czechoslovak question reference should be made to the admirable book of Mr. Seton Watson, *Munich and the Dictators*.

ness and good faith of the Dictators had been tried both with regard to Spain and Austria, with the result that in each case a complete triumph for the policy of force had followed. Evidently if the further development of the policy of aggression was to be avoided, something more efficacious than British remonstrances must be devised. At this juncture, Monsieur Litvinoff, speaking for the Russian Government on March 17th to representatives of the Press, said: — 'It may be too late to-morrow, but to-day the time has not gone by, if all States and the Great Powers in particular take a firm and unambiguous stand' for the collective salvation of peace. This statement was officially communicated to the Austrian, Czech, French and British Governments. The British reply was that the proposal was inopportune! There can be little doubt that, had it been adopted, Czechoslovakia would have been saved and the Hitler or Prussian policy would have been definitely checked. In his assault on Czechoslovakia Hitler stood practically alone.[1] Mussolini never actively helped him. Indeed, Italy cannot have desired to see the extinction of Czechoslovakia with whom she had no quarrel.

The policy of Poland was at this time very ambiguous, but it is unthinkable that she would have joined in an attack on another Slav people supported by Britain, France, Russia and such other countries as would have rallied to their standard. It may be said that this is all speculation and the facts might have turned out very differently. That is possible. But one of the main purposes for which the League existed was to set such doubts at rest. If, instead of snubbing the Russian Government by curtly saying that their proposal was inopportune, we had welcomed it and had summoned a meeting of the League Assembly, we could then have announced that the British, French and Russian Governments regarded as of vital importance the maintenance of the principle that no country must resort to war in breach of the Covenant, and were ready to take all measures necessary

---

[1] It must be remembered that the treaty of Alliance between Germany and Italy was not made till May 22nd, 1939.

to enforce it. I do not believe that any member of the League of any importance would have opposed such a movement. But if they did so, that would not technically have made any difference, since under Article 16 each member of the League is entitled and, as I think, bound to take whatever action may seem to it effective to arrest aggression. In practice the only important thing to know was whether we should have been supported by sufficient strength to make it impossible for Germany to have persisted in her policy.

This was, however, not the view adopted by the British Government. They still adhered to the plan of rebuking the German policy as creating a 'profound disturbance of international confidence', and declining to pledge themselves to take action to prevent attacks on Czechoslovakia or other States. To do so was said to be to commit the country to 'automatic' sanctions, by which was meant that if you state clearly what you will do in certain circumstances, you deprive yourself of the power of not so acting if the circumstances arise. That is so. But if you do not take this course, no amount of vague minatory phrases will produce any effect on people like Hitler and his advisers. Our Government recognized the truth of this observation with regard to the Eastern frontiers of France and Belgium. They were ready to give unambiguous pledges to defend them. But they failed to see, at this time, that the success of aggression in Central Europe inevitably weakened the whole structure of peace including the security of France and Belgium. Hence came the folly of saying that our frontier was on the Rhine and that no British interest was involved in the safety of Czechoslovakia and other parts of Central and South-Eastern Europe. I well remember the kind of talk that was popular in ministerial circles at that time, suggestions for the dismemberment of Czechoslovakia, the abandonment of her fortified frontier and even the cession of all the south-eastern countries to the domination of the Axis Powers. To such irresponsible language history has given the reply.

Meanwhile a fierce agitation was going on in Germany.

Hitler was talking of the 10,000,000 Germans in outside countries which must be united to the Reich, a phrase understood to mean the six and a half millions in Austria, which he had already taken, and the three and a half millions in Czechoslovakia which he meant to seize. This was coupled with violent attacks on the treatment of the German speaking minority in the northern part of Czechoslovakia, known as the Sudeten province, as to which it need only be said that it was incomparably better than the treatment of racial and religious minorities in Germany. The agitation on the subject was a mere blind to give a kind of pretext for aggression. Unfortunately, it was taken by the British and French Governments at its face value and the Czech Government was continually pressed to make concessions to the German minority, which men like the distinguished President of Czechoslovakia, Dr. Benes, knew would only be made the jumping-off ground for further German demands. It is a melancholy story which no decent Briton can read without acute discomfort.

On May 7th, the Dictators of Germany and Italy met in Rome and, while pouring scorn on the 'Utopias to which Europe had blindly entrusted her fate', celebrated the consolidation of the Axis, whereby a 'bloc of 120 million people' had been created 'to safeguard their eternal right to live and to defend themselves against all forces which might oppose their natural development'. This was followed, in the second week of May, by the celebrated luncheon at Lord Astor's house where the Prime Minister, Mr. Neville Chamberlain, conveyed the impression to a group of American and Canadian journalists that neither France nor Britain could or would fight for Czechoslovakia, which was advised to concede any reasonable German demand. The conversation, when published on May 14th in the *Montreal Daily Star*, was not admitted, but its substance has never been denied. Undoubtedly it was one of the main grounds for Ribbentrop's assurances to Hitler that whatever he did in Central Europe, the Western Democracies would not fight. This, indeed, was the line taken by many of the supporters of the British Government in our Press.

It is not necessary for my purpose to go through all the details of the approaching disaster through the summer. Sometimes an immediate attack by Germany was threatened, and when the menace was met by a more than usually determined reply by Monsieur Daladier, it was postponed and there was a temporary improvement. This was hailed by the advocates of appeasement as proof that their policy was succeeding. In July, Lord Runciman was induced to accept a mission to Prague to try to mediate between the German minority and the Czechoslovak Government. He was to have no specific instructions or authority, and the Government apparently believed that whatever he said or did, their position would not be affected. This mission the veteran statesman surprisingly accepted. Its only result was to strengthen the German conviction that they could rely on British acquiescence in their policy. To most observers it seemed clear that the international situation was getting worse. Had the negotiations been carried out under the League, in conditions of open discussion, the facts would have been unmistakable. As it was, the British Prime Minister was persuaded and declared that 'throughout the Continent there was a relaxation of that sense of tension which six months ago had been present'. That was at the end of July, and by the beginning of September, after the Czech Government had made concession after concession to the insatiable demands of Berlin, it became obvious that nothing short of complete submission was required. War seemed imminent and to avert it Mr. Chamberlain courageously but most unwisely flew to Berchtesgaden. He brought back terms for the dismemberment of Czechoslovakia and the abandonment to Germany of the whole of her lines of defence in Bohemia. He took with him, on his flight, no trained diplomat. Indeed the Foreign Office attitude throughout these proceedings seemed to be one of gloomy acquiescence. In vain the Czechs had appealed to their Arbitration Treaty with Germany.

That was brushed aside and the League of Nations was scarcely even mentioned. The obligations of the Covenant to 'preserve as against external aggression the territorial integrity and political independence' of Czechoslovakia were ignored. Indeed, it was commonly asserted that we had no treaty obligation to defend her — a statement that is entirely inconsistent with any reasonable reading of Articles 10 and 16.

I do not propose to travel over the well-worn ground of the interview at Berchtesgaden, where Hitler's demands were conceded; the interview at Godesberg where they were, in consequence, increased; the refusal to accept them and the final surrender at Munich which a section of the public — taught to believe that the avoidance of war on any terms was a great victory — enthusiastically accepted. Throughout, the treatment by the British negotiators of Dr. Benes and his Government could scarcely have been harsher if they had been defeated aggressors. They were not even consulted, though their representatives were present in Munich. Nor need I say anything of the dramatic intervention of Mussolini, no doubt arranged with Hitler, or of the celebrated foolscap promises of Hitler which he so easily signed and still more easily tore up. One incident which affected me personally I ought to mention. Before Munich, when the crisis was acute, Madame Benes rang me up from Prague on behalf of her husband to assure me that the Sudeten agitation was a put-up job and to ask me what I advised. I felt forced to reply that, much as I sympathized with her country, I could not advise her to rely on any help from mine. It was the only reply that could be made, but I have never felt a more miserable worm than I did when making it. To me and many others the transaction was as shameful as anything in our history. And yet the Ministers who carried it out were honourable men and many thousands of their fellow-countrymen acclaimed their conduct. They believed that the great blessing of peace had been purchased by the generous self-sacrifice of Britain! On both points they were mistaken. Peace — if by peace is meant freedom from international disturbance — was no more secure after Munich than before. Even the actual terms agreed on proved completely illusory. Much was said at the time about the great superiority for Czechoslovakia of Munich over Godesberg The territorial boundaries which on paper showed some improvement were so whittled away by a kind of drafting Commission set up to settle — as it was said — minor controversies, that actually the Godesberg terms were scarcely worse than the final result of Munich. Then there was a provision for a fresh guarantee of the relics of Czechoslovakia by France and Britain, in which Germany was later to join. How that guarantee was supposed to have any value if the guarantors openly announced that, whatever happened, they would not fight, it was not easy to see. In fact it can scarcely be said to have come alive. So far as it existed, it silently preceded the sheet of foolscap into Hitler's waste paper basket. Nothing was more painful in the whole of these subsidiary negotiations than the constant threats of the Germans to enforce by arms any of their demands which were resisted, threats to which we instantly submitted. So that even the peace between Germany and Czechoslovakia was of a very precarious character. Nor did Germany show greater moderation in her general policy. Seizing upon the murder by a young Jew of a minor official attached to the German Embassy in Paris as a pretext, ruthless decrees were enforced in Germany depriving the remaining Jews there of practically the whole of their property. There was no pretence of justice about the substance of the decree or the loathsome torture by which its enforcement was accompanied. To this day it is a matter of doubt whether its object was simply to replenish the German war chest or to satisfy the sadistic passion of Hitler and his extreme anti-semitic supporters. Finally, as we all know, Germany after various nibblings at Slovakia and Ruthenia, throwing off all disguise in March 1939, invaded Bohemia, occupied Prague and declared the whole country annexed to the German Reich. This finally convinced the advocates of 'appeasement' that

that policy must be given up, and the British Government reverted — not even then to the League of Nations, the members of which were thought to be too panic-stricken to be capable of action — but to the ancient policy of armaments and alliances. No doubt in substance this was the only policy open to the Western Democracies though it is a question whether, even so, it would not have been more efficiently carried out through the machinery of the League. However, by this time war conditions had practically been reached. The 'Great Experiment' in the maintenance of peace, with which this book deals, had for the time being been suspended, and an examination of the preparations for war would not help in its elucidation.

The policy of which the climax was the Munich surrender therefore failed to preserve peace. It did worse than that. It gave the impression that we were so anxious to keep out of war that we were prepared for almost any sacrifice to secure that object. In a way, it was just that atmosphere of sacrifice which attracted so many of our fellow countrymen. It satisfied our longing for an idealistic basis for our policy which used to be sneered at as the nonconformist conscience — a sneer as unworthy as it was inaccurate, for luckily nonconformists have no monopoly of idealism in this country. Looked at from the purely personal point of view, there were good grounds for admiring the self-sacrifice of a Minister, no longer young, making three flights to Germany in less than a fortnight, in the hope of securing the peace to which he was passionately attached. There was a note of chivalry about the effort which struck a responsive chord in our highly emotional people. But that is not the way it appeared abroad where people naturally cared little for the personal as distinct from the international aspects of the policy. They asked at whose expense was this policy carried out? Who paid the bill? Not France or the British Empire — they believed that they were paying nothing, and for the time being that was true. Any suggestion that we might offer to surrender some portion of the British Empire in order to buy Hitler off was indignantly rejected, as it had been when we were trying to save Abyssinia from Italy. What the Western Powers did was to force Czechoslovakia to abandon to Germany a great part of her territory and practically all her means of defence, prepared with the utmost skill and at great expense to save her from just the fate to which she was afterwards compelled to submit. And this was done by two Powers one of whom had given her the most express and definite pledges to defend her, and both of whom had entered into the general treaty known as the Covenant of the League of Nations whereby they were bound 'to respect and preserve as against external aggression' her 'territorial integrity and independence', and to take all the measures — diplomatic and economic, and if necessary, military — that might be required for that purpose. It may be said that they never actually refused to discharge their treaty obligations to Czechoslovakia. But they had clearly given her to understand that if she resisted Germany they would take that course. It is also urged that they were powerless to do anything themselves and that they did not believe that Russia could be relied on to help. The Russian Government plainly said they were ready to fulfil their treaty obligations. In any case, months before the crisis reached its very acute stage, Russia proposed a conference to decide on joint action, which Britain and France rejected. Had they kept the League in vigour and referred the controversy to it, all this could have been cleared up. Further, if they felt powerless to do anything to help the Czechs, what right had they to press her to make concessions? What justification was there for the Runciman mission? They had a right to interfere only if they recognized their undertaking to protect. A more plausible defence was, perhaps, that in the interest of Czechoslovakia herself it was best to compel her to give way. But surely that was a matter for Czechoslovakia to decide. We had promised to 'preserve her territorial integrity and independence'. Unless and until she released us from that promise we were bound by it. If there was any serious doubt on the subject, there was the institution at Geneva at which the whole question might have been discussed at any time during the spring and summer of 1938. The Russian proposal of March in that year opened the door wide for such a discussion. The opportunity was not taken because it was believed that in spite of Hitler's character and the Prussian tradition of which he was the unrestrained exponent, he could be persuaded to abandon his policy. The plan failed, and it deserved to fail, for it was not founded on any intelligible principle. It was a house built upon sand.

In spite of the fact that Hitler never made the slightest response to the Munich gesture, the policy of appeasement was further applied to the other member of the Axis. On January 11th of the new year, our Prime Minister and Foreign Secretary proceeded to Rome in order to give formal recognition of the Italian conquest of Abyssinia, and we read of two British Ministers solemnly drinking, at a State banquet, to the extinction of the independence of a country that we were pledged to protect. As to what else passed on that occasion we have received little information. It was not treated very seriously by Mussolini, I should think, since according to press accounts he took pains to show his indifference to the representatives of the British Empire by absenting himself from Rome during a considerable part of their visit.

If it was hoped that this paying court to the Italian Dictator would prevent the outbreak of war, events falsified that aspiration. It is true that Ministers still cherished the illusion that the danger of war had been removed. They even seemed to think that the Munich policy had had a good effect on the moral opinion of the world in our favour. As far as published facts are concerned there seems no ground for this belief.

I have no more to say about international events up to the outbreak of war. As Johnson said of the murder of Desdemona, 'I am glad I have finished my revisal of this dreadful scene. It is too much to be endured'.

The Assembly did meet in September, 1938, but its proceedings were entirely overshadowed by the Munich crisis and the League's only important contribution to those proceedings was the speech of Monsieur Litvinoff in which he repeated the proposal he had made in March. There were also discussions about the reform of the Covenant, which had no definite result except to show that some of the smaller Powers had become gravely discouraged.

CHAPTER V

CONCLUSIONS

IT is commonly said that the League of Nations has failed. It must be admitted that the chief purpose for which the League was created was the maintenance of peace, and within twenty years of its inauguration we have been plunged into a major war which is in itself the climax of several other wars. That, however, is not the whole truth. In attacking the problem of the prevention of war, the Covenant proceeds on two lines. There are the Articles 10 to 17 which seek to restrict directly the right of nations to resort to war, and there are also a number of provisions which aim at removing those conditions of international life which are evil in themselves and tend to keep alive international jealousies and hostilities. The means by which this object was to be achieved was by the promotion of international co-operation. Thus the Preamble of the Covenant begins: — 'In order to promote international co-operation and achieve international peace and security'. So, too, the Resolutions of the Peace Conference on January 25th, 1919, stated the objects of the proposed League to be: to promote international co-operation, to ensure the fulfilment of international obligations and to provide safeguards against war. The conception was that if the nations were encouraged to work together for objects of common interest, they were less likely to fight.

A very large part of the activity of the League has therefore been devoted to this purpose and, by universal consent, work of this description done by and in connection with the League, in economic and social questions and in other ways, has been extensive and successful.

Recently a strong Special Committee of the League under the Chairmanship of Mr. Bruce, the eminent representatve of Australia, has issued a report reviewing the past economic and social labours of the League and making proposals for their intensification. The report points out that more and more as the improvement of communications and the growth of a common life has brought the nations nearer together, it has become increasingly difficult to solve the problems involved, by national effort alone. In the early years of the League, an effort was made to lay down the limits of international activity, but it was found impossible. The actual subject over which the question arose was the provision of swimming baths for children, which at first sight certainly seemed to be a matter of strictly national interest. But on close consideration it was found that even in such a matter as that, the 'interchange of experience and the co-ordination of action between the national authorities' was of the greatest value. The result has been that the sphere of action of the League has grown greatly, and recently more than half its too restricted expenditure has been devoted to these questions.

I do not propose to attempt any detailed account of this part of my subject. But if the causes of the League's 'failure' are to be accurately diagnosed something must be said about it. From the outset its importance had been fully recognized. At the same time as the Committee of the Paris Conference was sitting under the Presidency of Mr. Woodrow Wilson, to draw up the Covenant of the League, another Committee, presided over by Mr. Samuel Gompers, was elaborating the International Labour Organization. Nine guiding principles were laid down for regulating and improving world industrial conditions, and an organization was created, called the International Labour Office, to promote international action in the directions so indicated. Constitutionally, the I.L.O. was 'established at the seat of the League as part of the organization of the League', and its expenses are paid out of the general funds of the League. But its administration is, in other respects, not controlled by that body. The League's financial authorities discuss and determine what sum shall be annually allotted to the I.L.O., but neither they nor the League itself interfere with the expenditure of that sum. Members of the League are automatically members of the I.L.O. But other countries may join the I.L.O. without joining the League, and the U.S.A. have in fact done so. Indeed, a State that withdraws from the League may decide to remain a member of the I.L.O. — Brazil has taken this course, and there are three or four other States which have given notice of their intention to imitate her.

Though, therefore, closely connected with the League, it is quite autonomous. Nor is its constitution the same. It has, indeed, an Annual Conference of the Members of the I.L.O., a smaller selected committee called the Governing Body, and an International Office presided over by the Director, which roughly correspond in function to the Assembly, the Council and the Secretary General and Secretariat of the League. In one respect there is an important difference between the two institutions. The persons attending the Assembly and Council of the League are representatives of the Governments. The analagous individuals in the I.L.O. represent governments, employers and workers. Thus, in the Conference, each country is entitled to four delegates, two representatives of the Government, and one each of the employers and the workers. The arrangement has been very successful, except in respect of the totalitarian countries where independent representation of anything but the government has been impossible. Both Germany and Italy have accordingly now withdrawn from the I.L.O. as well as from the League. Certain consequences have followed this method of representation. One is that each delegate votes individually, so that it often happens that the representatives of the Government and those of the employers or of the workers are found in different lobbies. This further involves that decisions do not require unanimity to be valid. The results of the system have been very good, and I have often wondered whether some system of the same kind could be applied to the League itself. Certainly the atmosphere of the Assembly is apt to be too governmental. When, as I have recorded, the late Mr. George Barnes, being one of the delegates of the

United Kingdom, expressed views which were not shared by his government, he was told the next year that he must undertake to conform to bureaucratic direction or he could not attend at Geneva. He refused, and the nations lost the considerable advantage of hearing the opinions of a typical Briton with a large measure of the national characteristic of being right. At the same time, the difficulties of any change are very great, and I can only commend the matter to the consideration of those who will have to frame the new international organization after the war.

The most important work on the part of the I.L.O. has been the formulation of Conventions dealing with industrial difficulties of which it has succeeded in securing the acceptance of no less than sixty-five, concerned with the work of women and children, social insurance, hours of work, conditions of employment at sea, and a number of other similar subjects. This great achievement has been reached by the general co-operation of all those interested and has been immensely assisted by the three directors who have held office — Monsieur Albert Thomas, a very remarkable personality, a great orator and a man of titanic energy; Mr. Harold Butler, in his way as valuable an international servant as Monsieur Thomas; and the present director, the American, Mr. Winant.

Admirable as has been the work of the I.L.O., it has only dealt with a portion of the non-contentious co-operative work of the League. I have had occasion to call attention to the labours of the various League Committees appointed by the Council or Assembly. They have made recommendations and obtained results in many matters. On the humanitarian side, a real advance has been made in such matters as the protection of women and children from horrors like those connected with the so-called white slave traffic; and the control of opium and other narcotic drugs. The machinery of the League has been of the first importance both because it has worked far more rapidly than the old diplomatic methods, an example of which we have watched in the Committee for Non-Intervention in Spain, and because by the pressure of publicity it has thrust aside the obstruction of interested Powers. Slavery and forced labour have, in the same way, been tackled, the last in conjunction with the I.L.O., and those two hoary old abuses have been almost extirpated, apart from the recent proceedings in territory occupied by the Hitler Government.

The same methods have been applied to health questions, where great improvements have been made in dealing with epidemics and other diseases; to questions of transit and communications by sea, and by rail and road on land; to the question of nutrition and to the investigation of crucial questions of economics like unemployment and tariffs, which will be of undoubted value when settled peace permits them to be taken up again. A very interesting enterprise has been the Committee of Intellectual Co-operation, presided over by that great protagonist of peace, Dr. Gilbert Murray. It has done excellent work in bringing together the intellectual activities of the different nations.

Then there have been other problems affecting particular nations, such as the rescue of Austria and Hungary and Bulgaria from their financial difficulties, partly by assisting them to make administrative reforms and partly by using the credit of the members of the League in order to enable them to raise the necessary funds. So, too, the League has provided experts to advise countries like China how to overcome the accumulated difficulties of a system of government unsuitable to modern conditions. But for the criminal invasion by Japan, China would by now have been far advanced on the road to prosperity. One of the most strikingly successful of these efforts was the help given to Greece in coping with the tremendous task of finding homes for her compatriots when they were expelled from Asia Minor as a result of the Greco-Turkish war. In this connection the League's exertions to find a solution of the refugee problem must not be forgotten. Its earlier work of this kind under the inspiring leadership of Dr. Nansen was remarkably successful because, broadly, all the nations were ready to co-operate in providing for these miserable people. Later, especially in trying to aid the Jewish and other refugees from Germany, less has been achieved. The systematic ruin and expulsion without regard to age or sex of German citizens against whom nothing but their race or their liberal opinions was even alleged, was carried out on such a scale and with such a refinement of cruelty as to make it humanly impossible to deal with them completely. Something has, indeed, been done, but not enough.

The Bruce Commission has proposed the consolidation of all these activities under a new General Committee of the League which is designed to separate them from political passions and preoccupations. The proposal is certainly attractive, particularly as emphasising the very great importance of this part of the League's work.

In addition to the work which I have called non-contentious there have been certain matters which can scarcely be so described but which have not been concerned with acute international disputes. There were, for instance, the international administrations of the territories of the Saar and of Danzig. These were tasks outside the Covenant, and accepted by the League at the suggestion of the Paris Conference. The Saar, after a rather stormy beginning, settled down under its international government peacefully and prosperously. By the Treaty, it had to be given the right to decide by ballot after fifteen years whether it would choose to go back to Germany or not. Elaborate precautions were taken by the League to secure a fair and quiet vote. An international police force was entrusted with the control of public order and the inhabitants voted by an enormous majority for reunion with Germany.

Danzig was less successful. It is, or was, a predominantly German town, lying in a mainly Polish region. There were League High Commissioners who were supposed to keep the peace between these two nationalities, with an appeal to the Council of the League. It was an impossible task and it resulted in failure. As far as I could observe, there was no real desire on the part of either Poles or Germans to make it a success. The High Commissioners were hard-working and some of them very able men, but they could do nothing effective in the circumstances. The moral of these two cases is that nowadays artificial arrangements of territory by treaty will not succeed if the population concerned are opposed to them.

One device tried to deal with difficulties of this kind was to give to racial, religious and linguistic minorities in those countries which were created or greatly enlarged by the Treaties of Peace, rights to be impartially and justly governed under the protection of the League. This also was a duty not included in the Covenant and imposed on the League by special Treaties. The principle is as old as the Treaty of Berlin in 1878, and though the device has only been a partial success, to ignore the rights of minorities or leave them to fight for what they can get has not produced better results. I believe the machinery for enforcing minority rights might be improved, but I should be sorry to see it abandoned.

In the somewhat parallel case of Mandates, international supervision has worked very well. There, the treaty entrusting to a mandatory power the administration of certain territories laid down in some detail the principles of government which the mandatory was to pursue. Though the conditions of the mandates varied according to the territory dealt with, roughly, they were the same as prevailed in our Crown Colonies until the Tariff fanatics included the latter within the British protective system. The mandate system was part of the Covenant, and to carry out the necessary supervision a strong permanent Committee of experts was created which receives annual reports about the mandated territories indicating how the conditions of the mandate have been performed. There is no coercion beyond publicity provided for, and on the whole the plan has worked very well. It has raised the standard of Colonial administration without causing serious friction. It is therefore regrettable that the British Government should have affronted the mandatory jurisdiction of the League in its recent Palestine policy. Action of that kind weakens the authority of the League without any compensatory benefit.

On the whole, then, the action of the League apart from actual international disputes has been an outstanding success. The words of Mr. Cordell Hull, the American Secretary of State, on February 2nd, 1939, on this point may be quoted: — 'The League of Nations has been responsible for the development of mutual exchange and discussion of ideas and methods to a greater extent and in many more fields of humanitarian and scientific endeavour than any other organization in history'. That is true, and he is also right when he adds that 'each sound step forward in those fields is a step towards the establishment of that national and international order which is essential to real peace'. But it is necessary to add that these activities must be supplemented by direct action to preserve peace if the fabric of civilization is to be maintained, without which no progress or security is possible. Indeed, the marked success of the League's non-contentious work followed by the recrudescence of European war, is glaring evidence of the mistake made by those who urged that the League could be made to work as a peace-keeping machine without its coercive powers.

International co-operation in this sense has done much good work but it has failed to keep the peace by itself. What, then, of the more direct action of the League for the prevention of war? Certainly much has been done. The conception that 'any war or threat of war is a matter of concern to the whole League' and indeed to the whole world is very generally, though not universally, accepted. The old idea that international law did not forbid war, whether just or unjust, is more and more discredited. The fact that the Kellogg-Briand Pact which laid down the contrary rule, which, in the American phrase, outlawed war, was almost universally accepted, is an advance in international opinion which should not be underrated. Nor have the efforts of the League in the same direction been meagre or ineffective. The establishment of the Permanent Court of International Justice at the Hague at the very outset of the League's life was a great achievement. It has decided thirty-one disputes, and under its special powers of advising the League it has given twenty-seven advisory opinions. In no case has any decision by the Court been disregarded. Some of the decisions have been criticized, and it has been alleged that the judges have been actuated by national feeling in their judgements. The only prominent case in which this has been charged was that as to the legality of the proposed *Zollverein* between Germany and Austria in 1931. I have already explained why I think the charge is unsustainable.[1] On the other hand, in more than one instance judges have given judgement, in cases in which their nation was a party, contrary to the argument put forward on its behalf. It would be absurd to suggest that a judge of the International or of any other Court is unaffected by his feelings and even his prejudices as a man. But the Hague Court has an excellent record in such matters and has shown that its members do habitually, in giving their judgements, earnestly and successfully strive to act with rigorous impartiality. That is the international reputation which they enjoy. I hope that every fair opportunity will be taken to extend the jurisdiction of the Court.

But it is true that the international disputes which are most dangerous to peace are precisely those which are not amenable to judicial decision. The Covenant does not provide for the decision of such cases. It confines itself to saying that justiciable disputes should be decided by arbitration or by the Hague Court, and that with respect to all disputes no resort to war shall take place until a delay of six to nine months has taken place and all the resources of negotiation, mediation and arbitration have been exhausted. No case has arisen in which war has taken place after these measures have been adopted. But there have been a certain number of cases in which hostilities have broken out in breach of the Covenant before their adoption. Of these, there were, up to the autumn

[1] See page 219.

of 1931, some thirty of forty which came before the League. Generally speaking, they were satisfactorily disposed of, that is to say, a reasonable settlement was reached by pacific means and was so genuinely accepted by both parties that little or no ill-feeling was left behind. Two exceptions are often quoted — the Polish and Lithuanian dispute over Vilna,[1] and the Greco-Italian quarrel usually called the Corfu[2] controversy. The Vilna question was discussed and re-discussed. But what finally defeated the League efforts was the fact that neither of the parties would accept its decision, so that in the end the dispute was left unsettled. In the Corfu case, it was common ground that Italy had suffered a great wrong in the murder of Italian officers engaged in international duty, for which Greece was liable to make compensation. But Italy quite unjustifiably seized on Corfu in order either to put pressure on Greece, or as was commonly believed, in order permanently to possess herself of the island. In the end Italy withdrew from Corfu but Greece had to pay more than most of us at Geneva thought right because she had agreed to accept the decision of a body called the Ambassadors' Conference which then sat at Paris. The result, though not ideal, did save for Greece that for which she cared most, namely Corfu, and so far as it was unjust that was not the fault of the League.

Up to 1931, therefore, the work of the League in gravely contentious matters had been successful. It was said that all the questions so dealt with by the League had affected only Powers of minor importance, except the Corfu case. That is true, and for the reason that it was a simple matter for the Council of the League to enforce on the smaller Powers abstinence from war. The actual use of force never became necessary. But it was there in reserve, ready to be used if required. Take any of the cases in which the intervention of the League was successful. Take, for instance, the invasion of Albania by Yugo-Slavia[3] in November, 1921. The Council met within a few hours of the report of hostilities.

[1] See page 128.   [2] See page 148.   [3] See page 128.

An immediate message was sent calling upon the parties to stop fighting, and it was known that strong measures would be taken against that one of them which showed itself to be the aggressor. There followed a sharp fall in the securities of the invader, negotiations took place, a settlement was reached and, since submission had been to an international authority, it left no soreness behind it.

Similar, if rather more elaborate, action produced the settlement of the Greco-Bulgarian[1] dispute in October, 1925. In that case, as I happen to know, preliminary enquiries had been made by the British Government as to how naval action could be taken if it became necessary. In one case where there was a failure to secure a settlement — the Polish-Lithuanian dispute — the practical difficulties of forcible action were well-known and perhaps encouraged a recalcitrant attitude on the part of the countries concerned.

It was the same thing in the more serious and definite failures of the League after 1931. In those cases, for various reasons, force was ruled out. In the Manchurian question, for instance, every species of remonstrance and persuasion was tried. The opinion of the whole world was mobilized against the aggressor. The causes of the dispute were most fully and impartially examined Recommendations for a settlement were made which took full account of the legitimate interests of both sides. But when Japan refused to desist from hostilities the members of the League made no attempt at coercion and the wrongdoer carried off its booty and prepared for the further aggression which followed a year or two later. No doubt there were difficulties. Two of the Great Powers who were most interested in the Far East — Russia and the United States — were not members of the League. There was also the possible danger to Hong-Kong and Shanghai, which loomed so large in the minds of British statesmen. But the fact remains that every effort of persuasion and remonstrance was tried, to induce Japan to refrain from aggression. The opinion of the whole world was arrayed

[1] See page 174.

against her without effect because, as the history of the case shows, she was satisfied that the peace powers would not use force, and force alone would have turned her from her purpose.

Another point in this question should be noted. It seemed to establish that the British Government would risk nothing to preserve peace in a quarrel which, as they believed, did not affect British interests — that is to say, British subjects or British territory. Not only was force not used to restrain the aggressor, but the reason given for not using it reduced League action to fatuity or worse. The whole object of the members of the League should have been to stop the aggression, not because it was a threat to the territory of this or that power, but because it endangered the peace of the world. That is the very essence of the League system. The consequences of the British attitude were quickly seen. Japan proceeded with her aggression. She utilized what was at first a relatively trifling incident to inaugurate the conquest of four Chinese provinces as large as Germany and France put together. Still worse, she set a precedent followed three years later by Italy and then by Germany, which has brought upon us all the sufferings of the last few months.

The Abyssinian question was even more disastrous to the League system than the Manchurian. As early as the autumn of 1934, it was known that the Fascist Government was preparing for the invasion of Abyssinia, and the British Government — and, no doubt, the French Government also — received information to that effect. I personally among others drew the attention of the Government to the Abyssinian news and urged that the League should take action. Nothing was done. Then came the series of appeals by the Ethiopian Government to the League in which they pointed out the increasingly hostile attitude of Italy and asked the Council to secure the pacific settlement of the dispute through arbitration or by mediation. In each case the Western democracies secured, or acquiesced in, the decision that the discussion should be adjourned or that, if any kind of enquiry was allowed, it should be in substance abortive. Italy was, intentionally or otherwise, induced to believe that if she proceeded with her aggression she need not fear any serious opposition from Britain or France. So she proceeded with her preparations for war, while Abyssinia, under her then existing treaties, was practically precluded from making similar preparations. By August it was clear that the Italian invasion was imminent and when the Assembly met early in September, the new British Foreign Minister, Sir Samuel Hoare, in his celebrated speech of September 11th declared that his Government believed in collective security and were prepared to take their share with other members of the League in preventing Italian aggression. The statement was quite definite and was received with general approval in this country. Other Ministers made similar declarations both then and a few weeks later in connection with the general election which was pending. The action in support of these strong statements was, to put it mildly, disappointing. No attempt was made to break off diplomatic relations with Italy or even to withdraw the heads of missions of the League Powers — the course indicated by the Assembly resolution of 1921. On the contrary, the Ministers both of France and Britain were continually saying we had no quarrel with the Italian people or even, apparently, with the Italian Government, but that, as a matter of international decorum, we felt bound to disapprove of the invasion of one member of the League by another! Slowly and reluctantly some of the less effective economic sanctions were imposed on Italy and were by her disregarded. All this time it would have been perfectly easy for the French and British fleets to have cut the communications between Italy and Africa, which would have forced a stoppage of the war. It was hinted at the time and since that we had an insufficiency of shells or of some other essential weapons. Admiral Fisher, in command of the Mediterranean fleet, knew nothing of such pitiable weakness. But even if it were really true, that is no excuse for adopting an attitude of support for the League, meaning all the time to do nothing to make that support effective. The truth must be that these suggested explanations of the policy of the Anglo-French Governments are quite mistaken. The real fact is that, as in the Manchurian case, neither Government believed that it was justifiable to use such force, on behalf of the maintenance of the new international law, as might lead to war. Had Italy attacked some piece of British or French territory, the reply would have been instantaneous that the attack must be withdrawn or war would follow. But the conception that the maintenance of peace was of far more importance than the integrity of our territory had not then been accepted by the majority of the British or French Cabinets. That is and was in itself deplorable. But it was made far worse by the Geneva speech of September and by the imposition of incomplete sanctions on Italy in which the great majority of the members of the League were induced to join.

There followed the Hoare-Laval Treaty in effect abandoning Abyssinia and disregarding our treaty obligations under the Covenant of the League. Our people were rightly indignant and insisted on changing our Foreign Minister, Sir Samuel Hoare, for Mr. Eden. But that did little to induce the Cabinet to adopt a more vigorous foreign policy. Addis Ababa consequently fell, the conquest of Abyssinia was claimed by Italy, the sanctions were withdrawn, and those countries which had followed our lead in imposing them were profoundy discouraged. A little more than two years later, the Italian Empire of Abyssinia was acknowledged by Britain, and, as I have said, the Prime Minister, Mr. Chamberlain, and Foreign Secretary, Lord Halifax, went to Rome to drink to the success of the Italian achievement. The consequences of these proceedings have been deplorable.

In March, 1936, Germany re-occupied the Rhineland as the first step in her policy of aggression. She and Italy combined to overthrow the democratic government of Spain in order to instal one which they believed would be more favourable to their policy. Then came the absorption of Austria and the melancholy history of the betrayal of Czechoslovakia, not to speak of the annexation by Italy of Albania. Finally, the German invasion of Poland convinced even the most sanguine supporters of the policy of appeasement that German ambition was for universal domination and France and England went to war in defence of the liberty of themselves and of all other nations, small and great, and for the rejection of the claim that only force counts in international affairs. In none of these matters was the authority of the League invoked or its machinery utilized. Now at last it has been recognized that the only alternative to international chaos is international co-operation for peace. It is on that principle that the League was founded and as long as it guided the policy of the Great Powers, Europe — and the world — advanced steadily towards Peace and Prosperity.

It must be admitted that the League system has been seriously impaired and we have now to consider what should be done to replace or restore it. In the first place, let us be clear what is the cause of our present troubles. All sorts of special reasons have been put forward. We hear of the unfairness in the world distribution of territory as between the Axis and the League Powers. Much, too, is said about the injustice of the Treaties of peace. If by injustice is meant that the vanquished powers did not fare so well as the victors, that is obviously and necessarily true. If it is meant that the vanquished powers were the victims of a 'Carthaginian' peace, the charge is absurd, conclusively disproved by the fact that within less than twenty years Germany became again the strongest military power in the world. Moreover, of the chief three aggressive powers, Germany, Italy and Japan, two were victors and each of them received at Paris considerable increases of territory.

I am far from saying that the arrangement made at Paris in 1919-20 was ideal. I did not think so at the time. I do not think so now. But I am convinced that that is not the cause of the recent aggressions. Nor do I believe that it is to be found in the controversy as to the merits of one form of Government or another. Japan is nominally a Parliamentary

Monarchy, yet she is one of the chief aggressors. Portugal is governed by a Dictator, yet she constantly insists on her loyalty to the Anglo-Portuguese alliance. We should have been quite ready to work for peace with the Russian Government, although we do not agree with its constitutional form nor its views on economics or religion. When people deplore the conflict of ideologies they are either the victims of a phrase or they mean something much more than a divergence of opinion on constitutional questions. There is, in fact, a conflict of ideologies of great importance. But it concerns not the internal government of the various states but the external policies which they pursue. On the one side there is the view that the only thing that counts in international matters is force, that, quite literally, the only legitimate test as to which of two sides of an international quarrel is right is to ask which is the stronger, and that all talk about essential justice and perpetual peace is just the sentimental balderdash with which the weak try to conceal their inferiority or the strong to palliate their aggression. This position has been openly asserted by the spokesmen of Germany and Italy. Thus Hitler, in *Mein Kampf*, says, at page 208: — 'The only earthly criterion of whether an enterprise is right or wrong is its success', and Mussolini, in the *Sunday Sun* of October 20th, 1930: — 'Imperialism is the eternal and immutable law of life'. It is quite true that Hitler and Mussolini often claim that theirs is the policy of peace and revile the League Powers as the real disturbers of tranquillity. But an Axis peace means a peace after the unspecified demands of the Axis Powers for reunion of race, space to live and strategic safety have been granted, and no limits are or can be placed on these demands.

On the other side is an increasingly definite challenge to this whole system. To us, the Totalitarian gospel of force is a gospel of anarchy. The triumph of the German conception means the destruction of all that we hold as essential to civilization. We believe that underlying all human relationships, national not less than individual, are certain fundamental principles of right and wrong and that it is only on the acknowledgement of this truth that any tolerable international system can be built. Force is doubtless (in our view) necessary but it must be controlled by machinery devised to secure justice and not left to the haphazard and necessarily prejudiced direction of the parties to any dispute. That is what we mean by the supremacy of law, the existence of some standard superior to individual nations, to which they all must bow. No doubt that involves a limitation of national sovereignty since it abolishes the unrestricted right of war.

There is nothing novel in this controversy. Right through the centuries there have always been the two currents of opinion, those who believe that patriotism must have a moral basis, and those who do not. Indeed, the German view was more or less predominant in most countries until quite lately. The pursuit of *la gloire* was popularly held in France to be a sufficient defence for a war. And in England many believed that patriotism required us to say 'My country, right or wrong', just as the German patriots say *Deutschland uber Alles*.

We ought, then, to be cautious about indulging in unsparing condemnation of our opponents, but we may legitimately claim that, whatever may have been our actual shortcomings, we do desire our Government to stand firm for the principle that no nation should attempt to take the law into its own hands and resort to aggressive war to enforce its 'rights'. Aggressive war *is* an international crime, and it is the duty of all peace-loving and law-abiding states to prevent or stop it. That is, or ought to be, the fundamental tenet of our international creed. It should be easy for us to take this line since we have long established the principle of the supremacy of the law in our own country.

It is, then, in accordance with our general political ideas that we should have been the defenders of the League of Nations in its purpose to bring law and order, right and justice into international relations. That is its central object. The first step must be the abolition of aggressive war. So long as that exists all international progress is precarious. If and when the unlawfulness of aggressive war has been firmly established, other progress may be possible. That is the real issue. It is not a question whether this or that international arrangement is satisfactory, but whether any nation desiring a change shall be entitled to attempt to carry it out by main force. If the advocates of force succeed in imposing their ideas on the world, the outlook is black indeed. A world composed of warring nations struggling to destroy one another and inevitably destroying themselves in the process can only lead to the annihilation of our civilization.

Aggressive war wherever it occurs is a danger to the peace of the world. As such, it is a far graver attack on British interests than any injury to British trade or territory unless that attack is also the result of aggressive war. We ought, therefore, to be ready to join with other peace-loving nations in stopping such war, if necessary by force, since it has been established that no remonstrance, however weighty, can be trusted to restrain an aggressor. Action in restraint of aggression should be based on the conception that it is an international crime and a breach of the supremacy of law in international affairs. Every precaution should therefore be taken to secure that force should be used by the peace powers only against a country clearly shown to be an aggressor.

How, then, should these principles be made effective? Some believe that the use of force, however limited, is illegitimate and that the only way out is to declare that in no circumstances will we fight, to abolish all our warlike armaments by land, sea and air, and to accept whatever consequences such a policy may bring as preferable to war. That is the full Pacifist position. I am unable to accept this view. The case for it is put in two ways. Firstly, war is said to be essentially immoral and un-Christian. Secondly, it is contended that war is futile and, above all, incapable of producing peace. As to what may be called the ethical objection, I cannot agree that if an unjustifiable attack is made or threatened against a State, which can be stopped by other States, they do wrong if they join that State in exerting sufficient force to prevent or stop the attack. Such action is not a case of arbitrary violence or even self-defence; it is the forcible prevention of injustice. It may be true that it is impossible by force to improve the morals of the aggressor. But that is not the point. I cannot think that, if a bystander has the power to stop a crime, by force if necessary, and does not do so, he is free from blame. Nor can I see anything in the Bible which conflicts with that view. No-one would, I presume, contend that the Old Testament condemns the use of force in all cases. Nor, in my view, is the teaching of the New Testament in this respect inconsistent with that of the Old. Certainly no specific reversal of the Old Testament rule can be cited. If I understand rightly the argument of the Pacifists, they do not rely so much on any specific text but rather contend that Gospel morality is based on love, and war is inconsistent with love. To go into this argument fully would require a book by itself. I can only hope to state the barest heads of my reply here and now. I would say, then, that the use of force does not in itself seem to me inconsistent with love. If I knock a man down to stop him from throwing another over a cliff, I do him no real injury, and what applies to individuals applies equally to nations. But it is said the cases are not parallel. Force applied to prevent a man from committing a crime affects only the would-be criminal. War injures and slays thousands of people including helpless invalids and children, who have no kind of responsibility for aggression committed by the Government of their country. That may be so, but if you belong to an organized group, you must share its responsibility. If it were not so, no coercive international action would ever be possible. When we cut off imports from Russia in order to compel the Russian Government to release British subjects who had been wrongfully arrested, no doubt the merchants and others immediately affected were guiltless of the arrest. But they were Russian subjects enjoying the protection of the Russian Government and receiving the benefits which any organized administration confers on those who are subject to it. Corporate responsibility is a necessary consequence of corporate life. Granted that a Government is engaged in aggression on an innocent neighbour and that the only way of stopping the aggression is by force, I cannot think that the fact that innocent subjects of the aggressive Government may suffer makes it wrong to take the forcible action necessary to protect the victim State. But we should recognize that war is in itself a horrible thing, that it should only be employed in the last resort when no pacific means of settlement is available and then only when sanctioned by some properly constituted international authority.

The final pacifist contention is that war is useless, that it never does any good and that to try to maintain peace by making war is palpably absurd. It is said to be as absurd as Beelzebub casting out devils — so drifting back through a complete misapplication of a passage in scripture to the ethical argument which I have already discussed. War, from the point of view I am now dealing with, is only a kind of force. Is then force never of value to stop a wicked or criminal action? Of course not. Human civilized society is largely based on the contrary hypothesis, of which the policeman is the embodiment. When George III called out the troops to stop the Lord George Gordon riots, the operation was instantly successful. When the Powers represented at the Nyon Conference declared that their fleets would sink any submarine indulging in piratical action, no further action of the kind took place, and indeed history is full of instances where the use of force has been completely successful in preventing lawless or criminal action. No doubt it is seldom of use except negatively. You can force a man not to do something easily enough if you have sufficient power to do so. It is very much more difficult to compel him to do something, and impossible to make him think anything.

And if force is not to be used to stop aggression what do the pacifists propose in its place? Sometimes they suggest that if, by international action, you can show that an aggressive act is generally reprobated, that will deter the aggressor. It is not so. Experience points the other way. Japan went on with her Manchurian enterprise in 1931-32 though practically every civilized country disapproved it. Italy consummated her invasion of Abyssinia though it was unanimously condemned by the States represented in the Assembly of the League of Nations, as well as by the United States, and was definitely approved by no country.

Another pacifist suggestion is that a totally disarmed state would not be a threat to anyone and therefore need not fear aggression. This is pure delusion. An aggressor State enjoys trampling on the defenceless. Czechoslovakia, after being deprived of her fortifications and her arms, was invaded by Germany, her territory occupied and her population enslaved, and the recent cases of Finland, Norway, Denmark and Holland are even more in point. The present Lord Russell, when he was still a strong pacifist, was surely more correct when he argued that if we disarmed ourselves, the Empire would be taken from us and we should have to obey the behests of our armed neighbours.

For these reasons, which could be multiplied, pacifism furnishes no solution to the problem. Still less can I believe in armed isolation, which means either pure national cowardice — reluctance to accept the responsibilities of our position — or is based on the strange doctrine that we can by our own unaided strength maintain our Empire and its trade. Certain it is that if we will not help others they will not help us. In view of the avowed belief in aggressive force in Germany and some other countries, armed isolation can only be regarded as a particularly foolish form of national suicide.

The truth is that the British Empire is and must remain part of the general community of nations. It cannot reject the responsibilities of that position, neither can it discharge them unaided. That has been true, more or less, for a long time past. But in former days it was obscured by the fact that the British Islands and indeed almost the whole of the Empire seemed to be immune from direct attack so long as we held command of the sea. Even so, we were forced into closer and closer relations with other countries as the effectiveness of our sea defences was gradually diminished by the progress of invention. Moreover, our unavoidable and increasing dependence on foreign trade, coupled with our very genuine, though sometimes tactless and unpractical, desire to take our share in the struggle for international justice compelled us to take an active part in the life of the nations around us. Then came the World War of 1914 and the demonstration that the development of submarine and air warfare had enormously increased our vulnerability. It was no longer safe for us to trust to the sea to give us time to improvise defence against a sudden danger.

It had become clear that preparedness in some form or another was essential for national safety. Continental nations with no sea to protect them had long realized this. They had sought safety in arms and alliances. But those expedients were unsatisfactory. To make a nation secure, armament must make it stronger than any probable enemy. That means that its probable enemy will become relatively weaker and in consequence be in danger. Hence the inevitable armaments race with all its attendant evils. Alliances are only another way of increasing armament. To meet them, the only resource is to form counter-alliances, with the result that two or more groups of countries are created, anxiously watching one another and each justifying the growth of its armaments expenditure by dwelling on the enmity of its neighbours.

We saw the process in full operation before 1914 and again in the last seven or eight years before the outbreak of the Polish war.

It was to meet this situation, after it had produced the catastrophe of 1914-1918, that the League of Nations was proposed. It was no new idea. Something of the kind had been repeatedly suggested. But the colossal scale of modern war made it urgent to find some means of national security. Here, then, was a plan by which might be obtained all and more than all the security given by alliances without the very grave disadvantages that ordinary alliances lead to. Let the peace-loving nations combine, not against this or that Power, but against all aggressors. Let them form, as it were, an international mutual assurance society.

It was an essential part of this conception that, in the last resort, adequate force should be on the side of those who were attacked. In such a defensive force we must play an important part. That meant that we might have to join in resisting aggression in any part of the civilized world. Here was the difficulty for us as for other nations. Immediately came the cry that it was unreasonable or even immoral to ask that British blood and treasure should be expended to defend distant countries like Manchuria or Abyssinia or Czechoslovakia. What, it was asked, does it matter to us what happens to people who dwell in such places? Let us, then, avoid 'commitments' to act in defence of others and confine ourselves to the protection of our own so-called interests. Evidently such a view struck at the very foundation of the League of Nations or indeed of any international organization of peace. Unless it is agreed that peace is essential to us as it is to all civilized peoples, and that any serious breach of it wherever it occurs is a threat to the peace of the whole world, no world co-operation for peace is possible. Conversely, if these propositions are admitted, then resistance to aggression is vital to our interests wherever in the civilized world that aggression may take place. At the Peace Conference in 1919, this proposition had been easily accepted. We had all just been through four years of agonizing warfare, embracing almost the whole world, which had originated in a political murder in the extreme corner of the south-east of Europe. Evidently what had happened once might happen again. Peace *was* indivisible and the new structure for peace should if possible extend all over the civilized world. Perhaps the representatives of the nations in 1919 over-estimated the value of experience. Perhaps they ought to have limited the obligation to take the first active steps for peace to those nations who were nearest to the outbreak of war. Certain it is that only by vigorous and courageous leadership could the Governments of the world have been kept up to their essential duties under the Covenant. As we have seen, that leadership failed. Till 1931 the League had not to deal with crises of the first importance. Accordingly, the important States operated its machinery with great success. Then succeeded a period of great economic difficulty and consequently of great reluctance to take risks. Hence, in the Manchurian, the Abyssinian and, later, the Czechoslovakian disputes, as well as in the Disarmament Conference, the policy of the French and British Governments, the natural leaders of the League, seemed to be dominated by the desire to avoid immediate responsibilities whatever might be the ultimate consequences. To their countrymen and still more their countrywomen, naturally disposed to accept official guidance in foreign affairs, our leaders boasted that they had kept us out of war. They did not add that, so far as that object had been achieved, it had been at the cost of the Chinese, the Abyssinians and the Czechs and, alas! of our national reputation for courage and good faith. And the policy was not even successful in its immediate object.

In order to resist the aggression on Poland, we then reverted to the old policy of alliances together with offers of negotiated concessions. It was probably the only possible policy at the time it was begun. But it is open to the objections already pointed out, nor does anyone pretend that it can permanently succeed in maintaining peace. Its most convincing advocates represent it as a stage in the return to a policy based on some League or Association of Nations. But what is that to be?

Recently, a demand has grown up for a Federation of the democracies of the world. This, of course, is as old as *Locksley Hall*. For a poet writing in the middle of the nineteenth century, in the full tide of the Victorian belief in representative institutions, it was natural enough to see a great vision of the Parliament of Man, the Federation of the World. And it is much to be hoped that in the future something of the kind may be possible. But we have to deal not with ultimate aspirations but with immediate practical necessities:

How can we prevent war? We must therefore look rather carefully at any actual proposition such as 'Union Now'.[1] The plan is this: — Let us have an international constitution on the model of that of the United States. There would be a House of Representatives, elected by the different countries on a basis of population. Even on this point obvious difficulties arise, since some of the least warlike countries, like China, have the largest number of inhabitants. In order to correct such inequalities, there would be a Senate elected by States. These Houses would decide by majority on such questions as peace and war, tariffs, currency and the like, which are of major international importance, so that a great country like the United States or Great Britain might find herself committed to war, or to free trade, against its own desires, by a combination of other states. I have difficulty in believing that American opinion would tolerate such an arrangement. I am afraid that English and Dominion opinion would be equally hard to convince. Some years ago, a group of able young men — for they were young then — with the countenance of Lord Milner set about constructing a federal constitution for the British Empire. They called themselves the Round Table and they had considerable financial and literary backing. With great industry and imagination they drew up a sketch of the proposed constitution. It was a most attractive scheme and enquiries were set on foot as to what support it would have. In Great Britain the atmosphere was friendly if a little sceptical. But when the project was mooted in the Dominions, it was so decisively rejected that its promoters regretfully abandoned it. They found that there was an insurmountable conviction among all Dominion statesmen that their countries would never agree to accept the rule of any Imperial legislature or executive in which they would each of them have only a minority voice.

If that is the feeling in the British Commonwealth, with

[1] *Union Now*, by Clarence Streit, published in London and Toronto, by Jonathan Cape, 1939.

all the unifying influences and sympathies which exist in it, how much more would it appear in a number of States separated in many cases by language and literature and even general culture and in all cases by great and proudly-held historical tradition? It is to be noted in passing that, as far as the British Empire is concerned, no difficulties of this kind have occurred in the League of Nations. On the contrary, an organization in which the Dominions have complete freedom and equality and by which they can co-operate with other peace-loving countries, including the United Kingdom, in the maintenance of international law and order has been, as far as the unity and good-fellowship of the British Empire are concerned, an unqualified success.

If, then, we are to seek any model for an International Constitution, there seems at least as much to be said for the British Empire as for the United States. After all, is it not true that even in America the sentiment for State Rights was long a great danger to national unity and led to a terrible Civil War? How far it exists at present I do not know. But the careful checks and balances of the Constitution show how keenly the framers were alive to that danger. Nor has the result been altogether encouraging internationally. America is, I doubt not, admirably governed in domestic affairs. But the extreme conservatism of the Constitution does create difficulties in the way of international action. I remember an American statesman explaining to me at considerable length how, with its constitution, it was really impossible for America to have any foreign policy at all! That may have been an exaggeration. But it points to a grave danger in trying to apply such a system to an International Constitution which would deal exclusively with foreign affairs. I do not see how there could be an International President, or an International Administration of the American type. Yet without those two elements, would the American Constitution have worked at all? I should have thought not, for they seem to supply almost all the motive power for progress, the constitutional functions of Congress and the

Judiciary being mainly to check innovations. However that may be, is it not manifest that the problem of organizing world peace is so different from that of creating a Constitution for the American States or even the British Dominions that analogies from the British Empire or the United States are almost certain to be misleading?

I do not forget that the author of *Union Now* proposes that his scheme shall apply at first to the democracies, and that other countries shall only be admitted when they become democracies. In other words, he proposes to Federalize the peace bloc, with the addition of the United States.[1] I am afraid that the immediate result of this would be the crystallization of a counter-group of those countries which believe in some form of autocracy. Must we not still be content to make only such an advance as may effectively unite the powers for peace without disturbing more than necessary the passionately held doctrine of National Sovereignty? Mr. Streit is, I agree, perfectly right in believing that this doctrine is the great enemy of International Co-operation. It must be so, and I would like to assure Mr. Streit that we were well aware of it at Paris. Had we doubted it, we should have been speedily disillusioned. At every stage we were warned by British and still more by American critics that we must keep clear of a super-state. Senator Lodge and his appropriately named Battalion of Death denounced the relatively slight invasion of National Sovereignty involved in limiting the right of war, not because it did not go far enough, but because it went too far. The whole clamour raised against the League by its British mercantile and bureaucratic critics has been based on the charge that British policy has been made subservient to Geneva. If it is true that the League failures from 1931 onwards have been chiefly due to the unchecked resurrection of National Sovereignty in its most extreme form, it certainly seems very optimistic to believe that it is at present practicable to induce the Powers to accept a much more drastic invasion of Nation-

[1] I rather gather that other advocates of the scheme have dropped America.

alism such as would result from the adoption of a Federal Union. I should be afraid, on the contrary, that the isolationists would welcome such a movement as demonstrating the inevitable result of any approach to international co-operation and would use it as a justification for their attack on any League or Association.

Surely if, with Tennyson and Mr. Streit, we believe that the Federation of Mankind is the ultimate goal to aim at, the proper course is to proceed step by step. That is the plan which we in England have pursued for some centuries, not without success. There is no method of reform open to humanity which can proceed without disturbance, and that disturbance, unless great care is taken, produces evils of various kinds. Nor can we hope that any change, however beneficial, will be carried through with unbroken success. I have tried to show in the preceding pages that, until 1931, the League had operated with growing efficiency and authority. I have urged that its three great failures in Manchuria, Abyssinia and Czechoslovakia — especially in the last two cases — were due to the existence in France and England of Ministries unwilling to fulfil their solemnly-assumed obligations under the Covenant. I do not say that the League system is incapable of improvement; I agree with President Wilson's presentation of it at the Conference in Paris: — It is a 'living thing' capable of growth and decay. But even now it is a great improvement in many ways on any form of peace-keeping machinery that preceded it. What is wanted is that the decay should be arrested and the powers of the League revived and in certain respects intensified. As regards sanctions, the general principle that an attack on any of the members of the League is a matter of concern to all of them is sound and should be retained, provided it is clearly understood that action suitable in one case is not necessarily suitable in all. To that I will return directly. With respect to the other powers and duties of the League, there is very widespread agreement that what I have called the non-contentious work of the League has been very successful and should be continued and indeed vigorously developed, whether it has been done by the I.L.O. or by the Assembly or Council of the League and their Committees. This is equally true, as I have also pointed out, even of the minor contentious or semi-contentious work, which has come before the League or before the Permanent Court of International Justice. For all this kind of work, a world-wide organization is almost essential. The general framework of the League, including the Council, Assembly and Secretariat, and the analogous organs of the I.L.O., should therefore be maintained; and that is equally true of the Hague Court.

Nevertheless, this does not alter the fact that the League has not prevented, in several very important cases, a 'resort to war' in circumstances forbidden by the Covenant, of which the war in the Far East and the series of totalitarian aggressions are the gravest and most dangerous to world peace.

An examination of League history in this respect shows two things. The first is that remonstrance, however general and well-founded, will not alone stop an aggressive power from carrying out its policy. Secondly, there has been a lack of solidarity, of *esprit de corps*, in the League Powers which should have induced them jointly and almost automatically to resist an attack on any one of their number. That is partly due to want of imagination caused by geographical remoteness or other considerations, partly to the unfamiliarity of the truth that peace is in itself the greatest of national interests, and partly to the want of vigour and precision in the League organization. I believe that all these defects would be lessened if there was, inside the framework of the League, a confederation or confederations of geographically related powers with appropriate confederated organs.[1] The most obviously necessary of these bodies would be a European Confederation. There is a movement in this direction and it should be continued and developed after

---

[1] It will be observed that in many respects the proposals which follow are substantially the same as those known as Pan-Europa.

the war into what should become a definite Confederation of European States, the central object of which should be the preservation of European peace. It should be open to European members of the League who fully accept the principle that aggression is an international crime and are prepared to use all their strength to protect victims of it in Europe. A European International General Staff and a Secretariat would be needed, and possibly other organs. The Confederation would be autonomous in the sense that it would not be subject to the control of any other international authority. But it would remain in close touch with the League and would notify the Council and Assembly of its proceedings. There must be no rivalry between the two organizations, but, on the contrary, the closest co-operation.[1]

Obviously what has been said is a mere indication of the underlying idea. Much else would require elaboration with the object of increasing and emphasizing the Confederation's corporate life. Questions of social and economic progress, including possibly a common currency and a common tariff policy and, it may be, a Confederation flag, would doubtless arise. If, as is vital for permanent peace, a scheme of international limitation of armaments is adopted, it might probably involve an international air force under the control of the European General Staff.

This still leaves non-European questions to be dealt with, such as Japanese aggression in the Far East. No doubt the obvious plan would be to have Confederations for other regions, similar to that proposed for Europe. But it is doubtful whether that is practicable in either Asia or America. I submit that for all places outside Europe, the best course would be to leave the Covenant of the League as it is, subject to some clarification of the provisions of Article 16 and the limitation of the requirement for unanimity (if it exists) under Article 11. Article 19 which deals with the pacific correction of unsatisfactory international conditions should also be reconsidered and, if found necessary, strengthened.

[1] Definite proposals on this subject will be found in Appendix III.

CONCLUSIONS

As regards Article 16 the point that should be made clear is that, though the obligation to take action against an aggressor rests on each member of the League individually, yet the action contemplated is joint action. In other words, it is an individual duty to take common action. Further, the action is to be preventive rather than penal, and is only obligatory if it is reasonably likely to be successful. With modifications on these lines, I believe the League might still be very useful where no special Confederations exist.

All this, it may be said, is only another piece of machinery. After it has been created, the fundamental difficulty will remain. No machinery can do more than facilitate the action of the peoples. Unless they and their Governments really put the enforcement of the law and the maintenance of peace as the first and greatest of national interests, no Confederation or Federation can compel them to do so. But I believe that Confederation — that is, the constitutional union of independent States, inside the general framework of the League, may help to make men realize that it is only by international co-operation that peace can be preserved. Beyond that, we pass from the region of political reform to that of spiritual regeneration. Discussion of that kind is outside the scope of this book. I will only venture to express the hope that my fellow-countrymen will, in these momentous matters, recognize their duty to themselves, their country and their God.

APPENDIX I

MEMORANDUM ON PROPOSALS FOR
DIMINISHING THE OCCASION OF FUTURE
WARS
(*Autumn, 1916*)

IT is estimated that the total number of killed and wounded in this war approaches 50,000,000 — more than the population of the British islands — and that of these 7,000,000 have been killed. These numbers include the women and children of Armenia, Syria and the occupied territories, but by far the largest part consists of young men in the prime of health, strength and ability. We have so far spent between 2000 and 3000 millions of pounds. Assuming our Allies have spent as much and our enemies half as much again the total expenditure has been not less than some 8000 or 9000 millions, and may well have been much more. Some part of this has gone to the nourishment, lodging and clothing of the troops and other personnel. But a very large proportion even of this expenditure is due to war conditions. It is safe therefore to say that the total sum actually wasted is now many thousands of millions. In addition a considerable amount of fixed property, shipping, and goods have been destroyed, representing certainly many millions more, and there have been no doubt other incidental losses. Taken altogether, the impoverishment of the world by waste of life, waste of labour, and destruction of material has been appalling. Human suffering has resulted on a scale unprecedented in the history of the world. Apart from the spectacular horrors, such as submarining, Zeppelin raids, the atrocities in France and Belgium, the Armenian massacres, the cold-blooded starvation of the Syrian population and the cruelties to the Poles, Serbians, and other inhabitants of conquered countries, the ordinary incidents of modern warfare are terrible. A small battle recorded as the capture of a few yards of trench involves the death by torture of hundreds, perhaps thousands of young men, the maiming or blinding of as many more, and for the lucky ones horrible wounds inflicted by jagged fragments of high-explosive shells. Perhaps even harder to bear are the anxiety, the grief and the bereavement which fall on the women at home.

This is not all. People talk of the self-sacrifice and courage of those who fight, and it is indeed magnificent. But they forget the other side of the shield. Crimes of cruelty, lust, dishonesty, drunkenness have marked the advance of almost every victorious army in history. German outrages in the early months of the war differed only in degree from the proceedings of other armies in similar circumstances. Nor do the evil results of war stop with the fighting. On the whole, there is little evidence that the civilian population at home have been sobered by the magnitude of the catastrophe or are bracing themselves to meet the fearful social and economic problems which will confront us when peace at length arrives. It may well be that, when the war is over, we shall be only at the beginning of our troubles.

All this is very trite. My excuse for setting it out is to emphasize how disastrous is war in general and this war in particular. It is not too much to say that it has endangered the fabric of our civilization, and if it is to be repeated the whole European system may probably disappear in anarchy. It is surely, therefore, most urgent that we should try to think out some plan to lessen the possibility of future war. Even if we succeed in destroying German militarism, that will not be enough. Militarism exists everywhere, even in this country. If the militarism of Germany is destroyed, what security have we that some other country may not take her place? Nor can we hope that the settlement after the war will remove all causes of quarrel. Whatever shape the territorial arrangements may ultimately take, we can see enough of them already to be certain that they will not be final. Assuming it to be true that a territorial settlement should be based on nationality, how can we defend the allotment of Constantinople to Russia, of Dalmatia to Italy, or Macedonia to Serbia, of the Banat to Roumania, or even of the German parts of Alsace to France? And there will be many other causes of quarrel. Poland may not improbably be bitterly disappointed. Hungary will be restless under spoliation. Austria will be torn by political fear of, and racial sympathy for, Germany. Germany herself will be sore and unquiet. It is not improbable that Russia will be in serious domestic trouble, from which a military despotism may well emerge. The South-East of Europe will be, as heretofore, a prolific breeding-ground for every kind of civil and military disturbance.

What then can be done? The only possible way out appears to be to try to substitute for war some other way of settling international disputes. Two expedients suggest themselves: arbitration and conference of the Powers — European Concert. The difficulty of arbitration is to discover the arbitrators to whom sovereign Powers will be content to submit questions of vital importance. The same objection does not apply to conferences. But, as was found in the present war, no machinery exists to force unwilling Powers to agree to a conference and await its decision. It would be simple to include in the Treaty of Peace a general agreement to that effect. But if a group of Powers were determined on war, how are they to be compelled to enter a conference? In other words, what is to be the sanction? A provision that all the Powers shall combine to punish by force of arms a breach of the treaty will probably by itself be ineffective. As far as Europe is concerned, there will always be a tendency for the Powers to form themselves into two groups more or less equal in strength, and if one of these becomes aggressive it may and probably will ignore all treaties. Under these circumstances the risks of war are so great that few countries would enter it merely in support of treaties and international right, and the settlement of the dispute will be left to war between the Powers immediately concerned. If, however, an instrument could be found which would exert considerable pressure on a recalcitrant Power without causing excessive risk to the Powers using it, a solution of the difficulty might perhaps be found. I believe that in blockade as developed in this war such an instrument exists. No doubt for its full effect an overwhelming naval power is requisite. But much could be done even by overwhelming financial power, and with the two combined no modern State could ultimately resist its pressure. Suppose in July 1914 it had been possible for the Entente Powers to say to Germany and Austria, unless the ultimatum to Serbia is modified or a conference is called, we will cut off all commercial and financial intercourse from you, it is very doubtful whether the Central Powers would have proceeded. If the United States could have been induced to join in such a declaration, the effect would have been enormously increased. And though it is certainly hopeless to expect America to fight in a European quarrel unless her interests are directly affected, it does not seem so certain that she would refuse to join in organized economic action to preserve peace. It is assumed as a necessary condition of this proposal that a territorial settlement of a reasonable sort is arrived at in the treaty, and its maintenance is guaranteed by the signatory Powers. It would enormously help if some effective agreement for the limitation of armaments could also be arranged; and in the first draft of this paper I had suggested provisions with that object. But, in view of the convincing criticism by Sir E. Crowe, I have decided to abandon that part of the scheme.

I append a rough draft to explain the working of the scheme.

PROPOSALS FOR MAINTENANCE OF FUTURE PEACE

The High Contracting Powers further agree that the territorial arrangements hereinbefore set forth shall remain unaltered for the next five years. At, or if any of the High Contracting Powers so demands then before, the end of that period a conference of the High Contracting Powers shall be summoned, and any rearrangements of territory which have become necessary or desirable shall be then considered, and, if agreed upon, shall be forthwith carried out.

If any difference or controversy shall arise between any of the High Contracting Powers, with respect to the meaning of any of the articles of this treaty, or with respect to the rights of any of the parties thereto, or with respect to any other matter, a conference of the Powers shall forthwith be summoned, and the controversy shall be submitted to it, and no action shall be taken by any of the parties to the controversy until the conference has met and considered the matter, and has either come to a decision thereon or has failed for a period of three months after its meeting to come to such a decision. Any decision agreed upon at such conference shall be maintained and enforced by all the High Contracting Powers as if it were one of the articles of this treaty.

Each of the High Contracting Powers guarantees and agrees to maintain the provisions of this treaty if necessary by force of arms, and in particular undertakes that if any Power shall refuse or fail to submit any controversy to a conference as provided in the last preceding article of this treaty, or shall otherwise infringe any of the provisions of this treaty, each of the High Contracting Powers shall thereupon cut off all commercial and financial intercourse with the wrongdoing Power, and as far as possible shall prevent such Power from having any commercial or financial intercourse with any other Power, whether a party to this treaty or not; and it is hereby further agreed that for the purpose of enforcing this provision, any of the High Contracting Powers may detain any ship or goods belonging to any of the subjects of the wrong-doing Power or coming from or destined for any person residing in the territory of such Power, and with the same object may take any other similar step which may seem desirable or necessary.

APPENDIX II

My Dear Prime Minister,

I am sorry to say that I have arrived at the conclusion that I ought to resign my office.

Let me in the first place assure you that this conclusion is not due to any personal difficulty. On the contrary, I feel that I owe you and all my colleagues much gratitude for your kindness and consideration. Least of all have I any grievance against Bridgeman. He will, I hope, have already told you that throughout our time at Geneva we worked together in the closest agreement. Apart from one or two questions of procedure, I do not think that we had any differences of opinion. Certainly we had none with respect to the policy to be pursued at the Conference. It is true that in technical matters I had to rely chiefly on the advice given to us by our naval experts. Here again we were extremely fortunate in having as our chief adviser so able and wide-minded an officer as Admiral Field.

The difficulty is, I am sorry to say, much more serious, for I cannot conceal from myself that on the broad policy of Disarmament the majority of the Cabinet and I are not agreed. To quote a well-known phrase, we 'do not mean the same thing'.

I believe that a general reduction and limitation of armaments is essential to the peace of the world, and that on peace depends not only the existence of the British Empire but even that of European civilization itself. It follows that I regard the limitation of armaments as by far the most important public question of the day. Further, I am convinced that no considerable limitation of armaments can be obtained except by international agreement. On the attainment of such an agreement, therefore, in my judgement, the chief energies of the Government ought to be concentrated. I do not say that it should be bought at any price. But I do say that it is of greater value than any other political object.

Much that happened during the session last spring of the Preparatory Commission for the Reduction and Limitation of Armaments was to me of a disquieting nature. Over and over again I was compelled by my instructions to maintain propositions in the Commission which were difficult to reconcile with any serious desire for the success of its labours. For the most part these instructions turned on smaller points, but the cumulative effect on the minds of the Commission was very unfortunate, and was largely the cause of its comparative ill-success. In particular the representatives of the Admiralty scarcely concealed their opinion that the whole of the Commission's proceedings were futile, if not pernicious.

I do not say that the majority of the Cabinet shared the views of the Admiralty in this respect. But they certainly seemed to take very little interest in the success or failure of the Commission which was to me of the utmost moment.

Nevertheless, when you were good enough to ask me to be one of the British representatives at the recent Conference, I gladly accepted. I thought that there was little doubt of agreement being reached. The only snag that I could see was the celebrated question of 'parity' between the United States and ourselves, and on that matter we were given full authority to accept the American point of view. It is true that we were urged if possible to avoid any limitation of the number of smaller cruisers, but even here we were given discretion. Indeed, to have gone to a Conference on the limitation of armaments and to have refused to allow one of the principal categories to be limited would have been hopeless, as no doubt my colleagues saw.

I repeat, therefore, that I regarded agreement as almost certain and I believed that agreement between the three great naval powers to a reduction of their armaments would be of great assistance in facilitating the efforts of the Preparatory Commission for general limitation. Its failure would of course be a corresponding disaster. But I did not contemplate that.

When we reached Geneva, it quickly became apparent that we had been much too sanguine. In particular, there was no hope of agreement unless it included a limitation of the smaller cruisers, and an unqualified acceptance of the principle of parity. So clear was this, not only to us but to the Cabinet, that we received an urgent telegram from them directing us to agree to parity, which as a matter of fact we had already done. Parity in our minds and in those of the other negotiators meant what is now called 'mathematical equality'. But this was not apparently realized by some of our colleagues. As soon as they did realize that we had agreed to it in this sense, they became much disturbed. But for some time we were allowed to go on with the negotiations, doubtful and difficult as they were.

At last it seemed that we were well on the road to an agreement. At the suggestion of the Americans we had been in consultation with the Japanese and had arrived at a common formula with them. This we had presented to the chief American delegates and they had told us that there was no insurmountable difficulty in agreeing to it except on one point, namely, the question of whether the smaller cruisers were or were not to be allowed to carry an 8-inch gun. Even on this question suggestions for a compromise had been discussed between us which seemed to furnish good hopes of success. But it was just the prospect of success which was agitating those of our colleagues who had come to believe that what is now called mathematical equality between us and the Americans of the smaller cruisers was a danger to the Empire, and accordingly, notwithstanding our protests, the Cabinet sent us a peremptory summons to come home.

You will remember the discussion at the first Cabinet after our return over which you presided. The whole contention of those whose opinions I have been describing was that since we were pledged to parity we should somehow or other avoid an agreement.

The majority of the Cabinet, however, decided that we should be authorized to continue the negotiations broadly on the lines on which we had begun, subject to such modifications as the Admiralty and the Cabinet might think essential.

Accordingly another Cabinet was held three days after your departure to consider these modifications. Meanwhile two things had happened: In the first place, news had come through from Washington saying that the Americans attached vital importance to the permission to mount 8-inch guns in the secondary cruisers; secondly, a proposal had been made to meet the view of the opponents of an agreement that we should suggest that the agreement could only be until 1931 when a Conference under the Washington Treaty is due, and until that time all parties should enjoy complete liberty as to the size of gun to be mounted in the secondary cruisers, it being understood that the whole of the questions involved should come up for discussion again in 1931. Of this proposal the Chancellor of the Exchequer, who was the leader of those who feared the results of an agreement, was a vehement supporter. But when the matter came to be considered by the Cabinet he changed his attitude, avowedly because he thought such a proposal would not improbably produce an agreement with the Americans which he was determined if possible to avoid. The majority of the Cabinet, though most of them did not accept his reasons, agreed with his conclusions, in spite of the opposition of the First Lord of the Admiralty and myself, who felt that without some latitude there was no hope of success in the difficult negotiations before us.

No doubt the adoption of the 8-inch gun as a normal weapon for the secondary cruisers would be a great misfortune. But if the Americans insist on so arming them we cannot prevent it. Surely it would have been far better to have obtained such limitation as we could get even if it did not extend very far. In any case, I thought, and think, the breakdown of the Conference is little short of a catastrophe.

I accordingly informed the Cabinet that if, in consequence of this decision, the Conference broke down, I must reserve my full liberty of action.

We returned to Geneva. As soon as we arrived it became clear that without a compromise on the 8-inch gun question there was no hope of an agreement, and I so informed the Cabinet. At the same time we suggested as a possible way out of the difficulty the adoption of a 7-inch gun. In reply we received a telegram rejecting this suggestion and telling us in so many words that were we not to offer any compromise on the 8-inch gun. A day or two later the Americans put forward the suggestion that if any party so utilized its rights under the Treaty as to cause anxiety to another party, a Conference might be held, and if no agreement were come to, the Treaty should terminate. We were anxious to reply by giving to this suggestion a more specific reference to the 8-inch gun. The effect would have been to postpone the decision of the question until the Americans actually decided to arm the secondary cruisers with 8-inch guns. This also the Government rejected.

I observe that in a recent speech the Chancellor of the Exchequer, brushing away amiable insincerities as to the partial success of the Conference, declares quite bluntly and truly that it has failed. That is undoubtedly the fact. He goes on to say 'We are not able now — and I hope at no future time — to embody in a solemn international agreement any words which would bind us to the principle of mathematical parity in naval strength'. And later he goes on to suggest that we may be able to come to a practical agreement without the aid of a 'paper formula'. I am afraid that in plain English this means that the speaker is not prepared to enter into any further Treaty with the United States for the limitation of naval armaments upon terms which have any prospect of being accepted in America.

What then is the position? I cannot doubt that it means that during the lifetime of the present Government there can be no prospect of a successful negotiation with America for the further limitation of armaments. If that is so, can the League Preparatory Commission usefully meet in November as had been proposed? It is, at best, doubtful. I do not even know whether under the circumstances the American delegates would attend. Even if they did, we should have to admit that for the present an agreement for naval limitation was out of the question, and certain of the Continental Powers have always maintained that limitation of land and air forces must be accompanied by limitation at sea.

It is noteworthy that the extreme nationalist papers in

Paris are already rejoicing in the prospective defeat of disarmament by international agreement. I think they are wrong. I believe it is true that the nations must either disarm or perish. I have great confidence that when the people of this country realize what the issue really is they will share that opinion, and that the peoples of other countries will follow their lead. But for myself I am convinced that inside the Government I can do no more to help disarmament by international agreement. In the late discussions the issue was joined between those in the Government who are devoted to that policy and those who oppose it, and the latter won. All that remains is for those who were defeated to submit or resign. In my view the issues are far too serious to make it legitimate to adopt the first alternative and I must therefore try whether outside the Government I can do more for the cause I have at heart than I have been able to do in my present position.

No reply was received to this letter, owing, no doubt, to Mr. Baldwin's absence in Canada, and on August 25th I sent a further letter, enclosing a Minute summarizing my previous letter and having this additional paragraph: —

What, then, of the future? I look back on the refusal to accept the Treaty of Mutual Assistance, the unconditional rejection of the Protocol, the Ministerial declaration against compulsory arbitration, the partial failure of the Preparatory Commission, and now the breakdown of the Three Power Conference. An advance in the direction first of security, then of arbitration, lastly of disarmament itself, has been tried, and in each case has made little progress. In each case the policy advocated has been more or less completely overruled. As it has been in the past so will it be in the future. The same causes will produce similar effects. For the truth is, however unwilling I am to recognize it, that in these matters my colleagues do not agree with me.

10 Downing Street,
Whitehall.
August 29th, 1927.

My Dear Lord Cecil,

I deeply regret that you have reached the conclusion that you ought to resign your office. It is, indeed, a source of satisfaction that your resignation is not due to any personal difficulty, and I am glad to add my witness to the good personal relations which have always existed between us.

I am concerned at your statement 'that on the broad policy of disarmament the majority of the Cabinet and I are not really agreed'. When, however, I examine the statement of your views on this question I incline to the opinion that, having decided upon resignation, you exaggerate any differences that have arisen, whether recently cr in the earlier days of the Government. Shortly after we came into office our own views on the broad question were stated by the Secretary of State for Foreign Affairs at Geneva in a speech on the subject of the Geneva Protocol in terms previously discussed and approved by the whole Cabinet. From it I take the following extract: —

> 'It is unnecessary to lay stress upon the sympathy felt throughout the British Empire with any effort to improve international machinery for maintaining the peace of the world. Arbitration, disarmament and security are the main themes of the Protocol, and on all these great subjects the British Empire has shown, by deeds as well as words, that it is in the fullest accord with the ideals which have animated the Fifth Assembly of the League. Successive Administrations in Great Britain, with the full approval of the Dominions, have not only favoured arbitration in theory; they have largely availed themselves of it in practice. They have not contented themselves with preaching disarmament; they have disarmed to the limits of national safety. They have taken their full share in creating and supporting the League of Nations

and the Court of International Justice; while the immense sacrifices they have been content to make in the cause of general security are matters of recent history.'

In essence, and apart from emphasis, this policy does not appear to differ materially from your own views even as now stated by you. We have pursued it ever since with results on the peace of the world and on disarmament which, as I shall presently show, have not been inconsiderable.

It is not, I think, on the broad policy of peace and disarmament that our differences, so far as there are differences, arise, so much as on the means by which that policy can be most effectively forwarded. Even here there was at least a large measure of agreement.

As regards the work of the Preparatory Committee of the League you presided over the Sub-Committee which prepared the British case and practically drafted your own instructions, and in your absence your place as Chairman of the Sub-Committee was taken by a colleague whom you certainly will not accuse of luke-warmness in the cause.

As regards the recent Conference of the Three Powers. I will enter into no details at this stage since you refrain from doing so, though here again I think you exaggerate whatever difference existed between the Government and yourself. But this much I must say. I can take no blame for its failure either to myself or to my colleagues who, after my departure and up to the very moment when a telegram from the delegation at Geneva informed them that the Conference was at an end, were still working for such a compromise as might yet attain the twin objects of limitation of armaments and national security which the Conference was summoned to achieve.

As to the future, I refuse to share your pessimism. It is true that no great progress has as yet been made on the lines of the great World Conference to which you refer. The Geneva Protocol did not commend itself to us any more than did the Treaty of Mutual Assistance to our predecessors. But, as I have already noted, progress has been made by other if less ambitious methods. The Washington Conference, the Locarno Treaty, and the settlement with Turkey have all led to some measure of disarmament and indicate that progress can be made on the lines we are pursuing. Year by year our own aggregate expenditure on armaments has fallen, and year by year in the world at large the importance of this question is becoming more deeply felt alike by Governments and peoples. I am not without hope that even the Three Power Conference, notwithstanding its apparent failure, may yet result not only in a possible early reduction in naval armaments, but in the long run in a better understanding of each other's problems and difficulties by the nations concerned. I do not underrate the difficulties. They are, as we have always known, many and great, but that is not in my opinion a reason for throwing up the sponge. It is the task of statesmen to learn from failure no less than from success, and this is more especially the case in an age-long problem that has hitherto baffled all efforts to find a permanent solution. I can only regret that you are no longer willing to continue as our principal representative in the international discussions on disarmament and that I must now seek elsewhere for the help for which I have hitherto turned to you.

Yours very sincerely,

STANLEY BALDWIN.

[The statement that I drafted my own instructions is based on a misunderstanding, which I explained in the House of Lords.]

APPENDIX III

Prepared, by Lord Cecil, for the consideration of the
League of Nations Union

(*September, 1940*)

INTRODUCTORY

We entered the present war to rescue Poland and other
countries from the cruel and unjust attack by the Nazi
tyranny which, if it were to triumph, would endanger the
Liberty and Happiness of all the World. We seek no enlarge-
ments of our territory or economic privilege. We desire that
international relations should be governed not by brute force
but by Freedom, Truth and Justice, in the benefits of which
all nations should equally share. To attain these objects we
believe that the settlement after the War should be on the
following lines.

PRINCIPLES OF WAR SETTLEMENT
PRELIMINARY

1. At the end of the war a conference of the belligerents
must be held to deal with the special issues raised by the war;
such as — the restoration of occupied territories, financial
measures concerned with war damage, provisional measures
to prevent the renewal of a policy of aggression by Germany,
Italy and their allies.

2. As soon as an agreement on these points has been reached
invitations should be issued for an international congress
consisting of the belligerents and some at least of the neutral
States, to decide on the terms of a world settlement including
such financial and territorial arrangements as may be desirable for the establishment of good relations between all
nations.

3. Whatever territorial or financial arrangements are made,
the two vital problems to be solved will be the Maintenance
of Future Peace, and Economic and Social Reconstruction.

4. These problems are closely related. Peace is essential to Reconstruction; Reconstruction is vital to Peace. Both depend on the Supremacy of Law.

5. The Supremacy of Law in this connection does not mean so much obedience to particular rules governing international intercourse as the recognition that the sovereignty of nations should be limited by certain fundamental principles such as good-faith and justice and the rejection of force as the sole arbiter of international rights.

PEACE-KEEPING

6. If international good-faith and justice are to be observed some authority must be brought into existence which can declare in any particular case what good-faith and justice require. Similarly, if mere force is not to be allowed to determine international controversy, in other words, if aggression is to be prevented, some authority must be entrusted with the duty and given the power to prevent it.

7. It is on the question of what is to be that authority that the fundamental international controversy arises. The Germans hold that there can be no limit to the sovereignty of a State except its power to enforce its will. They think, therefore, that as they claim to have the supreme military power in Europe, they have a right to do whatever they think desirable on that Continent.

8. We, on the contrary, hold that no nation can be trusted to be judge in its own cause, and we point to the events in the Far East, in Abyssinia, in Austria, in Albania, in Czechoslovakia, in Poland before the war, and in other cases since the war began, to show what horrible injustice and cruelty are produced by the German theory.

9. It seems clear that if we reject the domination of a single Power we must look to a combination of Powers, which will both have moral authority to declare what justice and good faith require and will be sufficiently strong to prevent international aggression.

10. That was the main idea underlying the League of Nations. It failed because its members were not prepared to run the risks inevitable if powerful aggressors were to be coerced into abandoning aggression.

In other words, the League Powers did not take their Covenant obligations to keep the peace seriously. A change of attitude on this point is essential if peace is to be preserved by international co-operation.

(*a*) If the British and French Governments with the other members of the League had been prepared forcibly to prevent the Italian invasion of Abyssinia in 1935, we should probably not have been compelled to witness the attacks by the Dictatorships on Austria, China, Czechoslovakia and Albania; nor should we have been driven in circumstances of much greater difficulty to take up arms on behalf of Poland in 1939.

(*b*) That seems obvious to us now and indeed the danger was clear enough to many people at the time. Why, then, did we and others act as we did five years ago?

(*c*) The answer is, in the first place, because we were still thinking in terms of British interests, that is, the trade and territory of Britain. It was said, for instance, that we were not interested in Abyssinia, forgetting that we were deeply interested in the maintenance of peace and in the support of the machinery which had been constructed to maintain it.

(*d*) Secondly, it was said that other members of the League would not back us up. The allegation was in the main unfounded; but whether true or false, it created an atmosphere of hesitation.

(*e*) Thirdly, there was the view that if, in defiance of our obligations under the Covenant, we allowed Italy to conquer Abyssina she would be more likely to help us against Germany.

(*f*) Further, difficulties were caused by the wide extent and consequent vagueness of the League obligations. Each of the fifty odd members of the League was in form bound to carry out against an aggressor in any part of the globe the onerous duties imposed by article 16. Nor was it quite certain what those obligations were.

(*g*) It was partly due to this vagueness of League obligations that the members of the League were lacking in *esprit de corps* and were inclined more and more to look at aggression from a rigidly national standpoint —

an inclination very much increased by the world-wide nationalist movement exemplified by Fascism and Nazi-ism.

(*h*) There was in consequence a tendency to minimize by explanation the meaning of Article 16, and to fall back on condemnation of the aggressor and appeals against him to the public opinion of the world. Many people indeed contended that this was a better way to keep the peace than by imposing sanctions. The experience of the Manchurian and Abyssinian cases ought to have convinced all impartial people that this was a mistaken view.

RECONSTRUCTION

11. It is impossible to say what will be the economic condition of the world at the end of the war. But all are agreed that it is likely to be extremely serious and may be catastrophic. To meet these conditions there will have to be emergency provisions designed to mitigate starvation and set going again the machinery of credit and exchange.

12. But temporary measures will not be enough. A determined attempt to break down economic nationalism must be made. Tariffs must be lowered and other devices which have hampered trade must be abolished.

13. The work done in the last 20 years by the League and the I.L.O. must be continued and speeded up. This is true of the economic and industrial and also of the social and humanitarian work. It may well be that far-reaching changes will have to be made in the conception of State co-operation in, control of, and assistance to trade and industry. If so, such changes may be international in character and will have to be dealt with by the international authority.

14. Two other subjects will require courageous action; the racial, religious and linguistic minorities, and the administration of Colonial territories. A great deal of experience has been gained in both matters by the work of the League which must be continued and expanded. We do not think it possible at present to go more into detail on these questions, and we will only say that the principle of equality should be one of the governing considerations in their solution.

MACHINERY

15. The International Authority to be set up should consist in the first place of an institution as nearly representative of the civilized world as possible.

16. Whether this should be an entirely new organization or an altered and improved League must depend on the conditions prevailing at the end of the war. We believe, however, that there should be in either case an Assembly, a Council and a Secretariat on the same lines as in the League. We do not think that any closer organization such as Federal Union is practicable at present.

17. The functions of the Authority should be the same as those of the League, that is to say, its business should be the maintenance of peace, and the improvement of the economic and social life of the world, through international co-operation.

18. The I.L.O. or some analogous organization should also be maintained.

19. So also should the P.C.I.J., with jurisdiction to advise the International Authority on any question submitted to it and to decide any international dispute of a justiciable character or even of a non-justiciable character if the parties agree.

20. If any member submits to the International Authority that the provisions of any treaty or other international conditions have become dangerous or inapplicable, the Authority should examine the matter and recommend such steps as may be desirable. If this recommendation is adopted unanimously, except for the votes of States immediately interested, it should be binding on all States Members of the Authority. If it is adopted by a majority it should be binding on those who voted in the majority.

21. The provisions for dealing with international disputes contained in Articles 10-17 of the Covenant should apply to the new organization except that they should be redrafted so as to make it clear that while all members agree that aggression is an international crime and that it is part of the duty of every member of the organization to do all it can to put a stop to aggression, and in no case to assist the aggressor, the extent of the coercive action, political, economic or military, to be taken by each member should be decided by that member.

22. In addition to the larger body, there should be one or more standing Regional Committees consisting of members who are prepared to utilize their whole strength in preventing aggression in particular regions, such as Europe. They should expressly agree that they not only regard aggression as an international crime but also that they are prepared to use all means in that region, military as well as economic or diplomatic, to restrain the aggressor.

23. Machinery in the nature of Confederation of the Governments represented on each Regional Committee should be established which should include at least a Regional General Staff.

24. Apart from special measures to prevent Germany and Italy from again plunging the world into war, a general reduction and limitation of armaments should be carried out by international agreement as soon as possible after peace has been made. It should be part of that scheme to abolish all national armaments specially suitable for aggression, including particularly national air forces. Such reductions would be carried out under the strictest supervision of the International Authority. As part of this disarmament, an International Air Force should be created to assist in keeping the peace. Regional divisions of this force should be available for regional Committees.

25. A Committee on the lines and with the powers of the recently-formed Bruce Committee should be constituted by the International Authority to deal with Economic and Social questions. Where possible any such questions affecting particular regions should be transferred to the Regional Committees.

26. Similarly, questions dealing with Minorities or Refugees might also be transferred.

In conclusion, it is essential to insist that neither the system for keeping the peace here proposed nor any other can succeed unless the nations genuinely accept the view that peace is the greatest of national interests and are consequently ready to maintain with all their strength a Peace approved by international authority as being founded on Freedom, Truth and Justice.

INDEX

INDEX

INDEX

Butler, Harold, Director of International Labour Office, 98

Butler, James: on Lord Cecil's staff at Paris, 1919, 66

Butler, R. A.: succeeds Cranbourne as Under-Foreign Secretary, 1938, 301

Buxton, Major A.: Geneva, 110

CABINET MEMORANDUM by Lord Cecil, 1915: inception of League, 47, 59, 61, Appendix I

Campbell-Bannerman, Sir H.: Prime Minister, 30

Canada: Membership of League, 85, 87; supports Simon's defence of Japan, 1932, 234

Cannes Conference, 1922: downfall of Briand, 133

Carr, William, 17

Carson, Sir Edward, 45

Castlereagh, Lord: Quadruple Alliance, 54; Congress of Aix-la-Chapelle, 55; Quintuple Alliance, 56-8

Cecil, Lord: legal reminiscences, 18-23; Party-political position, 30, 101-2, 115, 133, 178, 189-90, 236; Under-Secretary for Foreign Affairs, 1918, 40; offer of resignation to Lloyd George, 45; Minister of Blockade, 1916. Assistant Foreign Secretary, 1918, 46; Cabinet Memorandum: inception of League of Nations, 1915, 47, 59, 61, Appendix I; resignation over Welsh Disestablishment, 61; British Representative for League questions, Paris Peace Conference, 61; Expert Advisory Committee on the Covenant, Paris, 66; speech in support of first draft Covenant, Paris Conference, 97-8; South-African Representative, Assemblies 1920-21-22, 109, 116, 134

—— —— 1921: leaves Government side of House: co-operation with Liberals, 115; Member of Temporary Mixed Commission, 124

—— —— 1922: returns to Conservative side of House, 133; speech at Assembly, 1922–Treaty of Mutual Guarantee, 140-1

—— —— 1923: visit to U.S.A., 143-4; Lord Privy Seal, charged with League affairs, 145; misunderstandings with Curzon, 145-6; views on European outlook, 146-7; represents Great Britain at Assembly, 147; difficulties over Baldwin's Protectionist policy, 155; peerage, 155

—— —— 1924: visit to Scandinavia and Holland, 157; Chancellor of Duchy of Lancaster, 163; difficulties with Sir A.

Chamberlain, 163; Rector of Aberdeen University, 163; awarded Woodrow Wilson Peace Prize: visit to U.S.A., 163-4

—— —— 1925: British Member of Preparatory Commission, 171

—— —— 1926: Admission of Germany to League: differences with Cabinet over procedure; resignation tendered and withdrawn, 178

—— —— 1927: Member of Composition of the Council Committee, 178; protest at Government attitude to Draft Disarmament Convention, 184; Member of Conference on extension of Washington Naval Agreement, 185; views on naval limitation: threat of resignation, 186; resignation: causes of differences with Government, 186-9, Appendix II; relations with Bridgeman, 189

—— —— 1929-30: visit to Madrid–Paris–Frankfort–Berlin, 198-9; British representative at Geneva, 200; relations with Foreign Office–Henderson; Dalton, 200-1; difficult relations with MacDonald, 207; Member of League Committees: Secretariat, Covenant, Preparatory Commission, 208-9; presentation of portrait, 212

—— —— 1931: visit to Vienna–Prague–Heidelberg, 216; Delegate to Assembly and Council meetings, 219, 227; visit to Rome: interviews with the Pope and Mussolini, 224; Report on League procedure over Manchuria: Reading's disapproval, 225-6; visit to Paris: Trocadero meeting, 228; views on Japan and Manchurian affair: dissatisfaction with Foreign Office, 228

—— —— 1932: Delegate for last time, to Assembly, 234; Independent Conservative support for Government, 236; invited to serve on Disarmament Conference: considerations involved: reasons for refusal, 236-8; proposal for Abolition of Aggressive Weapons: speech to Disarmament Conference, 236-7, 238-9; views on disarmament question, 237-8

—— —— 1933: review of situation: confidence in League, 248; visit to Montreux, 248; refusal to attend Assembly, 248; visit to Toronto: Empire Conference, 249, 250-1; Chairman of Governing Body, High Commission for Refugees, 252

—— —— 1934: visit to Brussels–visit to Ireland [Belfast and Dublin], 256-7

377

INDEX

INDEX

INDEX

INDEX

Spain: original non-Permanent Member of League Council, 99; demand for Permanent Seat on Council, 177; threat of resignation: acceptance of League plan, 180; withdrawal of resignation, 197; civil war, 281; London International Committee advocates non-intervention, 282; appeals to League against Italo-German aggression, 282, 290-1, 305; Italian piracy: Nyon meeting: Anglo-French action: piracy abandoned, 291-2; results of Chamberlain policy, 1938, 300, 302; Non-intervention Committee: German and Italian obstruction, 301; Italian intervention: bombardment of Barcelona, 303; Republican collapse: Franco victory, 1939, 307; celebration of Franco's victory in Rome and Berlin, 282, 307

Steel-Maitland, Sir A.: slavery, 173

Stimson, Mr.: intervention in Manchurian affair, 1932, 228-9; letter to Senate supporting China, 1933, 232, speech in support of League action against Japan, 233

Stresa: Anglo-French-Italian meeting 1935: European situation: German rearmament: no mention of Abyssinia: MacDonald repudiates further responsibility for peace, 266; guarantee of Austrian independence, 309

Stresemann, Dr.: rapprochement to France, 1925: Locarno meeting, 1925, 166-7; speech on admission of Germany to League, 180; death of, 1929: his contribution to the League, 206

Suffrage Movement, 37-8

Sully: 'Grand Design', 50

Sweden: dispute with Finland over Aalands Islands, 1920, 108, 127

Swinfen-Eddy, Mr. [Lord Swinfen], 18

Switzerland: acceptance of Covenant, 84

System of Politics [Kant], 52-3

Tardieu, M.: approves plan to prohibit aggressive weapons, 239

Tariff Reform, 25-6, 31, 36, 102

Temporary Mixed Commission for Disarmament, 95, 114; membership of, 124-5; work of, 138-41; report to Assembly, 1922, 139; meetings of, 1923, 151; Draft Treaty of Mutual Assistance submitted to Council and Assembly: terms of, 152; partial success over Traffic in Arms, 1924, 157; abandonment by Britain: end of Commission, 1925, 171; responsibility of bureaucracy and armament firms for its demise, 171

te Water, Mr.: President of Assembly, 1933: appeal to Great Powers for a lead, 251

Thomas, Albert: International Labour Office, 98

Tokyo: Lord Cecil's visit to, 28

Treaty of Mutual Assistance [or Treaty of Mutual Guarantee]: Lord Cecil's speech to Assembly, 1922, 140-1; Draft Treaty entrusted to Temporary Mixed Commission, 141; terms of: consideration and presentation to Assembly by Dr. Benes, 152-3; turned down by Labour Government, 1924, results of its rejection, 157-8

'Triple Alliance', 1830, 56

Turkey: settlement of Mesopotamian frontier question, 1925, 174; tendency to co-operation with League, 1928, 198

Unanimity Rule, 72, 93-5

Unionist Free Traders, 26

'Union Now': Mr. Streit's proposals: objections to, 345-6, 347-8

United States of America: attitude to Blockade, 41-4; entry into war, 1917, 46; isolationist attitude to Covenant: refusal to ratify Peace Treaties, 74, 82, 99; opposition to admission of Dominions and India as League members, 86; approach to and co-operation with League, 87-8, 198; membership of International Labour Office, 87; hostility to League, 1920, 112; invitation to Washington Disarmament Conference, 1921, 132; Naval Ratio, 9-Power Treaty, 134; financial relations: war debts difficulties, 142; Lord Cecil's visit, 1923: American interest in League, 143-4; views on European diplomacy, 154; 164; inquiry into German capacity to pay Reparations, 154; offer to co-operate over Traffic in Arms, 1924, 162; Lord Cecil's visit, 1924, 164; refusal to participate in Permanent Court, 1926, 181; Naval [Coolidge 3-Power] Conference, 185; Anglo-American relations strained by British policy, 1928, 194; trade depression, 1929, 207; proposal for war debts moratorium, 1931, 220; promise of diplomatic support for League over Manchuria, 223; Prentiss Gilbert sent to Geneva as 'observer', 1931, 225; Stimson's interventions on behalf of China, 1932-33, 228-9, 232, 233; endorsement of League action: Roosevelt's offer of co-operation, 1933, belittled by British delegation, 235, 247; no co-operation in oil sanction against Italy, due to Hoare-Laval

DATE